THOMAS S. BURNS

THE OSTROGOTHS

HISTORIA

ZEITSCHRIFT FÜR ALTE GESCHICHTE · REVUE D'HISTOIRE
ANCIENNE · JOURNAL OF ANCIENT HISTORY · RIVISTA
DI STORIA ANTICA

EINZELSCHRIFTEN

HERAUSGEGEBEN VON
HEINZ HEINEN/TRIER · KARL STROHEKER/TÜBINGEN
GEROLD WALSER/BERN

HEFT 36

FRANZ STEINER VERLAG GMBH · WIESBADEN
1980

THE OSTROGOTHS

KINGSHIP AND SOCIETY

BY

THOMAS S. BURNS

FRANZ STEINER VERLAG GMBH · WIESBADEN
1980

CIP-Kurztitelaufnahme der Deutschen Bibliothek

Burns, Thomas, S.:
The ostrogoths : kingship and society / by Thomas S. Burns. – Wiesbaden : Steiner, 1980.
   (Historia : Einzelschr. ; H. 36)
   ISBN 3-515-02967-2

To Carol

TABLE OF CONTENTS

LIST OF ABBREVATIONS

CFHB	Corpus Fontium Historicae Byzantinae. Ser. Berolinensis
C.I.L.	Corpus Inscriptionum Latinarum
MGH	Monumenta Germaniae Historica
MGH.AA	Monumenta Germaniae Historica, Auctores Antiquissimi
JRS	Journal of Roman Studies
P.L.	J. P. Migne, Patrologia Latina
R-E	Realencyclopädie der klassischen Altertumswissenschaft
S.H.A.	Scriptores Historiae Augustae
Settimane di Studio	Settimane di Studio del Centro Italiano di Studi sull'Alto Medioevo

PREFACE

The Ostrogoths, like numerous others during the *Völkerwanderungszeit*, were itinerants never pausing long enough to send out roots in any abode before they reached their settlement areas in Italy. Today the path of their migration crosses linguistic frontiers unknown to the Roman world. Each modern nation from the Soviet Union through the Balkans and into Italy and Austria properly regards the Ostrogothic sojourn, however brief, as a part of their heritage. The secondary literature reflects the international interest in the Ostrogoths and has forced me to rely heavily upon summaries in western European languages of Slavic language studies. When summaries were not available and the work was pivotal, I consulted others more knowledgable in east European languages. Mr. Andrew Papiz, a graduate student in Russian history at Emory University prepared translations of the Russian material. I would like to acknowledge the special assistance given me by friends and colleagues. I thank my mentors Sylvia L. Thrupp and John W. Eadie for patiently sharing their wisdom during the seven years of work on the Ostrogoths. I also wish to express my gratitude to George P. Cuttino and Robert A. Smith for reading drafts and to the librarians at The University of Michigan and Emory University.

Emory University

Thomas S. Burns

INTRODUCTION

The Ostrogoths were always tribesmen. When they ceased to be tribesmen, they ceased to be Ostrogoths. At first glance "tribal" conveys a popular image of undifferentiated primitiveness and barbarity tempered by the timeless qualities of the noble savage. But this picture is false. Helpful comparative insights into the nature of all tribal societies have emerged from the maelstrom of recent anthropological publications. These scholars have destroyed the myth of unchanging simplicity and, in fact, have all but abandoned "tribal" as a precise descriptive term. Tribal societies undergo continuous modification as internal and external pressures alter degrees of segmentation and create new social and economic conditions, and these in turn lead to corresponding changes in all aspects of life. In almost every case tribal evolution from more or less amorphous groupings to a chiefdom proceeds as a result of outside stimuli. From these interpretations analogies to the development of the Germanic societies buffeted by Rome are manifest. They are "tribal" indeed but "tribal" in continuously evolving ways until they cease to be tribal at all.

Historians studying the long history of barbarian-Roman contact and confrontation have the advantage of time and perspective denied to most anthropologists. Compared with the relatively short histories embodied in the oral traditions of existing tribal groups, the Ostrogoths have a history spanning three centuries from the early contacts with Rome in the third century until the dissolution of their kingdom in Italy in 554. In the course of hundreds of years Ostrogothic society gradually transformed from small amorphous groups in the steppelands east of the Dniester River into a well-organized Italian-based kingdom. Finally the Ostrogoths, defeated if not humbled by Byzantine armies, quietly merged with the indigenous population of Italy.

The outline of the process is clear despite the limited source materials for several periods. During the third century the development of Gothic society accelerated in response to pressures from peoples long accustomed to influences radiating northward from the Roman Empire: among these were the Sarmatians, the Carpi, and Chernaikhov civilization in the Ukraine. Only after the initial raids into Roman territory did larger territorial groupings emerge around two peculiar topographic conditions. The Tervingi, as the name "people of the forest" implies, coalesced in the forests of Carpathia and central Moldavia; while the Greuthingi, "people of the steppes," developed a regional coordination east of the Dniester.

A leap to still broader groupings occurred in the eventful second half of the fourth century when the limited territorial groups confronted a revived and assertive Roman Empire before them and the fateful attacks of the Huns from behind. Forced to accept the military hegemony of the dominant regional powers, new and often non-Gothic peoples stood together for the first time in their history. By the 370's permanent leadership structures existed within two large confederations usually called the Visigoths and the Ostrogoths. On the eve of the battle of Adrianople, Visigoths and Ostrogoths remained loose assemblages of people most of whom spoke a Gothic tongue and shared similar customs and dress, but religion, politics, and tactical military operations remained the preserves of local and regional units. Great men like Ermanaric, Athanaric and Fritigern were overlords becoming kings. Caught in the vise between the Huns and the Romans, Gothic kingship developed quickly within the confines of a society still largely decentralized.

The road forked for the Ostrogoths after Adrianople in 378. Some participated in the great Visigothic victory and settled in Pannonia, but most succumbed to the Huns and served their new masters in victory and defeat until the dissolution of Attila's Empire. The Huns have intrigued historians since the middle ages, and recently several exciting studies have greatly furthered our understanding of their society. Yet only sparse information exists for subordinate members of their Empire. The themes of Ostrogothic kingship and social evolution remain obscure for the period when the Huns dictated much of the course of western European history.

Once liberated from Hunnic domination the Ostrogoths, no longer unified but under the two preeminent noble families, obtained settlement rights in the Balkans. The next thirty-five years were the formative period of Ostrogothic kingship and culminated with the dynamic, brilliant, and aggressive reign of Theodoric the Great. Again political events beyond Ostrogothic control created an environment suitable to rapidly centralized command structures over disparate groups of Germanic peoples.

An acute crisis virtually engulfed the Roman Empire as both the eastern and western spheres drifted into chaos. The West was firmly in the hands of Germanic condottieri, but the East gradually reestablished control over the Germanic components in its army and government as well as securing its northwestern flank by a revived federate system in the Balkans. Despite internal rebellions and periodic Germanic incursions into Thrace and elsewhere, Byzantium pursued a steadfast policy of intense diplomacy and occasional military expeditions directed at the Germanic peoples. The emperors Marcian, Leo, and Zeno repeatedly cajoled and coerced the Ostrogoths, whom they regarded as the key power lying between Constantinople and Italy. Under such trying circumstances the Ostrogoths had little choice but to unite behind their leaders more tightly than ever before. For the first time our records reveal kingship and society — their goals, strengths, and weaknesses — as each grappled with the seemingly endless chaos surrounding them.

By the autumn of 489 Ostrogothic participation in Byzantine Balkan policy was untenable for Greek and Goth alike. Theodoric, by then the sole claimant of a kingship based on tested bonds of personal leadership over all but a few recalcitrant nobles, set out for Italy with imperial blessings. Hence the problems of peace — settlement, defense, and government — assumed ever greater importance. But just as external pressures reenforced royal government in the unsettled decades after 454, the settlement in Italy territorialized the latent power of the nobility.

Within a mere six years of Theodoric's death in 526, the facade of unity resting upon the ancient pillars of segmented and localized authority began to crack. Fissures widened into open wounds as the Ostrogothic Kingdom reeled under the assault of Justinian's armies led by Belisarius and later Narses, but even in its bleakest moments Ostrogothic society displayed an amazing resiliency seldom witnessed in contemporary Europe. Underpinning Ostrogothic vitality lay a sturdy foundation of amicable relations with the indigenous inhabitants of Italy. Theodoric furthered such relationships through his government largely based on Roman administrative talent and tradition but lubricated at key junctures by the royal hand acting through his personal followers. The settlement thrust Goth and Roman together at many levels in situations of competitive cooperation while not destroying the effective strengths of either. The resulting fusion increasingly produced a bifurcated society divided between nobles and ordinary freemen with ethnic lines far less important than is customarily assumed.

To many Roman literati the barbarians were cultural assassins of the lowest order. Such self-proclaimed Valkyries looked down upon an all too simple battlefield of black and white, "we and they." Ostrogothic society rarely operated on principles of ethnic delineation. One virtue of tribal structure is the elasticity between members and aliens. Of course, fear and even hostility pervaded Ostrogoths facing the unfamiliar. They were as superstitious as their era, but during the crucial years in the Balkans, if not long before, they realized that all Romans, particularly the oppressed peasantry, were not enemies. Peace brought mutual respect born by facing the challenges of agriculture, government, and even defense, together. Violence erupted periodically but rarely from men whose roots were often scorched by service on the still restless frontiers surrounding Italy.

By focusing the monograph on the intimately related themes of kingship and social change, the prolonged impact of Roman civilization upon Germanic society emerges clearly. Modern scholarship usually has stressed the shortlived Ostrogothic Kingdom of Italy to the detriment of historical perspective and understanding. Sixth-century Ostrogothic society derived from a merging of the late Roman civilization of Italy and the end products of two centuries of excruciating migration and previous ill-fated attempts at settlement. Ostrogothic society in 490 mirrored not the Germanic world of Tacitus nor even that of Ammianus Marcellinus, yet roots deep in the past continued to bear fruit in Italy. Theodoric owed much to Roman statecraft but more to the basic substrata of a Germanic society forced to adapt to political, economic, and social forces transcending the narrow provincialisms of the third century.

Detailed political histories of the late Roman world at the time of the barbarian crisis often obscure the gradual but consistent evolution of Ostrogothic kingship and related tribal structures. Hence only twice will the reader find extended discussions of political and military events: the events of the late fourth century and the pivotal Balkans episode. During these years the inherited Ostrogothic society clearly accelerated internal change in response to political circumstances not well treated from the Germanic view in our literature.

The story about to unfold has no heroes, only people in search of solutions to problems whose complexity defied resolution. The Ostrogoths responded with a flexibility intrinsic to tribal societies. When they lost their adaptability, when they forsook their heritage, they ceased to exist as a people. The cutting-edge of change passed.

CHAPTER ONE

GOTH AND ROMAN FACE TO FACE

An Overview

Gothic society at the opening of the frontier period (ca. A.D. 200) was the product of largely unknown transformations in segmentation that had occurred during the early migrations. Already military alliances were transcending the original military obligations of kin. From this base Gothic society developed slowly towards still greater integration as the alliance system expanded to meet the challenge of the Roman frontier. By the middle of the fourth century large confederacies created from subtribal units existed and were led by men whose powers, if not always their titles, were near regal in scope. Although the confederate leaders usually could not order subunit leaders to undertake specific actions, they could direct them in unison in response to specific needs for concerted action. The positions of confederate leaders, particularly those of the Ostrogothic confederacy, gradually became powerful and permanent social features, but the transformation from subunit leadership to tribal kingship through confederation was never complete.

The tribal names, Visigoth and Ostrogoth, became meaningful political terms only after the creation of confederacies in the fourth century. Both tribal confederacies were built by allying subgroups that had already coalesced from smaller kinship units. There are no demonstrable distinctions between Ostrogothic and Visigothic social structures except the early development of a hereditary tribal leadership among the former. As a result, until evidence to the contrary is forthcoming, it is justifiable to use essentially Visigothic data to reconstruct the outlines of Ostrogothic social development during the fourth century.

The Goths first began to menace the Roman Empire in the early third century, but they did not simultaneously enter the survey of historical record. The paucity of contemporary historical literature for the third century contrasts sharply with the abundant materials of the fourth. Ammianus Marcellinus, the speeches of Themistius, and the fragments of Eunapius then join ranks with a diversity of other fourth-century evidence to provide a sound basis for the study of Gothic social structure. Gothic society of the third century, however, must be reconstructed largely from the retrospective hints of a few fourth-century Roman histories, of which none approach the reliability of Ammianus' account.[1] Epigraphical, papyrological, and numismatic evidence are only occasionally important outside a purely Roman context. The *Scriptores Historiae Augustae* and the *Caesares* of Aurelius Victor (the two principal sources bearing on Gothic history in the third century) are beset with problems.[2] The *S.H.A.* has generated such controversy that a continuing colloquium devoted to its study has been organized to answer such basic questions as its date, authorship, and reliability.

There is no question that the material concerning the barbarians, particularly the Goths, in the *S.H.A.* is generally consistent with what we know of Gothic society from other sources, including Aurelius Victor and Zosimus, and a few contemporary authors extant only in fragments. The major exception to the *S.H.A.*'s credibility regarding Gothic social structure occurs in the *Vita Claudii*. Claudius is said to have captured many kings (plerique capti reges), although tribal kingship does not seem to have developed until late in the fourth century. But the *Vita Claudii* is a panegyric, not a scholarly biography. Since Claudius was consistently known by his epithet "Gothicus," the fourth-century author thought it desirable to describe Claudius as capturing kings, even though Aurelian later encountered mere dukes (duces). Except for this observation of Claudius' royal captives, the *S.H.A.* depicts Gothic society as essentially amorphous. The leadership as actually described was ducal rather than royal, and the size of operational units in the migrations was much smaller than the units at Adrianople in 378.

---

[1] Wolfgang Seyfarth, "Nomadenvölker an den Grenzen des spätrömischen Reiches. Beobachtungen des Ammianus Marcellinus über Hunnen und Sarazenen," *Das Verhältnis von Bodenbauern und Viehzüchtern in historischer Sicht* (Deutsche Akademie der Wissenschaften zu Berlin, Institut für Orientforschung, 69, Berlin 1969), pp. 207–13 has concluded that Ammianus was sufficiently curious and well-informed about people on the fringes of the Empire that more comparative study should be directed toward his work, particularly the discussion of the Saracens. When Ammianus wrote, Theodosius was much more concerned with the Goths than either the Saracens or Huns. The amount of data and the number of eyewitnesses would have been proportionally greater for the Goths. Ammianus himself was probably not an eyewitness of Gothic society, although he was a contemporary. Most work on Ammianus has dealt primarily with his reliability for Roman history.

[2] For a detailed discussion of the *S.H.A.* and the barbarians see my "The Barbarians and the Scriptores Historiae Augustae," in: *Studies in Latin Literature and Roman History*, vol. 1 (Collection Latomus, 164, Bruxelles, 1979), pp. 521–40.

Roman dealings with the third century barbarians along the Danube, as recorded in *S.H.A.*, definitely took advantage of the lack of barbarian unity. But by the late fourth century the Goths had become much more cohesive. For example, Theodosius was able to detach Athanaric and his followers from the Gothic federation only after Athanaric had been cast out by the majority of the Goths in favor of Fritigern. This does not imply that a monolithic Gothic state existed in the late fourth century, far from it, but Fritigern did command larger groups, many of whom were themselves led by dukes, than did the third-century leaders in the *S.H.A.*

Little can be said about prosopographic problems in the *S.H.A.* in regard to Gothic leaders. "Cannabas sive Cannabaudes" (*S.H.A.*, *Vita Aurel.* 22.2) reveals an attempt to give the proper Germanic name for a very powerful third-century Gothic duke. But perhaps this is only a skillful ploy designed to show the author's concern for accuracy where in fact none existed. Cannabaudes is clearly a Germanic name and is neither a pun nor a name known from the fourth century. Unfortunately, Cannabaudes is known only from the *S.H.A.*[3] Whoever wrote the *S.H.A.*, or at least the *Vita Aureliani*, knew German names or had before him a source giving Germanic names. Without contradictory evidence, there is no reason to reject Cannabaudes as a historical figure of the late third century. Cannabaudes, like Respa, Vedue and Thurvar whose names are known only from the *Getica*, was after all a rather minor figure. If any of these *duces* had been the equivalent of the fourth-century confederate leaders, the later sources including Zosimus would undoubtedly have noted them.

Zosimus (ca. 500) is frequently the only authority who can be used to evaluate the picture of the third-century barbarians in the *S.H.A.* He certainly used the largely vanished works of Dexippus, Eunapius, and Olympiodorus (all considered reliable sources by historians working with their fragments), and his approach to history may have been influenced by Herodotus, Polybius, and Sozomen.[4] The similarity of Gothic social structure as portrayed in Zosimus' *Historia Nova* and that in the *S.H.A.* further support the reliability of the latter, especially since the two rarely overlap. Zosimus did not use the *S.H.A.*, or vice

---

[3] A. H. M. Jones, et al., *The Prosopography of the Later Roman Empire*, vol.1 (Cambridge, Mass., 1971), p. 179.

[4] Walter E. Kaegi, *Byzantium and the Decline of Rome* (Princeton, 1968), and Daniel C. Scavone, "Zosimus and His Historical Models," *Greek, Roman, and Byzantine Studies*, 11 (1970), pp. 57–67.

versa. Scattered references in the Latin panegyrics, Christian authors such as Gregory Thaumaturgus, and various Byzantine writers — the latter only rarely of independent value since the information they present is often too scanty even to establish a firm chronology — occasionally amplify the accounts given by Zosimus and the *S.H.A.*

There remains the controversial account in the *Getica*. Here Jordanes presents a curious blend of legend, history, and political propaganda. The relative social chronology revealed in the *Getica* is generally reasonable, even though it is the traditional Greco-Roman view of social evolution: kin to aristocracy to monarchy. First, Filimer led south a very loosely organized following, the migrants split under rival ruling families. Finally, the Amali family was established as a royal line. However, even if the *Getica* is ignored as a reliable source of Gothic history, the same stages in evolution are apparent from other sources. The archaeological evidence for the early migration suggests a kin-level enterprise for the first migration phase.[5] Fourth-century Roman sources also reveal that the aristocratic phase of the third century was superseded by the establishment of the "limited" monarchy in the course of the fourth century. Therefore, the *Getica*'s social chronology seems generally correct, but how accurate is this account in regard to specific names and events?

For the pre-238 (Emperor Maximinus) period Jordanes is well aware of the legendary nature of his evidence.

> Horum ergo heroum, ut ipsi suis in fabulis referunt, primus fuit Gapt, qui genuit Hulmul. Hulmul vero genuit Augis: at Augis genuit eum, qui dictus est Amal, a quo et origo Amalorum decurrit: qui Amal genuit Hisarna: Hisarnis autem genuit Ostrogotha; Ostrogotha autem genuit Athal: ... (*Getica*, 79).

But beginning with Ostrogotha he claims that he is drawing from the chronicler Ablabius, who apparently wrote a history of the Goths including the settlement in Scythia. Ablabius is unknown except for this reference, and he (if he existed) probably did not have any written sources for the third century. At any rate Jordanes, following Ablabius, declared that Ostrogotha was the king of the Ostrogoths, eastern Goths (*Getica*, 82). But elsewhere (*Getica*, 98) Jordanes states that Ostrogotha ruled both Gothic peoples, Ostrogoths and Visigoths. The apparent confusion over Ostrogotha's position is an indication of Jordanes' problems with the history of the third century. Jordanes, like Zosimus, had available the history of Dexippus (*Getica*, 113); further, Jordanes'

---

[5] The literature for the Scandza narrative in the *Getica* is immense. Some of this corpus is cited in the bibliography. For my views see "Pursuing the Early Gothic Migrations", *Acta Archaeologica*, 31 (1979), pp. 189–199.

references to Emperor Philippus (244—48) withholding tribute may have been based on Dexippus. Undoubtedly, the descriptions of third-century Gothic sieges were drawn from Dexippus. Unfortunately, in his extant fragments Dexippus seldom gives names, and never records the names of Gothic leaders. Hence, Jordanes may have had two completely dissimilar sources for the third century: the legend-based Ablabius who recorded names but little else; Dexippus who recorded the problems that the Gothic raids posed for the Romans but did not care to mention the Gothic leadership. By combining the two traditions, Jordanes created a synthesis in which possibly eponymous Gothic kings participated in verifiable actions in the third century. Even Jordanes betrays the fact that the Amali were not the paramount figures he would have his readers believe: they were not the only "kings," although the others went unnamed.

> Gothi, ut adsolet, subtracta sibi stipendia sua aegre ferentis, de amicis effecta sunt inimici. nam quamvis remoti sub regibus viverent suis, . . .(*Getica*, 89).

In spite of the presence of Gothic kings in the *Getica* account of the third-century Goths and the *S.H.A.*, no other evidence suggests that anything resembling the Ostrogothic monarchy actually dated from such an early period. The evidence, including the descriptive accounts in Jordanes, indicates instead an amorphous social and military structure, involving leaders (*duces*) not possessing the power and authority of fourth-century Gothic kings. This ducal nature of social organization is consistently portrayed in the sources, including the trouble-ridden *S.H.A.* and the *Getica*. Nevertheless and regardless of the overall similarity of the sources, it remains impossible to offer more than a tentative reconstruction of Gothic social structure prior to the late fourth century.

J. M. Wallace-Hadrill has recently reentered the murky waters of describing early Germanic kingship. As usual, he has brought order where before little existed.[6] Although it is hazardous to synthesize

---

[6] The problem of kingship and nobility in the early Germanic period has been investigated often, especially for the Franks. Still useful, although needing revision is M. Deloche, *La Trustis et l'antrustion royale sous les deux premières races* (Paris, 1873). Some of the more recent works include: Jan de Vries, "Das Königtum bei den Germanen," *Saeculum*, 7 (1956), pp. 289—309; P. E. Schramm, *Herrschaftszeichen und Staatssymbolik* (Schriften der M.G.H., 13.1, Stuttgart 1954); R. Sprandel, "Struktur und Geschichte des Merovingischen Adels," *Historische Zeitschrift*, 193 (1961), pp. 33—71; W. Schlesinger, "Herrschaft und Gefolgschaft in der germanisch-deutschen Verfassungsgeschichte," *Historische Zeitschrift*, 176 (1953), pp. 225—75; Hanno Helbling, *Goten und Wandalen* (Zürich, 1954); K. F. Stroheker, *Germanentum und Spätantike* (Zürich, 1965), which includes many useful articles by the editor; J. M. Wallace-Hadrill, *Early Germanic Kingship in England and on the Continent* (Oxford, 1971).

examples drawn from eight centuries and almost every Germanic tribe as Wallace-Hadrill has done, he has raised many crucial questions about Germanic social structure. He correctly stresses the functional inter-relationship of *rex, dux,* kin, and the whole people. Two notions warrant special attention: the flexibility of leadership and the syn-chronic importance of both war bands and kindreds in Germanic societies. Wallace-Hadrill concludes:

> "The Tacitean *dux* is not the tap-root but a specialized function of Germanic Kingship. Nothing suggests that the *rex* could not be a *dux* or that a *dux* could not acquire the traditional duties of a *rex*, or even that one was a much older office than the other. *Duces* rise and fall according to need, and so do *reges*. *Duces* who led confederations of warriors to victory and to new homes were either already of royal descent or soon found it desirable to claim that they where. The reason for this is that one cannot for long separate the war-band from the gens.[7]"

What little evidence is available for the third-and fourth-century Goths neither positively confirms nor denies this generalization, but the evidence does suggest that there was a difference between *rex* and *dux* in their relationship to the whole people. Wallace-Hadrill distinguishes between the sacral kingship, with its special and permanent responsibili-ties to the kindred units of the *gens*, and ducal leadership of a war band, which was usually an institution of free men exercising free choice. Other followings, including those with a large number of servile attendants, were known to the Germans along the Rhine, but free bands were more typical. Since nothing is known about the "selection" of Gothic dukes before the reign of Theodoric, it might be fruitful (but dangerous) to employ the Tacitean model in which military command was often bestowed by "the popular assembly." Further, the argument continues, the assembly itself was sacral, and its appointed war leader could draw upon its sacral role to support his own claims.[8] Unfortunate-ly, no such sacral body can be proved to have existed among the third century Goths, and the model must remain purely suggestive. An assembly of some kind may have decided many questions — leadership, division of booty, and legal disputes, but it is not until the fourth century that the actual existence of local assemblies and gatherings of nobles into a decision-making council can be demonstrated.

The concept of *gens* is troublesome and may be the crucial difference between Wallace-Hadrill's generalization and the actual social structure

---

[7] J. M. Wallace-Hadrill, *op. cit.,* pp. 15–16.

[8] O. Höfler, Der Sakralcharakter des germanischen Königtums," in: *Das Königtum, seine geistigen und rechtlichen Grundlagen* (Vorträge und Forschungen, 3, ed., Th. Mayer, Lindau, Konstanz, 1956), pp. 75–104.

of the third-century Goths. In every case the tribes mentioned by Wallace-Hadrill were in direct contact with the Empire for centuries. These tribes, as described by Tacitus, Sidonius Apollinaris, and others, had much more cohesive *gentes* than the newly arrived Goths of the third century. Several modern scholars have pointed out that the Romans applied the term *rex* to those holding sacral leadership over an entire *gens*, not to the leaders of warrior confederations.[9] In fact, this practice was not confined to the first century but was equally true of Ammianus Marcellinus and the *S.H.A.*[10] Therefore, it is not surprising that the sources for the third century Goths rarely employ *rex*. The Gothic leaders of that period, regardless of selection or possible sacral roles, were clearly not leaders of a Gothic tribe. In fact, "Gothic tribe" is itself a misnomer except in the broadest ethnographic sense.

The special relationship between *rex* and the *gens* and the kindreds within it is demonstrable for Theodoric and his successors in the fifth and sixth centuries, but should not be assumed for the early period. The role of ducal power in the creation of kingship among the Ostrogoths, although perhaps not a "tap-root," was highly significant. All the evidence suggests that Ostrogothic kings, as early as Ermanaric (ca. 376), expanded their power base by constantly incorporating war bands and subtribal groups into the *gens*, which looked to the *rex* for leadership.[11]

During two centuries of coexistence and often confrontation along the frontier, the power of certain families increased at the expense of others. The net result of this stratification was the superimposition of a more hierarchic order on the basically egalitarian kin network.[12] Kin obligations did not cease to exist, but they emerge very infrequently in the sources. Instead, the actions of the *duces* dominate the evidence. The size and permanency of ducal leadership increased gradually, until at the end of the third century the duke Cannabaudes was an imposing force along the Danube. Tribal unity subsequently increased slowly but discernibly in the course of a century of conflict with the Empire. The

[9] Walter Schlesinger, "Das Heerkönigtum," in: *Das Königtum, seine geistigen und rechtlichen Grundlagen*, pp. 110–21.

[10] R. Sprandel, "Dux und Comes in der Merovingerzeit," *Zeitschrift der Savigny-Stiftung für Rechtsgeschichte, Germ. Abt.*, 74 (1957), pp. 41–84. The title does not reflect the scope of the inquiry which begins with the fourth century.

[11] Much of the evidence will be adduced in Ch. 2. See R. Wenskus, *Stammesbildung und Verfassung* (Köln, Graz, 1961), pp. 482–485.

[12] Some comparative insight from the early Anglo-Saxons is available. See the provocative article by T. M. Charles-Edwards, "Kinship, Status and the Origins of the Hide," *Past and Present*, 56 (1972), pp. 3–33.

ability to utilize sophisticated Roman military and technological skills
also gradually increased. The Goths had entered a new sphere in which
their social structure and technological thinking were forced to change.
The Romans too were learning from and adapting to the Gothic
presence.

For the pre-confederate period four topics stand out: the problem of
terminology and the type of leadership; the possible borrowing of
military techniques to make up for inferior Gothic technology; the
changes in the material aspects of Gothic society; the controversy over
cultural borrowing. Cultural borrowing, first documented in the third
century, was an important mechanism for social change in the sixth
century, when adequate records become available. The four topics were
indeed interrelated. Gothic society changed concurrently, but the evidence usually reveals the result of change rather than the cause. The
dynamic tenor of frontier life established the milieu in which the
changes took place. Unfortunately, a causal relationship is beyond
reach. It is usually impossible to establish direct links between technological changes and social transformation. All that is here attempted is
to indicate those mechanisms for change demonstrable from the available evidence. Hopefully, the discussion of the problems confronting
the Goths and their manner of adaptation will suggest some factors at
work in the transformation from tribal to regal structures.

The Third Century: Expanding Confrontation and Cohesion

The major Gothic incursions into Roman territory in the third
century took place in three successive waves — 248–51, the 260's, and
at the end of the century. Accounts of the character and course of
these invasions, most retrospective, are vague, incomplete and sometimes contradictory, but together with archaeological evidence, are
sufficient to indicate developing tribal cohesiveness and increasing
adaptation to Roman culture. The Gothic invasions added appreciably
to the internal chaos of the Empire and diverted resources from the
grave Persian threat in the East. Rome managed to step back from the
abyss of total destruction following the death of Emperor Decius in
battle against the Goths and the capture of Emperor Valerian by the
Persians when a succession of able commanders took the reins of state.
Beginning in the reign of Gallienus (253–68) and accelerating under
Claudius Gothicus (268–70) and Aurelianus (270–75), Roman armies
reestablished order on all fronts and gave diplomacy a chance to work.

The success of restoration must have dazzled dumbfounded elders whose youths witnessed only darkness and foreboding.

In 238 signs of increasing unrest among the tribes north of the Danube precipitated Roman plans for a spring offensive into the area, but Emperor Maximinus died before he could launch the expedition.[13] Gothic expansion and the ramifications of the Gotho-Gepidic wars had already produced a series of tribal shifts and movements, much the same as the arrival of the Huns a century and a half later was to do. The Goths themselves had been junior partners in the early third-century invasions.[14] Newly arrived in the area north of the lower Danube, they were just one of several Germanic groups allied with the fiercely independent Carpi who refused to accept the Roman client system. The Carpi remained aloof living on the high terraces overlooking the rivers of Moldavia. Their settlements were small, consisting of a few huts, generally typical of Gothic and other Germanic sites in the Ukraine and elsewhere. But they differed from other tribes in that Roman material culture scarcely ruffled their domestic life.[15] The Goths, on the other hand, eagerly accepted Roman products. Nevertheless, the concentration of Carpic settlements along the Prut River combined with the pressure from surrounding peoples, including Rome, enabled the Carpi to unite with the newcomers into a manageable confederacy in the early third century. At this time the Goths were an amorphous group easily divided and detached from the alliance by Roman diplomacy. When the commander of Moesia, Tullius Menophilus, threatened to break up the Carp-Goth alliance by separate negotiations, the Carpi quickly sent an embassy to Menophilus demanding equal treatment. The Goths profited from their pact with the Carpi in the ensuing war against Rome in that they momentarily ceased fighting among themselves.[16]

By the middle of the century the Goths were the dominant power north of the lower Danube. In the period 248—51 the Goths and other groups ravaged Roman soil. In 248 they besieged Marcianopolis. Emperor Decius (249—51) moved quickly against the Gothic raids

[13] Herodian, vii, 2,9—2. Maximinus undertook two earlier campaigns: in 236 (after which he received the titles Dacicus and Sarmaticus) and in 237. See the notes to section vii, 8.4. in *Herodian*, Loeb edition, ed., C. R. Whittaker (Cambridge, Mass., 1970) V.2, p. 207.

[14] Jordanes, *Getica* 91 places Ostrogotha, king of the Goths at the head of a large confederacy numbering 300,000 including Taifali, Astringi and Carpi.

[15] Gheorghe Bichir, "La Civilisation des Carpes (IIe—IIIe siècle de n.è.) à la lumière des fouilles archéologiques de Poiana-Dulcești, de Butnărești et de Pădureni," *Dacia*, n.s. 11 (1967), pp. 177—224.

[16] Petrus Patricius, frag. 1. (Bonn ed.), p. 124.

south of the Danube partly because troops supposedly acting in response to the Gothic pressure had offered the throne to Lucius Priscus,
governor of Macedonia.

For the years 244–51, 94 multicoin finds have been discovered in
Bulgaria.[17] Some of these coins were buried in the wake of the Carpi
invasion of 245, but most date from 248 to 251 and bear witness to the
Gothic invasion in which the Carpi played little part.[18] The attack was
hardly coordinated. The first group attacked between Sexaginta Prista
(Ruse) and Augusta at the mouth of the Ogosta. They moved south
towards Nicopolis and Istrum, where Dexippus (frags. 22, 26) reports
that several towns were destroyed. This group seems to have penetrated
southeast into the interior along the Rusenski Lom river valley and
eventually linked up with other groups at Philippopolis in 250. B.
Gerov suggests that another group crossed the Danube at Sexaginta
Prista and followed the main Roman highways from Philippopolis to
Nova Zogora and Ognen. Still another Gothic group followed the
Roman road from Novae and Oescus to Philippopolis crossing over the
Trojan pass and another pass further west. A fourth group crossed the
Danube and ravaged the area along the Ogosta River. According to
Dexippus (frag. 26), the Goths besieged Philippopolis in 250. Excava-
tions in 1954/55 confirmed that at least a quarter of the city was
destroyed by fire at about this time.[19]

To the west the Goths coming from the northeast and east forayed
into the area of the upper Descus and Stryman Rivers. The Roman
fortifications in the Succi pass effectively barred large scale penetration
farther west. The defenses remained intact until the early fourth century. A few bands did manage to negotiate the pass or go around it, but
the main cities to the west, Serdica and Pantalia, were too stoutly
fortified for a few brigands to attempt. Scattered *castella* and road
stations were destroyed, but damage west of Succi was minor.[20]

After the Roman defeat near Beroea and the fall of Philippopolis,
both in late 250, nothing stood in the path of expanded plundering.
Decius must have stripped even the key pass defenses to strengthen his

[17] Boris Gerov, "Die gothische Invasion in Mösien und Thrakien unter Decius im Lichte der
Hortfunde," *Acta Antiqua Philippopolitana, Studia histor. et philolol., Serdicae,* 4 (1963), pp.
127–46. There is no need to repeat Gerov's detailed arguments on the critical dating of key
hoards and inscriptions.

[18] *Ibid.,* pp. 129–30 with full references to hoards.

[19] *Ibid.,* pp. 133–36. On Dexippus see Fergus Millar, "P. Herennius Dexippus. The Greek
World and the Third-Century Invasions," *JRS,* 59 (1969), pp. 12–29.

[20] *Ibid.,* p. 137. For the importance of the passes in the late fourth century see my "The
Battle of Adrianople. A Reconsideration," *Historia,* 22 (1973), pp. 336–45.

hastily assembled force. With the approach of winter, there was a flourish of raiding west, southwest, and north. The Goths going west followed the arterial highway to Naissus and Serdica. To the south they penetrated beyond Nicopolis and Nestum. In the north, Gothic bands crossed the Balkan passes into Moesia. When winter finally closed in most Goths wintered near Philippopolis, but a few remained north of the Haemus Range.

In the spring of 251 — April or May — the passes opened and the booty-laden bands began their exodus. As each group moved northeast at its own encumbered pace, the reduced Roman forces under Decius struck the vulnerable Goths. The Romans sought to capitalize on the situation, but in June 251, near the ancient town of Abrittus, the Roman forces were all but annihilated with their august leaders in the swamp. The Goths recrossed the Danube in the vicinity of Durostorum, just east of where they had crossed two or three years before.[21] The Carpi must have looked on in awe as the Gothic bands, wagons piled high with loot, slowly trudged on to their abodes east of the Dniester.

Three conflicting, and late, accounts survive of Decius' defeat in 251. According to Zosimus, Decius, urged on by the future traitor Gallus, his general, attacked the Goths drawn up in three lines bordering a swamp. The Romans were slaughtered while mired in the mud.[22] A line was not very complex, but among primitive groups it allowed the leaders a chance to control weak points and commit everyone to battle.[23] A triple battle line, as reported by Zosimus, was a notable advance over the simple line since it involves the concept of reserve units which the Germanic tribes consistently ignored. Unless Gallus also gave them their battle tactics, Zosimus spiced his account with tactics interesting to his contemporaries but foreign to third-century Gothic practice. Like many primitive peoples, the Germans, including the Goths, were masters of surprise, a tactic best used by small groups since it needs little command procedure. The Germans along the Rhine, for example, retreated into the swamps to ambush Maximinus in the area of Württemberg as he marched through their villages plundering the livestock and burning the

---

[21] B. Gerov, pp. 138–39.

[22] Sextus Aurelius Victor, 29,1–5; Zosimus, i, 23. Victor called these people Goths, but Zosimus used the more general term Scythians, which was no longer applied to any one tribe by fifth-century Greek writers. On Gallus, see Jordanes, *Getica,* 101. He was a Roman *dux.*

[23] H. H. Turney-High, *Primitive War. Its Practice and Concepts,* 2nd. ed. (Columbia, S.C., 1971).

grain.[24] Jordanes records that the Gothic "king Cniva" ambushed Decius near Beroea, just south of the Haemus range, where the Goths had fled when Decius entered Moesia. Decius' son was slain but Decius fought on, only to die near Abrittus.[25]

The *Tactica* of the pseudo-Maurice (written ca. 600) clarifies both Jordanes and Zosimus. Instead of a triple line of defense the *Tactica* reports that the Goths took advantage of their knowledge of the topography, placing themselves on solid ground along two or three pathways in the swamp. From these safe abodes they surprised the Romans strung out in the swamp. Stunned by the unexpected attack on their flanks, the Romans were utterly destroyed. After this our source goes on to report that the Goths crossed the Danube into Thrace and spread over Moesia.[26]

Without the troublesome addition of Cniva, whose career Jordanes may well have created by combining Ablabius and Dexippus, the ambush seems more plausible than the triple-line attack in Zosimus. Zosimus' version of Gothic tactics would have necessitated a central authority with the power to keep some men in reserve, thereby perhaps diminishing their chance for booty and honor. Ambush allowed all participants an equal share in the battle. The quality of ranks is reminiscent of the problems in primitive war in modern anthropological studies and appears quite applicable to the third century Goths.

Perhaps a certain Cniva did lead the Goths against Decius as Jordanes would have us believe. However, there is no support to such a statement, and the numismatic evidence makes it clear that there were at least four major groups of Goths involved. These groups crossed independently, months or even years apart. Much smaller groups did the actual plundering such as those destroying a few *castella* west of Succi before the Roman defeat at Beroea. It seems reasonable to assume that these bands were led by the spokesmen for the small Gothic villages east of the Dniester. There villages were little more than clusters of huts. Personal grave goods were often stunningly beautiful, but none rivalled

---

[24] Herodian, vii, 2.2–6. In the sixth century the Sclaveni frequently ambushed the Romans from their strongholds along the Danube, Procopius, *B.G.*, VI, xxvi, 18–19. On the use of ambush among the Germans see Hans Georg Gundel, "Die Bedeutung des Geländes in der Kriegskunst der Germanen," *Neue Jahrbücher für Antike und deutsche Bildung*, 3 (1940), pp. 188–96.

[25] Jordanes, *Getica*, 101–103.

[26] Mauricius, IV, 3.1 ed. J. Scheffer, *Arriani Tactica et Mauricii Ars Militaris* (Upsala, 1664; reprint 1967), pp. 109–110. See further Friedrich Lammert, "Zum Kampf der Goten bei Abrittus im J. 251," *Klio*, 34 (1942), pp. 125–26, who used the derivative *Problemata Leonis*, II,6 instead of the then unavailable Scheffer. The differences are very slight.

the great finds of the late fourth century.[27] The leaders of the small groups correctly would be called *duces* in Latin. To use the appropriate fourth-century term, *optimates*, obscures the poverty of the typical band leader.[28] Perhaps the distribution of booty was based on rank, and such a vast increase in material wealth went towards further solidifying leadership structures. The evidence is silent.

After the death of Decius, the political and military stability of the Empire further disintegrated. A vengeful press greatly distorted the travail of Emperor Gallienus, long blamed for much of the unrest. Revolts in Pannonia suppressed by Gallienus left the Balkans denuded of troops and allowed the Goths to advance unopposed into Thrace, occupy Macedonia and Achaea, and even cross into Asia.[29] The general Marcianus defeated some Goths in Achaea, but news of the opportunities for plunder brought others, including members of the Greuthingi, Leuringi, Gepids, and Herulians. These new forces were apparently quite different from the initial raiders, and ultimately far less successful, for during the campaigns of Claudius Gothicus the Gothic baggage train allegedly was captured and families were sold into bondage as agricultural slaves in the Roman provinces.

> There were three hundred and twenty thousand armed men. Add to these their slaves, add also their families, their wagon-trains, too . . . (*S.H.A., Claudius*, vi, 5–6).
> And so do we writers flatter Claudius! the man by whom three hundred and twenty thousand armed men were crushed, destroyed and blotted out, and by whom a wagon-train, as great as this host of armed men could fit out and make ready, was in part consigned to the flames and in part delivered over, along with the families of all, to Roman servitude. (*Ibid.*, viii, 2)
> The rivers are covered over with their shields, all the banks are buried under their swords and their spears. The fields are hidden beneath their bones, no road is clear, their mighty wagon-train has been abandoned. We have captured so many women that the victorious soldiers can take for themselves two or three apiece. (*Ibid.*, viii, 5–6)

In the fighting around Marcianopolis the scene was repeated.

> Many kings were captured, noble women of divers tribes taken prisoner, and the Roman provinces filled with barbarian slaves and Scythian husbandmen. The Goth was made the

---

[27] See especially the survey by N. Riépnikoff, "Quelques cimetières du pays des Goths de Crime," *Bull. de la com. impériale archéol.*, 19 (1906), pp. 1–80. More recent references can be found in A. R. Korsunskij, "Visigothic Social Structure in the Fourth Century," [in Russian], *Vestnik Drevnej Istorii*, 93 (1965), pp. 54–75.

[28] Olympiodorus, frag. 9, is explicit on the subcommand terminology for the late fourth-early fifth century. Ὅτι τῶν μετὰ Ῥοδογάϊσον Γότθων οἱ κεφαλαιῶται ὀπτίματοι ἐκαλοῦντο εἰς δώδεκα συντείνοντες χιλιάδας, οὓς καταπολεμήσας Στελίχων Ῥοδογάϊσον προσηταιρίσατο. L. Dindorf, Historici Graeci Minores, vol. 1, p. 452.

[29] Aurelius Victor, 33.1; *S.H.A., Gallienus*, v, 5; and Zosimus, i, 29.2. For an example of the treatment of Gallienus in the *S.H.A.* see *Claudius*, vii, 4.

tiller of the barbarian frontier, nor was there a single district which did not have Gothic slaves in triumphant servitude. How many cattle taken from the barbarians did our forefathers see? How many sheep? How many Celtic mares, which fame has rendered renowned? (*Ibid.*, ix, 3–6)[30]

Although this eulogy certainly exaggerated the size of the Roman victory, the general tenor of the campaign was similarly reported by Zosimus. In Zosimus (i, 46–48) the Goths were defeated piecemeal in a series of encounters while those seeking refuge behind their wagons were starved into submission. The Romans, having defeated the military threat, now welcomed the new source of manpower, recruiting some into the army and turning others into cultivators by giving them land. The rest of the Goths, weakened by these defections, retreated northward. These passages demonstrate that the early period of raiding had shifted to a migration of many groups drawn from many peoples. This point needs emphasis, for eventually the new level of Gothic activity brought about larger scale imperial responses. Faced with Roman escalation, men like Cannabaudes, the great Gothic duke in the *S.H.A.*, united several thousand men under their command. Such warrior alliances marked a radical departure from the previously typical bands of a few hundred, but the Goths still lacked anything approaching "tribal" unity. Emperor Probus soon brought more settlers across the Danube from the Gepidae, Greuthingi, and Vandals. His success reflects the weak tribal cohesion of these groups, for the bulk of each remained north of the river.[31] In the fifth century Theodoric refused to split his group for settlement, but in the third century there was no central authority or tribal cohesion. Throughout the third century the Romans took advantage of this amorphous structure[32] to obtain and disperse cultivators and to defeat the Goths piecemeal both along the Danube and in Asia Minor.

There is a basic similarity between *S.H.A.* (*Claudius, Probus*) and Zosimus in regard to the shifting character of the invasions from raids to migrations in which whole families took part. Both sources also reveal that some of the invaders were settled as cultivators. Therefore, a recent suggestion that the references in the *S.H.A.* to the settlement of

---

[30] Trans. by David Magie (Loeb. edition, 1932). Zosimus, i, 46 also recorded the establishment of the Goths on the land. Recall the panegyric nature of *plerique capti reges*.

[31] *S.H.A., Probus*, xviii, 1–2. Sed cum et ex aliis gentibus plerosque pariter transtulisset, id est ex Gepedis, Greuthungis, et Vandalis. . .

[32] Gallienus attempted to stabilize the Rhine frontier with new alliances with "selected chiefs," Zosimus, i, 30. The Romans were able to defeat the Goths piecemeal in the third century.

barbarians along the Danube are in fact modelled after the actions of Constantine and are not applicable to the third century is unacceptable.[33] The stylistic influence of Constantinian panegyrics is another issue, which primarily concerns the date of composition. The factual narrative in the *S.H.A.* meshes closely with Zosimus and cannot be lightly dismissed.

By 270, the Goths crossed the Danube in sizable numbers under dukes such as Cannabaudes, Respa, Vedue, and Thuruar.[34] Early fifth-century evidence provides a glimpse of a Gothic war band, which is probably a better model for the functioning of third-century groups than the Tacitean concept drawn from the northern Germans of the first century. Olympiodorus (fl. 420) attributed Alaric's rival Sarus with a band of 500 men, including a few nobles and the rest lesser men.[35] Cannabaudes, like Sarus, must have had others in a subcommand position, men who represented the various kin units within each band. A command structure of sorts was imperative if the dukes commanded thousands of people. The evidence for the existence of a subcommand structure (indeed of ranking beneath the *duces*) is a curious reference in the *S.H.A.* to Claudius capturing noble women.

Captae diversarum gentium nobiles feminae.[36]

But there is more to it than this casual comment at first indicates.

Aurelian, hoping to learn Gothic plans, gave one such woman (*virgo regalis*) to Bonosus, who later seized power in Germany. Many other Gothic noble women were kept at Perinthus by order of Aurelian. Bonosus and his bride Hunila were married at state expense.[37] Aurelian ordered the women to be fed in groups of seven, indicating a sizable number of these women. The names of only four Gothic dukes (listed above) have been preserved. There may have been more,[38] but within the context of significant military command, which the title ought to have conveyed, it is doubtful that there were a great many dukes among the Goths — too few to account for Aurelian's handling of the *opti-*

---

[33] Jacques Schwartz, "Le Limes selon l'Histoire Auguste," *Bonner Historia-Augusta-Colloquium*, 1968–69, (Antiquitas IV, 7, Bonn, 1970), pp. 233–238.

[34] Jordanes, *Getica*, 107, duces Gothorum.

[35] Olympiodorus, frag. 3, as preserved in Photius, *Bibliotheka*, codex 80, L. Dindorf, p. 451. On the reliability of Olympiodorus see E. A. Thompson, "Olympiodorus of Thebes," *Classical Quarterly*, 38 (1944), pp. 43–52.

[36] *S.H.A., Claudius*, ix, 4.

[37] *S.H.A., Bonosus*, xv, 1–6. Note again the terminology in Aurelian's order, ut optimates Gothicas apud Perinthum conlocares.

[38] Recall, *S.H.A., Claudius*, ix, 3, that many "kings" (plerique capti reges) were captured.

mates Gothicas, even if we assume that young and old alike were confined at Perinthus.

Therefore, "the noble women of different families (tribes?)" might reflect the ranking of Gothic society into common Goths, nobles, and dukes. In the third century, the distinction of duke was probably temporary. Admittedly, the case for ranking in the third century is weak; moreover, it is not until the 370's that the existence of a structured hierarchy can be proved. Yet the scope of the migrations, the magnitude of the efforts of Claudius and Aurelian, and the presence of more nobles than the ducal structure can explain, are more readily understood if we accept the fact that the Goths were becoming better organized by the process of ranking.

Of the four known dukes, Cannabaudes alone was defeated in the Balkan area (after he had recrossed the Danube). The others took ship to Asia Minor, where they raided the countryside, burning the temple of Diana at Ephesus and the suburbs of Nicaea and other cities before returning home.[39] Zosimus reveals that the Gothic incursions into Asia Minor were not migrations such as the incursion into the Balkan but a series of quick raids from 254 to 276, which attempted to take advantage of surprise. The Goths never remained in any one area long enough to be pinned down by the imperial forces.

The destruction wrought in Asia Minor was dramatic. Men were hanged on the gibbet and strangled. Yet the massive level of devastation, which followed the Goths and their allies across Asia Minor, was partly the product of released social tensions within Roman society. Many Roman Christians were forcibly taken back to the Gothic homelands, but other Romans freely enrolled among the barbarians and helped eliminate their fellow countrymen with "barbaric cruelty". Others served as guides. Still more took full advantage of the general breakdown of order to loot abandoned property or even to take outright possession. Some captives managed to escape from the Goths but were seized by their countrymen and placed in bondage.[40] Clearly major internal problems augmented the crises of the invasion period. For the Goths, supplies, pathfinders, and local unrest were all welcome, but their own goals were limited to booty and plunder. They did not enter the lists in behalf of any group or faction. Their leadership must have been hard pressed to move the raiders from one area to the next.

---

[39] Jordanes, *Getica*, 107; Zosimus, i, 35.

[40] Gregorius Thaumaturgus, *Epistola Canonica*, ed., J. P. Migne, *P.G.*, 10, cc. 1019–48. Gregory was an eyewitness to the events and was especially concerned with atonement for the sins committed by Christians on Christians during the chaos of the invasions.

Eventually hunger probably forced the scattered raiding parties to consolidate for further conquest along the roughly circular route they took through Asia Minor.[41]

The initial trans-Danubian incursions and those of Asia Minor were raids and nothing more. When these men found the land cleared, exploitable, and largely undefended, they changed from raiders to settlers and immigrants no longer seeking only plunder. The groups were members of various "tribes" — Tervingi, Greuthingi, Gepids, etc. — and were led militarily by dukes who topped a command built on certain "nobles," probably representing some federation of local groupings. The initial raids were small operations and could be pushed back by small forces. For example, Decius' hastily assembled force was relatively successful in spite of the loss of its commander. Later Emperors particularly Claudius and Aurelian, had a much larger problem — one that required several campaigning seasons to control. Control was sought first by military action but ultimately by the establishment of some Gothic people inside the frontier as agricultural settlers. The third-century Goths conducted larger scaled operations than those of the early migrations. In fact they seem more tightly knit under Cannabaudes and his fellow dukes than when the initial raiders ambushed Decius.

Although the nature of social change remains largely unknown, the Goths' experimentation with advanced engineering and military technology is better understood. The picture is incomplete, but enough parts are represented to justify several hypotheses about acculturation and the avenues of change. The conclusions drawn from the study of siege warfare are partially corroborated by the evidence of linguistic borrowing.

Goths living in small communities never before faced the task of taking a fortified city. Their attempts in the third century were often comical and rarely successful, but the problem of siege warfare demanded resolution or circumvention for any lasting success against Rome. Siege warfare introduces the problem of borrowing and the mechanisms for cultural exchange.

All "sackers of cities" had two tactical alternatives in siege warfare — blockade or direct assault. Blockade served well if the attackers could afford the time for the long investment process to starve the urbanites into submission. However, blockade had several drawbacks for the

---

[41] On the details of the march, its dates and progress, see M. Salamon, "The Chronology of Gothic Incursions into Asia Minor," *Eos*, 59 (1971), pp. 109–39.

Goths. First, the longer the besiegers remained (often years), the further the supply network stretched. Occasionally the besiegers starved before the besieged, as did Maximinus' troops before Aquileia.[42] Second an amorphous group such as the Goths could remain together for only short periods without internal conflict. Leadership disputes, supply, and perhaps a general yearning to move made extensive operations very difficult. As a result, the Goths rarely undertook a siege. When they did, the city was so strategically important that to leave it behind, harassing them at will, would have forced the Gothic leaders to consolidate their people for protection. Since consolidation in turn aggravated the supply problem, they stormed or blockaded few cities.

Tacitus' estimate of barbarian siege tactics in the first century was still true for the third-century Goths but not to the same degree:

> There is nothing of which barbarians are so ignorant as military engines and the skillful managements of sieges, while that is a branch of military science which we especially understand.[43]

At Marcianopolis in 248 the Goths attempted to pile stones before the wall, but their effort failed to take the city.[44] At Philippopolis in 250 the Goths took the city, but not because of their siegecraft of hide-covered wooden boxes wheeled to the city gates. The Goths at Philippopolis also pushed wooden-towers to the walls, but the defenders crushed the towers with boulders. The towers had no protective coverings and were quite crude. Towers were common in Roman siege warfare and the idea may have derived from Romans in alliance with the Goths. On the other hand, the simple devices depicted by Dexippus were probably not beyond Gothic capability. The Goths were more successful with a mound of dirt and wood placed against the wall.[45] At Side in Lycia the Goths employed wall-high towers with iron plates to protect them from the ballista, but again the defenders were victorious.[46] The use of iron plates is rather sophisticated and suggests that the engines at Side were influenced by Roman allies.

In 269 the Goths employed "machines" (towers are implied in the text) against Thessalonika and came close to success. Flaming missiles constructed from a woven wicker-type material soaked in olive oil

[42] Herodian, viii, 5.3, and for Alaric in Liguria, Claudianus, *vi.cons. Hon.*, 238.

[43] *Annals*, 12.45; cf. Dio Cassius, lvi, 22.2; Ammianus, xvii, 6.1; xxix, 6.12. The secondary literature is limited, see E. A. Thompson, *The Early Germans* (Oxford, 1965), and Peter Goessler, "Zur Belagerungskunst der Germanen," *Klio*, 35 (1942), pp. 103–114.

[44] Dexippus, frag. 25, Jacoby, *Fragmente der griechischen Historiker*, ii, A (Berlin, 1926), p. 466. Jordanes, *Getica*, 92. Jordanes was at least aware of Dexippus' work (*Getica*, 113).

[45] Jordanes, *Getica*, 102–3; Dexippus, frag. 27, Jacoby, pp. 470–72.

[46] Dexippus, frag. 29, Jacoby, p. 474.

thwarted the attackers, but the fire balls were effective only in large numbers. According to one account, the Goths dug reservoirs (ἔλυτρα) behind the engines to hold water for extinguishing the fires. Some of the engines were sheathed in lead (μολύβδινους στεγάνους) and would have been difficult to maneuver even without pits behind them. How the machines were withdrawn at night to prevent sabotage remains a mystery. In any event, fire destroyed most, and Thessalonika held.[47]

These examples are the only evidence for third century barbarian siegecraft. The most effective stratagem was to by-pass walled cities unless they could be taken by ruse. Unfortunate people in the open were abducted.[48] Marcianopolis and Philippopolis were besieged because both commanded strategic cross roads and contained garrisons, which could have severely harassed the Goths.[49] The success at Philippopolis perhaps strengthened Gothic resolve during the unsuccessful siege of Thessalonika a generation later. What was the origin of the idea of siege machines and their general design among the Goths?

Three alternatives suggest themselves: a purely Gothic origin, a skill learned by a few Gothic mercenaries and brought home, or the employment of Roman personel. The last seems most plausible and demonstrable. A Gothic origin cannot be ruled out, but the use of armored towers seems typically Roman and not something learned storming a laager of wagons — the typical defense for the Goths and later for the Avars. Roman smiths may have produced the iron plates used at Side, for no large Gothic iron working is known. The use of mounding after the machines failed at Philippopolis may indicate a lack of confidence in mechanized siege warfare or it may merely indicate that the Goths saw that mounding would work. Perhaps the ground was very uneven and totally unsuited for moving siege craft. The acquisition of siege knowledge by mercenaries has been cited as an explanation for the success of the Franks and Alemanni in the west. However, few Goths served as mercenaries until the fourth century.[50] Even in the fourth

---

[47] Zosimus, i, 43 confirmed the date of the siege and the use of machines. The details are found in a certain Eusebius, 101 F. 2, Jacoby, p. 481. This fragment is very confused because Eusebius was using an analogy of a contemporary third-century siege of Tours in Gaul to discuss Thessalonika, hence the extensive use of the optative mood.

[48] Pitza was taken at night while the gurads were revelling rather than watching from the towers. Fallen trees were used as scaling ladders. Zosimus, i, 32–33. For the abduction of field-hands see Zosimus, i, 43.

[49] Yanko Todorov, *Le grandi strade romane in Bulgaria*, (Roma, Istituto di Studi Romani, Quaderni dell'Impero, II, 16, Le grandi strade del mondo romano, 1937), pp. 19–21.

[50] P. Goessler, *loc. cit.* The use of Goths as auxilaries occurred ca. 270, Zosimus, i, 46.2, cf. Martin Bang, *Die Germanen im römischen Dienst* (Berlin, 1906), p. 104. This work has been

century no Goths serving in the Roman army are known to have operated siege craft, although a few certainly saw them.

The hypothesis of a Roman origin for Gothic siegecraft is more reasonable. The use of Roman personnel was a fairly common practice in the third century invasions. The Goths employed Roman captives as shipwrights and rowers in crossing the Black Sea and raiding Asia Minor.[51] Some of the Roman soldiers under Decius went over to the Greuthingi after being released from service, perhaps as a punishment for allowing the Goths to cross the Danube. With these deserters the Goths expanded their operations against Rome.[52] Occasionally men specifically skilled in the construction of siege engines were driven out of the Roman army and took service with brigands and rebels. Such a man joined the revolt of Lydius the Isaurian against the Emperor Probus.[53] If the alternative of employing Romans is tentatively accepted, then the third-century Goths began to utilize indigenous talent to supplement their own skills. The same borrowing of human resources characterized the initial phases of other Gothic attempts to live in the Greco-Roman world.

Much of the controversy surrounding acculturation along the frontier centers on the use of the linguistic evidence contained in the written Gothic language. Like the evidence of siege technology, the linguistic material is only suggestive of trends. It reveals avenues through which the more hierarchic Roman world influenced Gothic conceptualization of society. Although the Gothic Bible was first written in the late fourth century (the Bible is the principal Gothic document), the borrowing of Roman terms seems strongest in the third century when the suffix "tudo" was particularly prevalent in ecclesiastical Latin, and the "arius" suffix was commonly employed with civil offices. For example, second and third-century ecclesiastical Latin commonly utilized *multitudo* (Cor., II, viii, 2) and *magnitudo* (Paraph. of St. John, IV, 2). But the Gothic goes so far as to use *communitudo* and *aeternitudo* instead of the customary *communitas, aeternitas* (in Gothic the Latin *tudon* becomes duþi). From the Roman models of official nomenclature such as *arcarius, armamentarius, capsarius, cancellarius,* the Gothic modified words into offices such as:

---

largely overlooked by scholars interested in the barbarians, but his careful listing of tribes, military positions, dates and sources remains very useful for the pre-Constantine period.

[51] Zosimus, i, 33–34.

[52] Jordanes, *Getica*, 90.

[53] Zosimus, i, 70.

mota (toll)	motareis (toll collector)
liuþ (song)	liuþareis (singer)
laiseins (teaching)	laisareis (teacher, master)
boka (book)	bokareis (scribe)
vulla (wool)	vullareis (fuller)
sokjan (to search)	sokareis (investigator)[54]

No one has challenged the identification of "tudo" and "arius" as more typical of third-century Latin than fourth-century since Michel Breal made his study in 1892. The borrowed terms fell into three general categories: military terminology, particularly the command structure, ecclesiastical terms describing church offices, and terms closely associated with the Roman bureaucracy and trade. The common feature is hierarchy. Apparently the Goths had few words capable of rendering hierarchic divisions but understood the significance of the structure conveyed by the borrowed terms. If a third-century date for the borrowing is correct, the Goths quite early were acquainted with the structure of Roman society. There is no proof that Gothic social structure was consciously modelled on the Roman, yet the evidence suggests that there was a willingness to learn from the Romans. The fields of learning were the army, the church — probably through captured or exiled Christians some of whom were martyred under Diocletian (Christianity was brought into the Danubian area in the third century) —[55] and trade, which brought the Goths into contact with the imperial bureaucracy. Even if the linguistic analogies with the third century are rejected and the processes revealed are dated to the early fourth century when Christianity and the garrisons of the frontier

---

[54] Michel Bréal, "Premières Influences de Rome sur le monde germanique," *Mémoires de la société de linguistique de Paris*, 7 (1892), pp. 135–148, especially pp. 138, 140–142. Some Latin terms came to the Goths in their Greek or Celtic form, but Latin was the common vehicle of linguistic borrowing. For the Greek loanwords see also Ebel, "Die Fremdwörter bei Ulfilas in phonetischer Hinsicht," *Zeitschrift für vergleichende Sprachforschung*, 4 (1855), pp. 282–88, and Robert J. Menner, "Crimean Gothic cadarion (cadariou), Latin centurio, Greek κεν-τυρίων,"*Journal of English and Germanic Philology*, 36 (1937), pp. 168–75. For possible Celtic influence see Robert A. Fowkes, "Crimean Gothic Cadarion 'Miles, Soldier'," *Journal of English and Germanic Philology*, 45 (1949), pp. 448–49.

[55] Jacques Zeiller, *Les origines chrétiennes dans les provinces danubiennes de l'empire romain* (Studia Historica, 48, Paris 1918, reprint Roma, 1967), pp. 36–40, 105–20 (the martyrs in Moesia). M. Bréal does not confuse the borrowing of ecclesiastical Latin, which he dates to the third century, and the conversion of the late fourth century. Still troublesome is the fifth-century Arian, Philostorgius the Cappadocian, who states that the Goths were introduced to Christianity during a raid in the reign of Valerian and Gallienus (*Historia Ecclesiastica*, II, 5, extant only in the fragments preserved in Photius). Max H. Jellinek, *Geschichte der gotischen Sprache* (Berlin, 1926), p. 7. The Philostorgius reference is of dubious value; moreover, as late as 372, the Goths were still pagan.

system were more prevalent along the Danube,[56] the basic thrust of the argument still stands: Roman hierarchic concepts were introduced to the Goths by the army, the church, and the bureaucracy. It seems more than mere coincidence that Gothic society simultaneously became more hierarchic and consequently perhaps more receptive to the influences of Roman civilization.

The problems associated with cultural borrowing and siege technology point towards even more complex questions concerning the patterns of destruction and the continuity of civilization from the Black Sea far up the Danube. A detailed answer is premature and none will be attempted here. As barbarian expansion isolated each Roman community the inhabitants first sought refuge behind their walls. Gradually the strongholds along the Black Sea fell, but many revived and continued on a lesser scale until the great disruption of the Hunnic period. A few towns struggled on until the Avar conquests of the sixth century. The Goths struck Tyros in the 240's, but it continued to exist up to the fourth century. The Getae destroyed Olbia's central city in the first century, but the extramural settlement only ended in the mid-third century. In fact the rural villas around Olbia reached a peak in the early third century. In the Crimea, habitation at Termenous ceased in the third century. Ilourat, heavily fortified to protect the Bosporus in the first century, fell in the second half of the third. Around present day Fantalovskij (in antiquity an island northwest of Kepoi) eleven fortifications have been discovered to date. Here the crisis came in the second century, but the continuity of settlement continued until the Hunnic invasion. Others like Fantalovskij were severely damaged during the invasions, but later life returned until the late fourth century.[57] Along the Black Sea urban life was deeply wounded but in many cases not destroyed. The continuity of Greco-Roman civilization, although shaken, managed to endure.

Along the Danube the invasions of the third century introduced new ethnic groups into the area. When the client system broke down under the pressure from the north and east many groups, especially the Sarmatians, sought and eventually obtained reception into the Empire. Rome settled and dispersed them among the indigenous populations throughout the Empire, some as soldiers and others as peasant-culti-

---

[56] Some Goths served as *auxiliarii*, ca. 270; Zosimus, i, 46. See Martin Bang, *op. cit.*, p. 104.

[57] For a detailed bibliography of these sites see I. B. Brašinskij, "Recherches Soviétiques sur les monuments antiques des régions de la Mer Noire," *Eirene, Studia Graeca et Latina*, 7 (1968), pp. 81–118.

vators.[58] The net result of these receptions and settlements was a noticeable change in the ethnic and linguistic composition of the Balkans as the Germanic elements increased. Rather than being a break the shift was one of appreciable alterations in the population, which before had been Thracian, Roman and Greek. The change was most notable in the rural areas where Roman and Greek speech had progressed slowly against the indigenous dialects.[59]

The Dobrudga has left a similar record. The invaders swept through the Dobrudga in 250–251, 269–270 and again near the end of the century. At towns such as Histria, Dinogetia and Tropaeum Trajani the first destructions occurred under Commodus. The initial destruction was repaired and the cities flourished until about the reign of Gordian (238) when a new calamity struck. In most cases only the most meager signs of habitation reappeared prior to Aurelian. Walls were of prime importance, but they were hastily thrown up and were of inferior quality. At many sites, including Histria, there seems to have been a third level of destruction in the late third century. Towns with unusually stout fortifications suffered less and recovered more quickly. At Tomis the general mid-century devastations were limited to the suburbs, where numerous coins have been discovered. Tomis returned to normal under Aurelian.[60] The cities of the Dobrudga continued to function as trade centers and places of refuge well into the fourth century, usually until the reign of Valens.

Along the Black Sea coast, in the Crimea, the Chersonesus, the Dobrudga, and the lower Balkans the picture is clear even if the local details remain in dispute. The invasions of the third century did not break the continuity of Roman urban civilization but profoundly modified it. The towns survived — few in the north but almost all in the south. The countryside was far more affected. In the north the villa culture ceased to exist. In the south the population of the rural areas became increasingly Germanic. The ties between town and country continued but exchange declined as the cities themselves shrank. In the

---

[58] I. Barkóczi, "Transplantations of Sarmatian and Roxolans in the Danube Basin," *Acta Antiqua* 7 (1959), pp. 443–53. In general see András Mócsy, *Pannonia and Upper Moesia* (London, 1974), pp. 183–212.

[59] Boris Gerov, "L'Aspect éthnique et linguistique dans la région entre le Danube et les Balkans à l'époque romaine (Ie–IIIe siècle)," *Studi urbaniti di storia, filosofia e letteratura*, n.s. B, 33 (1959), pp. 190–91.

[60] For the complete reference to the archaeological reports see A1. Suceveanu, "Observations sur la stratigraphie des cités de la Dobrogea aux IIe–IVe siècles à la lumière des fouilles d'Historia,".. *Dacia*, n.s. 13 (1969), pp. 372–65. See also Halina Gajewska, *Topographie des fortifactions romanines en Dobroudja* (Wrocław, 1974).

fourth century surviving towns like Tira on the lower Dniester were important trade centers in the exchange of Gothic and Roman wares.[61]

The invasions created a new socio-cultural zone from the northern shores of the Black Sea as far south as Moesia. The poles were the Gothic peoples in the north living in scattered villages and carrying on some trade with Roman urban centers and, in the south, the Roman culture based largely on urban nuclei. Roman culture continued but with a decidedly Germanic presence in the army and in the countryside.

This dishevelled situation gave the Goths an opportunity to solidify local and regional hierarchies while gradually imbibing Roman culture from the disrupted and fractionalized Roman populations in the area. When Diocletian and the Constantinian dynasty reestablished a more systematic Roman presence, the Goths met the challenge by still further stratification. The more general impact of Roman civilization, already apparent in the third-century, continued apace.

---

[61] Korsunskij, *op. cit.*, p. 58.

CHAPTER TWO

THE GROWTH OF TRIBAL CONFEDERACIES

Gothic society entered the full light of day during the fourth century in a more stable Balkan situation than had existed in the third. The reestablished Roman frontier formed the backdrop for social change as a new environment rather than as an impermeable military barrier. Although the Danubian frontier frequently witnessed military conflict during the first three quaters of the fourth century, peaceful coexistence rather than warfare characterized life. As a youth Maximinus (235–38) reportedly had a customary exchange of gifts with barbarians coming to the river bank.[1] As late as 480 foodstuffs shipped upstream and traded along the Danube served to unite the Rugians and the "Romans" living in the river towns of Noricum. Throughout the fourth century the Empire tried to regularize relations with the Goths. One method was to limit trading points along the river; another was to offer regular employment to the Goths in the Roman army.[2]

Gothic society did not stand still. Gradually the Goths formed two large tribal confederacies each centered on a peculiar set of topographic circumstances. Those Goths west of the Dniester gradually coalesced into the Visiogothic confederacy concentrated in the woodlands of central Moldavia. At the same time, the Ostrogothic confederacy came into existence on the steppes east of the Dniester. In both instances the Goths lived in small villages while the few surviving Roman towns in their vicinity continued to decline in importance. To a certain extent the Goths became dependent on foodstuffs traded along the Danube,

---

[1] *S.H.A., Maximinus,* iv, 4–5. Traffic on the Danube continued even during the crisis of the early fifth century, Rutilius Numatianus, line 485. R. Syme regards this exploit, reported only in *S.H.A.,* as apocryphal, *Emperors and Biography.* Studies in the Historia Augusta (Oxford, 1971), p. 182.

[2] This policy was begun by Constantine and followed by his successors until the defeat at Adrianople altered the balance and forced Rome to deal with a much more powerful and hence troublesome assemblage. A good starting point of investigation of Rome's responses to the Goths is A. H. M. Jones, *The Later Roman Empire,* and the sources there cited. Goths were *auxilia* in Licinius' army at Chrysopolis, Anonymous Valesianus, 5.27 (Loeb Edition, 1964), p. 525; cf. *Getica,* 111–112. See also E. A. Thompson, "Constantine, Constantius II, and the Lower Danube Frontier," *Hermes,* 84 (1956), p. 376.

and in 367 they sued for peace after the commerce was disrupted and their own lands ravaged by Valens.[3]

The Danubian frontier was not static in spite of the dictates of geography. Constantine or Diocletian bridged the Danube, and strategic points north of the river were garrisoned[4] as Trajan had done two centuries earlier. Valens drove deep into Gothic territory.[5] Gothic bands, for their part, occasionally raided Thrace and Moesia. The Goths living in the lands above the river were not socially or politically homogeneous even by the end of the fourth century. Those settled along the Danube were involved in trade with the Empire and lived in fixed communities, whereas the groups in the interior were much less "civilized."[6] The Huns drove both types of Goths into the Empire, thereby further complicating the problems of command and settlement.

The Roman military reforms of the early fourth century created a stable frontier garrison population which intermingled with the native inhabitants (Celts, Germans, etc.) to a greater extent than troops had done previously. The area along both sides of the Danube gradually became a transition zone between the hinterlands of Roman and German much as the Rhine had long been. The disturbances of the third century had all but completely destroyed the Roman alliance network north of the Danube. With the return of relative peace, Diocletian and Constantine initated a long and successful effort to reestablish a client system. Many of the clients were new — the concept old. Traditional Roman diplomacy began to work. The Marcomanni, Quadi, and Sarmatians, long clients of Rome, inhabited both sides of the Danube; to these the Goths were now added. Inside the zone each side learned from the other, and as the Goths responded to Roman stimuli, the Roman garrisons along the frontier increasingly borrowed Germanic jewelry styles and, since jewelry and dress are often closely linked, perhaps personal dress. At many sites the quantity of distinctly Roman or Germanic artifacts (pottery and jewelry) gradually decreases and is replaced by local earthware and modified jewelry styles. One

---

[3] Ammianus, xxvii, 5.7: dein quod commerciis vetitis ultima necessariorum inopia barbari stringebantur, adeo ut, legatos supplices saepe mittentis, venialem poscerent pacem.

[4] Aurelius Victor, 41.15. Dating this event is impossible since both Diocletian and Constantine conducted campaigns in this area, Diocletian in 297 and Constantine in 332. See also Anonymous Valesianus, 34.

[5] Ammianus, xxvii, 5.6; Zosimus, iv, 10–11.

[6] Zosimus, iv, 20, 35. In the *Passion of St. Saba,* the optimates acted as enforcers at the village level, see E. A. Thompson, *The Visigoths in the Time of Ulfila* (Oxford, 1966). pp. 64–77.

such new creation was the "chip-carved" jewelry style, so called because of the technique of chiseling designs.

To date most scholarly attention has focused on the numerous examples from the Rhineland, but new discoveries along the Danube attest to the relative uniformity of frontier society on both rivers. Many of the finds are belt-fittings of the "facing-horse" style in which the abutting noses of the horses formed the "D" loop of the buckle. The slow method of construction and ornamentation was also employed in strap-ends and other small belt and jewelry pieces.[7] The style itself represented the finest of the personal jewelry styles. Many products of lesser quality usually accompany the finds. The evidence so far collected stresses that the style was characteristic of the frontier zone, for there are few examples from the interior of the Empire. The Ostrogoths, too, developed a taste for chip-carved ornamentation. Ostrogothic burials in Hungary and the Drava and Sava basins have revealed several examples dating to the late fifth century.[8]

The "chip-carved" metalwork represents a late Roman ornamental style confined to the frontier areas. The forces there, regardless of their treaty status (*laeti*, etc.), were primarily German. The style reflects the Germanic tastes of the men and their families who lived in Roman military settlements. Burial patterns also reveal the frontier-military in a Germanic garb. Burials in northern Gaul and the Rhineland dating from the last half of the fourth century and early fifth are generally uniform in the type of personal jewelry, weapons, and armor. It has been suggested that many of these burials represent Germanic elements because of the buried military equipment and the practice of mixing the graves of the rich and poor.[9] But the burying of such jewelry, weapons, and armor, as well as the lack of clear segregation by wealth, were common to both German and Gallo-Roman burials.[10] Although the lower Danube, where the Goth and Roman spheres first made

[7] Sonia Chadwick Hawkes, "Soldier and Settlers in Britain, Fourth to Fifth Century," *Medieval Archaeology*, 5 (1961), pp. 1–71, who compares continental and British styles. The initial article on the chip-carved style is G. Behrens, "Spätrömische Kerbschnittschnallen," *Schuhmacher-Festschrift*, hrsg. von d. Direktion d. römisch-germ. Zentralmuseums in Mainz (Mainz, 1930), pp. 285–94.

[8] J. Werner, "Studien zu Grabfunden des V. Jahrhunderts aus der Slowakei und der Karpatenukraine," *Slovenská Archeologia*, 7 (1959), pp. 422–38; notably at Kossino and Tiszalök.

[9] J. Werner, "Zur Entstehung der Reihengräberzivilisation," *Archaeologica Geographica*, 1 (1950), pp. 23–32.

[10] S. J. de Laet, J. Dhondt, and J. Nenquin, "Les Laeti du Namurois et l'origin de la civilisation mérovingienne," *Études d'histoire et d'archéologie dediées à Ferdinand Courtoy* (1952), pp. 149ff.

contact, has not received such intense archaeological investigation as has the Rhineland, even the excavations in Moesia have not produced the same depth of understanding; the problem of distinguishing Roman from Germanic sites is at least as futile along the Danube.[11]

The similarities between Goth and Roman, hinted at in jewelry, facilitated the interchange of ideas and customs already in the early fourth century. By the end of the fourth century the long military pressure, the influence of the Church, trade, and the overall structure of the classical world had more noticeably affected the Goths.

As long as they remained disunited the Romans worked with individual Gothic dukes at the expense of others. Centralization ran counter to the powers of duke and kindred and therefore was very slow in coming, but coming nevertheless. In an absolute sense Gothic society never overcame local or particularistic forces. Yet by the late fourth century Gothic kings, far more powerful than the early dukes, were supreme commanders in warfare, negotiated with the Romans in the name of the entire tribe, and were deeply involved in the sacral and social community. Ermanaric, Athanaric, and Fritigern were such figures, the first true kings of the Goths. All the evidence clearly makes them *primus inter pares* rather than absolute monarchs, and this is not at all surprising in light of the position of dukes and nobles among the Goths.

Little can be said with confidence about the period immediately following Aurelian's decision to evacuate Dacia.[12] Two points, however, are well established. First, part of Dacia had gone out of the Roman sphere decades before 275. In the area north of the Carpathian range the epigraphic record ends with Gallienus, whereas in the area southeast of Oltenia such evidence stops with Decius. Yet much of the fortification system in the south, especially along the river, was manned at least until the reign of Valens.[13] Second, the Goths and other peoples did not immediately occupy the evacuated areas. In fact all significant Gothic

---

[11] A late fourth century inscription found at Glava in Lower Moesia illustrates the problem. A veteran Valerius Vitalis, previously known as Tzita, had three sons; Florentius (*filius miles*), Vitalius (*filius miles*), and Laurentzio (*filio suo carissimo*). His sons apparently were soldiers too but were known only by their Roman names. *CIL*, iii, 12396; O. Fiebiger (1917) no. 171. The ethnic backgrounds, especially of the sons, could never be deduced from their names.

[12] On the problem of dating the evacuation see now Andrei Bodor, "Emperor Aurelian and the Abandonment of Dacia," *Dacoromania*, 1 (1973), pp. 29–40, who sets forth a late date of 275 after the tribes in the area had been subdued.

[13] Dimitru Tudor, "Preuves archéologiques attestant la continuité de la domination romaine au nord du Danube après l'abandon de la Dacie sous Aurélien (IIIe–Ve siècles)," *Dacoromania*, 1 (1973), p. 150.

artifacts discovered in Transylvania or Oltenia date after 300.[14] assuming, of course, that it is possible to distinguish Gothic or Geto-Gothic artifacts from a multitude of other artifacts whose ethnic identification is at best difficult to discern.[15]

The sources are very meager for these developments. The *III Panegyricus Maximiano Dictus* (291 A.D.) implies that a prolonged period of inter-barbarian warfare followed the evacuation of Dacia. The Tervingi Goths in alliance with the Taifali, a rather mysterious people, emerged from the wars as the most powerful single group. The Burgundians, Vandals, and Gepids retired westward and northward leaving most of Dacia for the Goths and their allies. Jordanes recorded a belief, perhaps rooted in the chronicler Ablabius, that the wars with the Gepids were important in establishing the Amali line, but such is only dynastic hearsay.[16] If we accept Jordanes on this point, then we must attempt to explain his chronology for the third century, which places the Gepidic wars before the Gothic invasion of Moesia, ca. 250. The panegyrist stressed that the Tervingi were the principal Gothic group involved in the fighting.[17] The Tervingi dwelled in the forest belt running from approximately Ploesti in the southwest to Copanca in the northeast — essentially the same area they still occupied at the time of the Hunnic invasions. Tervingi perhaps meant simply "men of the forest."[18]

In 290 the Visigothic confederacy, built around the Tervingi, did not yet exist. The Tervingi at this time allied with their southern neighbors the Taifali, rather than with other Gothic groups. There was no "tribal" leadership as such. Unless we accept Jordanes, there is absolutely no evidence that the Greuthingi participated in the expansion into Dacia at all. In short, the barbarian civil strife following the Roman withdrawal was basically a "non-tribal" affair in the sense that the Goths had no demonstrable tribal organization extending over large numbers of Gothic speaking communities. Yet there was some progress towards

---

[14] D. Protase, *Problema continuiţăţii în Dacia în lumina arheologiei şi numismaticii* (Bucureşti, 1966), pp. 139–40.

[15] A very useful summary is the recent contribution by E. Sturms, "Das Problem der ethnischen Deutung der kaiserzeitlichen Gräberfelder in der Ukraine," *Zeitschrift für Ostforschung,* 2 (1953), pp. 424–432, concerning the Dnieper area.

[16] *Getica,* 100.

[17] *III Panegyricus Maximiano Dictus,* xvii, ed. Galletier, v. 1, p. 65. Furit in uiscera sua gens effrena Maurorum, Gothi Burgundos penitus excidunt rursumque pro uictis armantur Alamanni itemque Teruingi, pars alia Gothorum, adiuncta manu Taifalorum, aduersum Vandalos Gepidesque concurrunt.

[18] From the Gothic "triu" meaning tree. See R. Vulpe, *Le Vallum de la Moldavie inférieure et le "mur" d'Athanaric* (La Hage, 1957), p. 25 with references.

regional groupings. The Tervingi were coalescing around a shared geographic and topographic environment. The Greuthingi too began to recognize their common geographic surrounding, for the root of the name appears to be philologically related to the Anglo-Saxon *greot* meaning flat, hence Greuthingi would mean "rulers of the steppes."[19]

The Constantinian involvement with the Goths, although important in the overall reestablishment of the Roman-German frontier, is unfortunately not sufficiently documented to provide any clues to Gothic internal developments. Suffice it to say that direct contact north of the Danube was reestablished if indeed ever severed. The imposing stone bridge erected over the Danube at Sucidava attested to Constantine's long-term determination to guarantee communication with Roman garrisons above the river. The abundance of pottery and Roman coins dating from the fourth century confirms an ample Transdanubian territorial presence by Rome early in the century.[20]

Between Constantine's death in 337 and 353, when the extant Ammianus Marcellinus begins, the sources are meager even for Roman history. E. A. Thompson in a tightly argued article has resurveyed every scrap of literary evidence relevant to the Goths in this period. His findings make it clear that there was a large scale Gothic thrust along the lower Danube during the 340s, probably in 346—47.[21] The peace concluding the struggle was not completely favorable to the Romans, who gave up most, if not all, of their Transdanubian strongholds. In return the Goths became allies of the Empire.[22] The most important revelation, however, is that for the first time in the records the Goths elected a *iudex* or δικαστής as a temporary war leader.[23] The anonymous *iudex* must have been elected by the Goths grouped around the Tervingi, who had emerged as a distinct regional group as early as 290. It seems unlikely that the Greuthingi living beyond the Dniester in the steppelands participated in the election.

---

[19] Vulpe, *loc. cit.*

[20] Dimitru Tudor, *Sucidiva, une cité daco-romaine et byzantine en Dacie* (Bruxelles, 1965), pp. 74—78.

[21] E. A. Thompson, "Constantine, Constantius II, and the Lower Danube Frontier," *Hermes*, 84 (1956), pp. 372—81.

[22] *Ibid.*, p. 380, from Libanius, *Or.* 59, 90 and 93. Their federate status must date from this peace and not from that of 332 when Constantine was victorious.

[23] *Ibid.*, p. 381, from Auxentius, *Epistola de fide vita et obitu Wulfilae* . . . , ed. Friederich Kaufmann (Strassburg, 1899), pp. 75, 21. Ubi et ex inuidia et operatione inimici thunc ab inreligioso et sacrilego iudice Gothorum tyrannico terrore in uarbarico cristianorum persecutio est excitata . . . The problem of the *iudex* will be picked up again, but it is undeniable that the title as employed by Ammianus and others in describing Athanaric denoted supreme military command.

From approximately the middle of the fourth century the character of the archaeological record changes for the area north of Sucidava. Gradually the inscriptions and coinage disappear. So too, the ruins of small houses probably occupied by farmer-soldiers and their families replace the carefully planned barracks and officers' homes. Local and Germanic wares are found increasingly in the late strata.[24] Whether Constantine's bridge was destroyed by barbarians, Romans, or the elements remains unknown. Valens had to cross a pontoon bridge when he attacked the Goths in 367.

The shadow of Ermanaric owes its origins to the troubled events east of the Dniester during the late fourth century. For all his fame, remarkably little is known about the first historical Ostrogothic king. Ermanaric took his own life in ca. 375 rather than lead his people into bondage to the Huns.[25] His suicide proved unpalatable to succeeding generations of bards faced with glorifying a hero whose death appeared inappropriate to the man. In its place they wove a story first of murder at the hands of irate brothers pursuing vengence for their sister Sundila drawn-quartered by orders of Ermanaric. Later in the middle ages even this personification faded as Ermanaric assumed the cloak of the valiant protector of Europe against the accursed Huns.[26] The man lying beneath the weight of legend warranted a gilded epitaph.

According to the royal genealogy in the *Getica*, Ermanaric was the first Amalian king for over a century. Four non-Amali had preceded him since the legendary Ostrogotha. His line was eclipsed in the third and early fourth centuries when the Greuthingi led by Ariaricus and Aoricus concluded their first treaties with the Empire in the wake of the Constantinian thrusts north of the Danube. Rome sought and obtained seasonal levies and offered a few warriors the honor of permanent recruits serving at the whim of the Empire. Obviously the Amalian line from Ostrogotha to Ermanaric was merely a ducal lineage not predestined for greatness:

Ostrogotha – Hunuil – Athal – Achiulf – Ansila – Ermanaric (*Getica*, 79)

---

[24] Dimitru Tudor, *op. cit.*, pp. 85–101.

[25] Ammianus, xxxi, 3.2.

[26] For the general outline of this legend see C. Brady, *The Legends of Ermanaric* (Los Angeles, 1943), pp. 1–18, who has overlooked the shifting subgroups within each tribe. See also O. Gschwanter, "Zum Namen der Rosomonen und an. Jonakr." *Die Sprache. Zeitschrift für Sprachwissenschaft*, 17 (1971), pp. 164–76, who rejects the Rosomoni as a distinctive name for an historical group but accepts the possibility that they may have been a war band antagonistic to Ermanaric.

Ermanaric (Aírmnareiks, reiks = prince) propelled his line to the leadership of the Greuthingi and created the Ostrogothic confederacy by extending his sway beyond the narrow focus of local power. Before the Huns pushed westward, he conquered and subjugated various neighboring peoples, many of whom antedated the arrival of the Goths: the Peucini, their savagery still legendary to the poet Claudian in the fifth century; several groups of Sarmatians; Celts long resident in the lower Danube and numerous groups of Goths.[27] Even the treacherous Rosomonni owed him allegiance. Sundila was a Rosomonni. Only a short stretch of the imagination is required to envisage the marriage alliances cementing the confederacy. Perhaps Sundila represents the plight of all reluctant brides whose beds cushioned the alliance.

Myth has clouded the operational details of the early Ostrogothic confederacy. Too far removed from the eyes of Roman historians to leave a full record, the Ostrogoths and Ermanaric fell early victims to the Huns. Historians must draw analogies from the better understood Visigothic confederacy of Athanaric and Fritigern. It is comforting that even Jordanes regarded the two confederacies as so similar that he began his discussion of the "divided Goths" after the battle of Adrianople in 378. A closeness between the two societies endured to the end. Another Fritigern fathered Aligern, the last great Ostrogothic duke and ally of Narses against the Franks.[28] The Visigoths, not the Ostrogoths posed the greatest problem for Rome in the last quarter of the fourth century.

In his discussion of the region of Valens and the events leading up to the crossing of the Danube in 376, Eunapius spoke of subunits called φῦλαι, classically a group united by blood ties and usually living in the same area. Each φυλή transported its own cult objects across the Danube in the care of its own holy men. The φῦλαι occasionally went together to form temporary confederations.[29] Eunapius makes no mention of Athanaric or Fritigern at this time. The reason for the omission is that prior to Valens' punitive expedition of 367 there was no one general Visigothic authority.

[27] *Getica*, 116. For the interpretations of the names of the conquered peoples see Irma Korkkanen, *The Peoples of Hermanaric. Jordanes, Getica, 116* (Suomalainen tiedeakatemian timituksia. Annales Academiae Scientiarum Fennicae, Ser. B, 187, Helsinki, 1975). Korkkanen suggests (p. 64) Rogas = Rugi, but the possibility exists that the Rogas were in fact the Rogi, a subgroup of the Ostrogoths not permanently incorporated until Theodoric.

[28] Agathias, *Historiarum Libri Quinque, CFHB*, 2, ed., R. Keydell (Berlin, 1967), A. 20.1.

[29] Eunapius, frag. 55, (ed. Dindorf, p. 248). E. A. Thompson has carefully mined this material in *The Visigoths in the Time of Ulfila*, pp. 43–63; however, Thompson's imprecise use of "clan," "kindred," and "tribe" as translations of φυλή confuses the discussion.

The *iudex* of the campaigns of the 340s was a very shortlived institution. Libanius, writing in 348–49, made no mention of such a leader, although he later gave Athanaric the title.[30] There was no *iudex* as late as 364, when Ammianus states that 3000 Goths were sent by their chiefs (*regibus*) to the usurper Procopius.[31] No one decision-maker organized the enterprise. Even in 367 Athanaric faced Valens with only his own war band, although the text implies that he could have assembled a larger force. He should have summoned the confederacy, for he was easily routed. The creation of the "Visigothic" confederacy was clearly a response to the Roman military threat.

Athanaric's position of confederate leader was clear to Ammianus, who never employed the title *rex* for Athanaric. Instead, Athanaric was "the most powerful judge, the chief of warriors, the judge of his people."

> Athanaricum ea tempestate iudicem potentissimum, ausum resistere, cum manu quam sibi crediderit abundare, extremorum meter coegit in fugam. . . (xxvii, 5.6)

> quae vehebant cum armigeris principem, gentisque iudicem inde cum suis, foederari, ut statum est, pacem. (xxviii, 5.9)

> Athanarichus, Theruingorum iudex. . . (xxxi, 3.4)

Ammianus frequently used *iudex* for provincial governors and other high Roman offices. This was common Roman usage and was still followed by Jordanes in his *Romana*.[32] In the third century, Odenathus received from the Romans the title *iudex*, among his other honors, although he was already king of the Palmyrenes.[33] In Roman eyes *iudex* may have taken precedence over *rex* or *dux*. Therefore, Athanaric's title may reflect a superior position to other Visigothic rulers, styled kings as the "regibus" in Ammianus' account of the events of 364 suggests. Athanaric himself seems to have preferred the title "judge" to that of "king" because the former stressed the wisdom of his leadership rather than the naked power of a "basileus". Saint Ambrose called him *iudex regum* implying that *iudex* was a superior title to *rex*.[34] The possibility

---

[30] *Ibid.*, p. 381. Libanus, *Or.* 59, 89.

[31] Ammianus, xxvi, 10.3.

[32] J. C. Rolfe, *Ammianus*, introduction, p. xxvi, note 2, and Jordanes, *Romana*, 363, 369, and 379.

[33] H. M. D. Parker, *A History of the Roman World A.D. 137–337* (2nd ed., London, 1958), p. 174 from Zonaras, xii, 23, 24.

[34] Ambrose, *De Spiritu sancto*, I. praef. In *C.I.L.* III, 6159, 7494, his is simply *rege Athanarico*. Themistus, *Or.* 10, ed. Dindorf, p. 160. Αἰσθανόμεθα οὖν πρὸς τοὺς λόγους τοῦ βασιλέως τὰ αὐτὰ τῶν βαρβάρων πασχόντων, ἃ πάσχειν οὐδὲν ἦν θαυμαστὸν ὑπὸ τοῦ δεινοτάτου τῶν τότε ῥητόρων τοὺς Ἕλληνας καὶ Ἀθηναίους, καί τοι γε προήγορον εἶχον οὐδετέρᾳ ληπὸν οὐδὲ ὥσπερ γλώττη βάρβαρον, οὕτω δὲ καὶ τῇ διανίᾳ, ἀλλ᾽ ἐν τῷ συνεῖναι μᾶλλον

exists that Ammianus, who may have consulted a Goth for much of his information, simply chose to substitute a phonetically and functionally similar Latin term for the like sounding Gothic equivalents.

By the end of the fourth century the Goths themselves distinguished ducal from regal authority. The *Gothic Bible* and the "Gothic Calendar," both products of the late fourth century, used the term *þiudans* in the sense of Roman emperor. Constantine is *Kustanteinus þiudanis*.[35] Matthew V, 35 is another example: *þis mikilins þiudanis* for τοῦ μεγάλου βασιλέως. The Greek βασιλεύς, when meaning emperor, usually is translated by *þiudans*. On the other hand, leaders such as Fritigern who were petty kings called *regulus* or *dux* in Latin and usually ἄρχων or ἡγεμών in Greek are Gothic "*reiks*" in the Calendar, 23 October. Such subchiefs were numerous in the tribal confederacies of the fourth century.[36] A domestic servant (οἰκείων) Doubius, assassinated Ataulf in the fifth century in revenge for his master's death at Ataulf's hand some years before. His master was a *reiks* of a subunit of the Goths.[37]

The similarities between Athanaric *thiudans* and Odenathus *iudex* are deeper than the mere phonetic similarities in their titles, for each was in fact more than a foreign king. They were the agents through whom the Roman government sought to establish a regional stability over several disparate groups. A weaker case could be advanced for references to *iudex* in Ambrose and Auxentius as examples of an established Latin translation for the paramount Gothic leader. The evidence cannot bear the weight of extended hypothesis, but if *þiudans* was rendered into Latin by *iudex* it certainly explains Athanaric's preference.

Regardless of his title, the confederate leader had little visible role in ordinary village life, for between him and the village lay his council and the regional nobility. The *Passion of St. Saba* describes the martyrdom of Saba in 372 in a Gothic village north of the Danube. Saba was probably a victim of the general persecution of Christians, which Sozomen credits to Athanaric.[38] Saba's persecutor was a visiting noble

---

σοφώτερον ἢ ἐν τοῖς ὅπλοις. οὕτω γοῦν τὴν μὲν τοῦ βασιλέως ἐπωνυμίαν ἀπαξιοῖ, τὴν τοῦ δικα-στοῦ δὲ ἀγαπᾷ, ὡς ἐκεῖον μὲν δυνάμεως, πρόσρημα, τὸ δὲ σοφίας, ἀλλ' ἐφάνη δὴ τότε λίαν τοῦ δικάζειν αὐτὸ τὸ δικάζεσθαι χαλεπώτερον, καὶ διηλέγχθη γελοῖος ὁ ῥήτωρ, ὁ κριτὴς ἄριστος εἶναι πεπιστευκώς. Obviously the real desires of Athanaric are subordinated to Themistius' wish to produce an ideal type – a combination of rhetorical persuasion and vigorous leadership – as a lesson for his readers.

[35] W. Streitberg, *Die gotische Bibel* (Heidelberg, 1908, reprint 1965), p. 472.

[36] See the detailed discussion of Richard Loewe, "Der gotische Kalender," *Zeitschrift für deutsches Altertum und deutsche Litteratur*, 59 (1922), pp. 245, 259–261.

[37] Olympiodorus, frag. 26, ed. L. Dindorf, *Historici Graeci Minores*, vol. 1, p. 460.

[38] Sozomenus, vi, 37, 12–13, ed. J. Bidez, *Kirchengeschichte*, v. 50 (Berlin, 1960), p. 296.

Atharid and his band carrying out a decision made by the leaders, *megistanes*, apparently in council. Atharid was the son of a chief, βασιλίσκος, named Rothesteus.[39] The village met and decided to shelter the saint by denying that any Christians were in the village, but Saba refused to hide his faith.[40] So too, Eunapius reveals that the leaders of the φῦλαι made decisions, perhaps in council, which the multitude then followed.[41]

The composition of subtribal councils varied within the confederacy. In some, the optimates dominated the decision-making process; in others, the council of elders exercised wide powers over younger men and ideas.[42] The division between elders and optimates was not clear. Undoubtedly many elders were considered optimates. The preeminence of particular members of the Gothic nobility rested on family ties, proven prowess, and perhaps wealth. Saba was not taken seriously by Atharid when he discovered that Saba was a humble man without means.[43] The size of an individual's retinue influenced his prestige and power but was at the same time a factor of family and prowess.[44] It seems likely that Rothesteus was the hegemon of a φυλή, and further that his family traditionally led the subgroup. Clearly Atharid was well established. The village was not the same as the φυλή but was a settlement within it. Atharid, not a member of Saba's village, was regarded as an outsider who could be deceived. The φυλή itself was an earlier response to the need for increased cohesion beyond the village level and stood between the developing kingship and the people. In most cases a regional nobleman, *reiks* in Gothic and Βασιλίσκος in Greek, still held actual power.

The closest Latin equivalent for βασιλίσκος is *regulus*, petty king.[45] Fritigern was a *regulus* prior to the crossing of the Danube. An example drawn from the contemporary Quadi tribal organization is illustrative of ranking leaders and enhances our perception of Gothic political evolution despite specific variations:

[39] *Passio S. Sabae*, 4, ed. H. Delehaye, *op. cit.*, p. 219. The importance of this source was not recognized widely until E. A. Thompson, *The Visigoths . . . Ulfila*, pp. 64–77.

[40] *Ibid.*, 5 and 6, Delehaye, p. 219.

[41] Eunapius, frag. 60.

[42] Eunapius, frag. 60, ed. Dindorf, v. I, p. 252.

[43] Olympiodorus, frag. 26; Claudian, *B.G.*, p. 482–85; *Passio S. Sabae Gothi*, ed. Delehaye, p. 218, line 14–15.

[44] Olympiodorus, frag. 26.

[45] E. A. Sophocles, *Greek Lexicon of the Roman and Byzantine Periods* (Cambridge, Mass., 1887, reprint New York, 1957), v. 1, p. 302.

Quorum regalis Vitrodorus, Viduari filius regis, et Agilimundus subregulus, allique optimates et iudices, variis populis praesidentes.[46]

Obviously the Visigothic *iudex* was vastly more important than the Quadi *iudices* who were probably local judges as were the Ostrogothic *iudices* of the sixth century. Such local *iudices* differed sharply from the Roman titles granted to preferred leaders and governors like Odenathus and Athanaric. The "variis populis praesidentes" suggests the existence of popular subunit organizations among the Quadi in which all tribesmen participated. These references, vague and conflicting as they are, to ranking and subunit structures are both indications of social transformations involving the consolidation of small segmentary units into larger organizations.

Such clear ranking cannot be proved for the Visigoths or Ostrogoths, but the confederate nature of both tribal groups probably produced some sort of tiered leadership. Rothesteus and Fritigern may have held equal positions within the Visigothic confederacy under the *iudex* Athanaric. Fritigern successfully reached for the top.

If Athanaric himself decided to persecute the Christians like Saba and to test them by requiring sacrifices before a statue ($\xi\delta\alpha\nu o\nu$),[47] then he was definitely an important sacral figure for the confederacy of Visigothic people. For Athanaric himself to conduct the test was a physical impossibility because the tribe was scattered over thousands of square miles. The $\xi\delta\alpha\nu o\nu$ test was probably conducted only within Athanaric's own domain,[48] elsewhere he had to rely on the nobility. There was no such test of Saba, who openly proclaimed his Christianity. Each leader may have conceived of a test for his $\varphi\upsilon\lambda\dot\eta$, for each apparently had its own cult objects. However, the infra-structure of persecution hardly negated the resounding decision made by Athanaric, a move obviously carried out with zeal by the nobility. On the other hand, politics may have motivated a persecution of potential dissidents rather than sacral concerns, and therefore the decision reveals little about Athanaric's sacral role as the confederate leader. Other evidence for the sacral position of the king is equally ambiguous.

Jordanes accepted without reservation that the first-century king Comosicus was king, priest, and judge.

hic etenim et rex illis et pontifex ob suam peritiam habebatur et in summa institia populos iudicabat.[49]

[46] Ammianus, xvii, 12.21.
[47] Sozomenus, vi, 37.12–14, ed. Bidez, p. 296.
[48] E. A. Thompson, *The Visigoths . . . Ulfila*, p. 61.
[49] Jordanes, *Getica*, 73.

But since Comosicus was a Geta not a Goth (Jordanes confused the two as had Cassiodorus), the statement reveals nothing except Jordanes' view of kingship. Comosicus was exceptional, for no other king in the *Getica* combined royal, priestly, and judicial functions.

In an anti-Arian tract, St. Ambrose rebuked Valens posthumously for allegedly wearing a pagan style neck ring and arm rings profaned by Gothic impiety "as do the idolatrous priests (*sacerdotes*) of the Goths."[50] One such ring was the famous gold Runic Ring of Pietroassa, measuring six inches in diameter and weighing 25 ounces. Scholars have offered numerous translations of the Runic inscription but agree only on its religious context. Saint Ambrose's testimony greatly strengthens the religious interpretation. Because of its great size and value many scholars believe that it was the property of a Gothic king or religious sanctuary. Some conveniently date the ring before A.D. 380, and have even associated it directly with Athanaric.[51] Royal items maybe, but St. Ambrose does not mention Gothic kings, only *sacerdotes.*

Ammianus' depiction of Burgundian royal responsibilities seems at first sight potentially valuable comparative evidence, but is dubious as far as the Goths are concerned.

> In their country a king is called by the grand name, Hendinos, and according to an ancient custom lays down his power and is deposed if under him the fortune of war has wavered, or the earth has denied sufficient crops; just as the Egyptians commonly blame their rulers for such occurrences.[52]

The Burgundian king was clearly associated with the sky and the weather. He was a sacral figure responsible for the gods' attitude towards the tribe as a whole. If he failed in this function he was replaced by someone more favorable to the gods of vegetation. Unfortunately, Ammianus omitted a comparison to the Goths. But if he had, he might have pointed out that the Burgundians also had a permanent and unremovable tribal priest acting exclusively for the entire *gens*, whereas the Goths are known to have had holy men only in

---

[50] Francis P. Magoun, "On the Old-Germanic Altar — or Oath-Ring," *Acta Philologica Scandinavia*, 20 (1949), p. 291, from Philippe Labbe und Gabriel Cossart, Giovanni D. Mansi, ed., *Sacrorum Conciliorum Nova et Amplissima Collectio*, 3 (Firenze, 1759), 617 c–d.

[51] *Ibid.*, pp. 288–90. See also Malcom Todd, *Everyday Life of the Barbarians. Goths, Franks, and Vandals* (Putnam, New York, 1972), pp. 134–135.

[52] Ammianus, xxviii, 5.14, trans. J. C. Rolfe, *op. cit.*, v. 3, p. 169. Apud hos generali nomine rex appellatur Hendinos, et ritu veteri potestate deposita removetur, si sub co fortuna titubaverit belli, vel segetum copiam negaverit terra, ut solent Aegyptii casus eius mode suis assignare rectoribus.

the φῦλαι, thus demonstrating the weakness of any Burgundian-Gothic analogy.[53]

There can be no doubt that eventually kingship became a special office among the Goths. After Theodoric's death men such as Wittiges and Hildibadus went through special ceremonies of kingship. Wittiges was raised aloft on a shield within a circle of swords.[54] Hildibadus was "clothed in purple" and hailed king.[55] Theodoric took over much of the role traditionally played by the Emperor in dealing with the sixth-century Roman church, but his exact position in the Arian church is unknown.[56] Yet it is incorrect to assign anything other than a vague sacral function to the confederate kings of the late fourth century. As representatives of their own subunit they had a sacral function: Athanaric's ordering out the ξόανον suggests some sacral power. Indeed they may have been regarded at the subunit level in much the same manner as the Burgundian Hendinos. The special sacral role of the king, recognizable to Jordanes, slowly increased as the kingship itself became a permanent tribal institution.

Between the Seret and the Dniester several earthen ramparts still snake their way across easily rolling steppelands. The Goths of the confederacy period are thought to have created at least two of the walls.[57] If we accept as a working hypothesis that the wall and ditch stretching between Brăhăsesti on the Seret and Stoicani on the Prut, a distance of 85 km., was in fact built by the Visigoths under Athanaric and similarly that the wall and ditch between Leova on the Prut and Chircăesti on the Dniester was of Ostrogothic construction, then several new questions about the leadership of Athanaric and Ermanaric must be raised. There is only slender evidence for such a hypothesis. Ammianus (xxxi, 3.5—7) reported that Athanaric, shocked by the speed of the Hunnic advance, ordered a wall to be built along his southern flank bordering on the lands of the Taifali and running

---

[53] E. A. Thompson, *The Visigoths . . . Ulfila*, pp. 60–63.

[54] *Variae*, x, 31.

[55] Procopius, *B.G.* VI, xxx, 17.

[56] See Georg Pfeilschifter, *Der Ostgotenkönig Theoderich der Grosse und die katholische Kirche* (Münster, 1896), still the basic treatment.

[57] Radu Vulpe, *Le Vallum de la Moldavie inférieure et le "mur" d'Athanaric* (La Hage, 1957). Vulpe writing in 1972 remains convinced of the arguments advanced fifteen years earlier when less work had been completed. R. Vulpe, "Les v a l l a de la Valachie, de la Basse-Moldavie et du Boudjak," *Actes du IXe congrès international d'études sur les frontières romaines* (Mamia, 6.–13. September 1972), p. 273.

between the Gerasus and the Danube.[58] Elsewhere Ammianus (xxxi, 3.5) mentioned a wall of the Greuthingi. The curious fact revealed only recently is that the so-called wall of Moldavia Inferior faces south with the ditch lying on the south side. The southern orientation provided a makeshift defense for the forests of central Moldavia, the heartlands of the Tervingi. There is no record of any Roman attempt to protect the interior of Moldavia from an invasion from the south. The builders, therefore, were non-Roman. Archaeology cannot date the wall even approximately: it might date from Herodotus to the Slavic invasions. Ammianus' report stands as an isolated testimony to large scale wall construction in the area.

How could the Goths accomplish such an undertaking within the confines of the confederate structure? Ammianus makes it clear that the wall was a hasty attempt to stop or divert the Huns, not a permanent solution. It is equally clear that Athanaric made the decision while among the assembled Gothic warriors after they failed to check the Huns and retreated into the forests. Presumably the decision was made in a war council probably similar to that which Alaric held some thirty years later during his invasion of Italy. According to the Roman court poet Claudian, Alaric's council consisted of elders and men of demonstrated military prowess. Athanaric in consultation with such men, probably representing the various φῦλαι of the confederation, decided to build a wall. But who did the spade work? Surely not leaders like Atharid or Rothesteus, the co-formulaters of the plan. The burden must have fallen on the humble members of Gothic society similar to those sheltering St. Saba. The humble Gothic men and women, plus the subject populations about whom so little is known, could have thrown up a "wall" within a month. No plans are reported for its defense. Presumably the mounted Huns would have had some difficulty breaching the wall, and the Goths could have assembled to attack when the invaders were temporarily divided by the narrow passageway. The wall itself may have been enough to detour Huns still unaccustomed to attacking defensive structures. At any rate, the combination of the wall and the easily defended forests in the interior proved effective. The Huns did not follow Athanaric into the forest, but eventually fear and hunger forced the isolated Visigoths to seek *receptio* in the Empire. The Huns did not route them in pitched battle as they did the Ostrogoths.

[58] The identification of the modern Seret River and the Gerasus is not beyond question but the arguments advanced by Vulpe, *loc. cit.*, are persuasive, J. C. Rolfe, *Ammianus* (Loeb edition), p. 398, believed the Prut to be the Gerasus.

The nature of the Visigothic confederacy and its leadership is well documented for the late fourth century. After Athanaric led his personal following into the mountains of Transylvania following his defeat by the Huns in 376, Alavivus and Fritigern brought the remaining tribesmen into the Empire.[59] Fritigern, the victor at Adrianople, was not originally king but a powerful duke, one of the *ducatores* (a *regulus* in Jordanes).[60] Alavivus alone commanded the Goths on the north bank of the Danube and negotiated with Valens for permission to cross.[61] His offer of peace to Valens, and if need be, of military service for land south of the river, was similar to the conditions establishing *laeti* or the treaty of *foederati* — indeed, quite like Athnaric's role in the negotiations with Valens in 367 in which the treaty was signed in boats on the Danube.[62] Alavivus was the leader of the confederation. The Roman agreement to allow free passage of the Danube applied to the entire Visigothic tribe; some Ostrogoths crossed but without permission. By negotiating with Alavivus, the Romans, in effect, recognized his position as tribal leader. Romans made treaties only with tribal chiefs, not amorphous groups of barbarians. The third-century practice of recruiting such amorphous barbarians into the army or settling them on the land as cultivators was applied to other groups as late as Justinian. Small groups usually posed no military threat and were easily repulsed at the frontier.

Fritigern's power was nearly as strong as Alavivus', and both were invited to dine at Marcianopolis with the Roman commander Lupicinus. Fritigern forever cautious, detected the assassination plot and escaped with his men (*cum sociis*)[63], but Alavivus disappeared. If Alavivus too escaped, then surely he would have taken part in the ensuing campaign. On the other hand, if he were slain at the banquet, why did Ammianus fail to mention it? The incident sparked the Goths to raise their war standards against the Empire. The murder of the

---

[59] Ammianus, xxxi, 3.6.–8, 4.1, 4.7. Eventually Athanaric was driven from his native land by a faction of his own following, and he accepted Theodosius' invitation to enter Constantinople – thus breaking his oath. There he was buried with royal honors. His forces remained loyal to Theodosius, Ammianus, xxvii, 5.10; *Getica*, 142–45.

[60] Ammianus, xxxi, 5.7; *Getica*, 135, Fritigernus Gothorum regulus.

[61] Ammianus, xxxi, 4.1 Itaque duce Alavivo ripas occupavere Danubi, missisque oratoribus ad Valentum, suscipi se humili prece poscebant, et quiete victuros se pollicentes, et daturos (si res flagitasset) auxilia.

[62] Ammianus, xxvii, 5.9. Sozomen is more definite about the embassy – an allotment of land in Roman territory in return for military assistance and lasting peace. *Historia Eccles.*, 37.5, ed. Bidez, p. 295. There was no land settlement with Athanaric in 367 but probably a recognition of the frontier.

[63] Ammianus, xxxi, 5.5–7.

confederate leader accounts for the massive scale of burning and pillaging far more readily than the near-miss of Fritigern.

Just prior to the battle of Adrianople, Fritigern was called king by Ammianus.[64] Even if Ammianus was inconsistent or imprecise in this one reference, the *rex* Fritigern, Fritigern's actions during the campaigns were those of the confederate leader. His kingship may date from any time after the banquet in the fall of 376. Indeed, the prospects of a war of this magnitude dictated his elevation, but his power was federate not autocratic. His position vis-a-vis other dukes was presumably strengthened prior to the demise of Alavivus by an agreement with Valens in which some Roman troops from Thrace were placed under Fritigern's command in his struggles with Athanaric.[65] If true, this is a clear example of Roman meddling in Gothic internal struggles, similar to intervention in German affairs along the Rhine in the first century.[66]

The nature of the raids and pillage, culminating in the battle of Adrianople in 378, clarifies the loose federate structure of the Gothic tribe. In this respect, Fritigern's power was similar to the Ostrogoth Ermanaric — i.e., both the Visigoths and the Ostrogoths had created a large federate tribal alliance comprised of Goths and other peoples frequently shifting their allegiance.[67] Each tribe was itself a loosely knit assemblage of people. The subgroups[68] often acted autonomously, attaching themselves to different allies, sometimes rivals of the remainder of the tribe. For example, one group of Alans, the Antes (perhaps meaning "outer Alans") went to war against the Ostrogoths while both were members of the Hunnic federation (ca. 400).[69] Or better still, in 377 Farnobius, an optimate of the Goths, concluded an

---

[64] Ammianus, xxxi, 12.9. Neither Eunapius, frag. 42, ed. L. Dindorf, *Historici Graeci Minores,* pp. 237–41, nor Sozomen gives the titles of any Goth, although the latter does discuss Fritigern and Athanaric. Therefore, the terminology for the kingship of Fritigern must be based entirely on Ammianus and the official nomenclature preserved in the Gothic language.

[65] Sozomen, 37.7, also suggested that in return Fritigern agreed to convert to Arianism, but he expressed the belief that the mission of Ulfilas was the important step in Christianizing the Goths.

[66] For the Rhine policy see E. A. Thompson, *The Early Germans* (Oxford, 1965).

[67] On Ermanaric's federation see above pp. 35–36.

[68] It is hard to accept E. A. Thompson (*Visigoths . . . Ulfila,* p. 63) that the φυλή organization was destroyed when the Visigoths settled inside the Empire after 376. Eunapius is explicit that it existed under Theodosius (frag. 60, Dindorf, p. 251).

[69] Jordanes, *Getica,* 247. The Ostrogoths were under Vultuulf, grandson of Ermanaric. If Vultuulf is the same person as Vithericus, the grandson of Ermanaric in Ammianus, xxxi, 4.12, then he was in tutelage at Adrianople in 378. The date of the Antes struggle would then be ca. A. D. 400. G. Vernadsky, "Note on the Name 'Antes'," *Journal of the American Oriental Society,* 62 (1953), p. 192.

alliance with the Taifali without any reference to Fritigern or other tribal leaders.[70] Late in Theodosius' reign two Gothic leaders, Fravitta and Eriulf, were at loggerheads over loyalty to the Emperor. Both men were important Gothic leaders and according to Eunapius were hegemonies of φῦλαι.[71] Prior to the appearance of the Huns the Gothic federations had coalesced: Ermanaric led the Ostrogothic (created around the Greuthingi), and Athanaric the Visigothic, located south of the Ostrogothic sphere and in direct contact with the Empire.[72] Athanaric's proximity to the Empire may explain his title *iudex*, which Ermanaric did not possess. Beneath the king lesser men continued to lead in their own manner.

Before crossing the Danube the Goths spread out in family groups to forage for food.[73] When the embassy of Alavivus was successful, they crossed under the scrutiny of the Roman garrisons. These groups were loosely organized under dukes. Fritigern and Alavivus were the most powerful, but others such as Sueridus and Colias operated independently.[74] After the incident at Marcianopolis the Goths split into small groups, some perhaps numbering a hundred or less fighting men and their families.[75] The size of each group depended upon the power and prestige of the leader and the available food supplies in the area. Bands of Goths spread out on both sides of the Haemus Range and into Thrace, and try as they might, the Romans could not effectively contain them. When Fritigern was in an area he did exercise an overall command, but while he pulled his forces together near Adrianople in Thrace (Colias and Sueridus were hopelessly besieging the city), other groups fought a major battle north of the Haemus near the town of Salices.[76] Even after the Goths abandoned the empty lands north of the

---

[70] Ammianus, xxxi, 9.3.

[71] Eunapius, frag. 60, ed. Dindorf, vol. 1, pp. 252–53. Eunapius is far from explicit on their position but the context of the passage makes it clear that Fravitta and Eriulf were in fact the leaders of the φῦλαι mentioned at the beginning of the fragment.

[72] The Greuthingi were "very far away" and were reached by Valens in 367 only after a long march (Ammianus, xxvii, 5.6).

[73] Ammianus, xxxi, 4.2. vagari cum caritatibus suis disseminantes. The small Gothic villages were abandoned at this time. Gerhard Bersu, "A Sixth-century German Settlement of Foederati," *Antiquity*, 12 (1938), p. 34, and I. Welkov, "Eine Gotenfestung bei Sadowetz (Nordbulgarien)," *Germania*, 19 (1935), pp. 149–58.

[74] Ammianus, xxxi, 6.1 Sueridus et Colias (Gothorum optimates) cum populis . . .

[75] In a minor battle with the Roman garrison of Dibaltum, the Goths did not have sufficient strength to surround the small force of defenders until the cavalry scouting forces returned. The Roman garrison was commanded by Barzimeres the *tribunus scutariorum*. His command could not have been large (Ammianus, xxxi, 8.9).

[76] Ammianus, xxxi, 6.3, and for the battle at Salices, xxxi, 7.1–16.

Haemus as the forces of Valens and Gratian closed the pincers, Fritigern needed several weeks to consolidate his forces at Cabyle before marching on Valens at Adrianople.[77]

Although the late fourth-century Gothic king could call his tribesmen together to confront a common enemy, each subgroup of the federation autonomously formed alliances with other subgroups for particular raids. The subunits were composed of families each capable of independent action, especially provisionment. Groups of families under noble or ducal leadership operated together for raids and plunder. Group solidarity was crucial in hostile territory where Roman garrisons could harass small bands and stragglers. The hit and run tactics of the Roman general Sebastianus before Adrianople were intended to compact the bands and thereby limit their plunder range and make foraging more difficult. The king was only able to limit the tribe's dispersion in order to facilitate regrouping when a strong force approached, but even in this area his authority was very weak. Until Valens brought his forces into Thrace, various bands were free to wander at will in search of food and booty. The strength of the king was his war band, composed of free warriors, servants, and kin.[78] He could muster these followers quickly and he personally led them in battle. The Romans fully appreciated the importance of the warrior band in Gothic society and eagerly pitted one against another. Valens may have given direct aid to Fritigern against the troublesome Athanaric. Later, Theodosius openly courted Athanaric against Fritigern, the great victor of Adrianople.

Among the Ostrogoths kingship was increasingly associated with one family: Vithericus, the grandson of Ermanaric, was king in spite of his minority. The bonds between men and their leaders, which held the tribe together, were strengthened in battle, but in peace the king and presumably the dukes retained their legal responsibilities and influence in Gothic society. Not all Germanic tribes developed a permanent central authority as quickly as the Ostrogoths and Visigoths. The Erulians had few contacts with the Empire, and their king was little more than a ritual leader even in the sixth century. Procopius carefully

---

[77] Ammianus, xxxi, 11.5, and for a detailed discussion of the process of calling together the nation see my article, *op. cit.*, p. 341, in which I attempted to show the various phases of Roman strategy toward the Gothic invasion.

[78] The exact composition of a war band would have varied. Athanaric included his kin. Sarus' band, as revealed by Olympiodorus, was made up exclusively of freemen. Servants were common in noble Gothic households, but the only contemporary evidence for servants in the war band is the Burgundian Code and may not be applicable.

distinguished the Erulian king, ῥῆγα, from the Gothic kings whom he consistently called βασιλεύς, even the short-lived Eraric.[79] More comparative study needs to be done before a conclusion can be reached concerning the relationship between the degree of Roman contact and centralization among the Germans, but the case of the Eruli and the Ostrogoths is suggestive of a direct correspondence.

The crisis of the late fourth century was a crucial phase in Gothic history, but to what extent did the tribe operate as a unit? Was there a sense of corporate identity? Could anyone, especially the king, speak for the tribe? The Visigoths and Ostrogoths never managed to achieve full tribal participation even during a crisis. Athanaric went to his mountain retreat with a large following when the others crossed the Danube. Some Ostrogoths shared in the Gothic victories in Thrace, while others became members of the Hunnic Federation, and still others remained in the Crimea and eventually became allies of the Empire.[80] In 400, Tribigild revolted from service with the Empire and caused severe damage to urban life in Asia Minor. With his Ostrogothic followers Tribigild freed a large number of slaves, many of them Goths. Zosimus thought that it was noteworthy that even among the dissidents:

> not one barbarian sided with the Roman cause, for in actual combat the barbarians would attach themselves to their fellow tribesmen and march against those who were Roman subjects.[81]

Tribigild's rebellion was based on the support of mercenaries and freed slaves and was in no sense a tribal event. Corporate identity remained vague. Yet according to Eunapius the Goths, before crossing the Danube, swore an oath to each other to struggle with all their might against Rome.[82]

---

[79] Procopius, *B.G.*, VI, xiv, 37–42; VII, i, 4.

[80] A. A. Vasiliev, *The Goths in the Crimea* (Cambridge, Mass., 1936), pp. 36–37. Vasiliev pointed out that despite his mistake of attributing a continuing contact between the Goths around Dory and those in Italy, Procopius was correct in asserting that a division of the Crimean Goths took place as well as an alliance with the Empire because of the Hunnish invasion (pp. 40–41). This situation was still evident at the time of Procopius although the invasion had occurred a century earlier. Procopius, *de Aedif.*, III, vii, 13–14; *B.G.*, VIII, v, 15–20.

[81] Zosimus, v, 15. trans. James J. Buchanan and Harold T. Davis. That Tribigild's forces were Ostrogoths is revealed by Socrates, vi, 6.5; Sozomen, viii, 4.2; Claudian, *In Eutrop.*, ii, 196; Thompson, "The Visigoths from Fritigern to Euric," *Historia*, 21 (1963), p. 109, n. 16.

[82] Eunapius, frag. 60. E. A. Thompson, "The Visigoths from Fritigern to Euric," p. 106, sees this as the first sign of factionalism among the Goths. Thompson's anti- and pro-Roman division suggest a common sense of purpose which did not exist. If it had, Theodosius would have been unable to split the Goths and pit one group against another. An interesting compara-

Eunapius' comment is hard to explain and impossible to accept since we know from Ammianus that the Goths were widely scattered' in family groups prior to crossing. Perhaps Eunapius should be regarded as one of the earlist fifth-century writers to reject the analogy of barbarian and pestilence so common in the third century.[83] It was obvious that something more complex than savagery had to account for the Gothic success in the Balkans. One alternative was a tribal vendetta of the Goths. But the attribution of any appreciable sense of tribal unity to the fourth century Goths misses the point of Fritigern's problems in Thrace and Theodosius' success in stabilizing the Balkan area by granting lands and playing one band against another.[84] In order to regard Roman society as the enemy, as the oath implies, the Goths first had to conceive of themselves as a unit — they did not. As late as 425 Philostorgius indicated that only recently had the Goths become a tribe distinguishable from the mass of Scythian peoples.[85]

Both Athanaric and Fritigern could have spoken for the tribe, but first they consulted with other leaders.[86] Either man could have negotiated for his own following without reference to the council but not for the tribe, since each subgroup leader clearly had the right to make his own agreements. After a council meeting, decisions were implemented by the king. This was especially true for a truce or alliance. Therefore Fritigern's private letter to Valens promising a preace favorable to Rome and future friendship, if Valens would show his forces and thereby quell the savagery of the Goths (xxxi, 12.9), was interpreted

tive case in the Chinese use of "surrendered" barbarians against their own tribesmen who had remained hostile to the Empire. See Ying-shih Yü, *Trade and Expansion in Han China*. A Study in the Structure of Sino-barbarian Economic Relations (Berkeley, Cal., 1967), p. 83.

[83] In *S.H.A., Claudian*, vi, 6, the barbarians drank the rivers dry and burned the forests. Furthermore, Ammianus' classic description of the Huns (xxxi, 2) who "warmed their meat against their horses" falls into the "plague concept" in which physical attributes and barbarities (often misunderstood as the case of "warming meat" which was in fact the treatment of saddle sores) are given as causal factors in success.

[84] The activities of Theodosius are very difficult to reconstruct, but his policy of settlement, fair treatment, and the employment of aggressive Gothic leaders in the Roman cause was reasonably successful. However, when he had to leave the East to put down the rebellion of Magnus Maximus in Gaul, the Goths were mistreated by the Roman garrisons and revolted. Zosimus, iv, 40, 56, 58; *Panégyriques Latins*, XII. Pacati Pan. Theodosio Dictus, 22.3, 32.3.—4, ed. Galletier (Paris, 1952). See further Otto Seeck, *Geschichte des Untergangs der antiken Welt*, vol. 5, 6, (2nd ed. 1921, reprint Stuttgart, 1966), pp. 84—134, and E. A. Thompson, "The Visigoths from Fritigern to Euric," pp. 105—26.

[85] Philostorgius, *H.E.*, xi. 8, ed. Bidez (Leipzig, 1913, revised ed. 1972), p. 138.

[86] Ammianus, xxvii, 9, may point to a council meeting prior to the action of Athanaric. The importance of the council is much more demonstrable under Alaric.

quite correctly by Valens (and Ammianus) as a ploy to buy time to further consolidate the Gothic army.[87]

At the risk of building a few bricks without sufficient straw, several general developments, all difficult to document, seem to have taken place concurrently with the evolution of larger military, political, and administrative units. Few institutions existed as permanent elements of society. The people and their leaders responded to immediate needs and once the crisis had passed, slipped back into the routine agrarian life of the village. Things were changing. By the end of the fourth century a "Gothic style" in personal dress and jewelry was established. The third century witnessed a very gradual Gothic absorption of styles borrowed from the indigenous populations and the Greco-Roman world via the Bosporus trade.[88] By the late fourth century the Goths had taken the initiative, producing fine pieces of cloisonne jewelry. Splendid examples of the use of glass and semi-precious stones were discovered in the famous Pietroasa Treasure.[89]

The Gothic Bible reveals a language with its own terminology for small regions, *garvi* for the Latin *pagus*.[90] The Goths also had words for market (*maþl*), discourse in public (*maþleins*), gain (*gawaurki*), the basic crafts such as workers in metal (*aiza-smiþa*), and various products including wool and leather.[91] The list could be extended, but what does an isolated occurrence of a word say about Gothic society? Philologists have answered and reanswered the question for centuries. The problem is exasperating for Gothic, for we basically possess the language of only one man, Ulfila. There is no certainty as to when words were created since the language in essence has no verifiable development. Even dating the entrance of loan-words is problematic. At the very least it seems

[87] But see E. A. Thompson who interprets this passage as proof of a division within Gothic society; i.e. that Fritigern was following a pro-Roman policy against the will of the rabble, "The Visigoths from Fritigern to Euric," pp. 106—8. If true, why would Valens refuse the offer? Such secret diplomacy had no chance of settling the problem and everyone knew it.

[88] M. Rostovtzeff, *Iranians and Greeks in South Russia* (Oxford, 1922); N. Riépnikoff, "Quelques cimetières du pays des Goths de Crimée," *Bull. de la com. impériale archéol.*, 19 (1906), pp. 1—80.

[89] Joachim Werner, "Die archäologischen Zeugnisse der Goten in Südrussland, Ungarn, Italien und Spanien," *Settimane di Studio*, 3 (1956), pp. 127—30; Alexander R. Korsunskij, *op. cit.*, p. 57; and David Brown, "The Brooches in the Pietroasa Treasure," *Antiquity*, 46 (1972), pp. 111—16.

[90] Mt. 8, 28. Mk. 6, 55. Lu 4, 14.8, 26.15, 14.15, G. H. Balg, *A Comparative Glossary of the Gothic Language* (Mayville, Wisconsin, 1887—1889), p. 132. A. R. Korsunskij, *op. cit.*, pp. 61—64, 73—74, places more trust in philological argument and hence has made more claims from the evidence.

[91] See Balg, *op. cit.*, for detailed citations.

safe to conclude that by the end of the fourth century the Goths were accustomed to regional units within their confederacy, that the public arena was often synonymous to the village market (witness St. Saba), and that the basic crafts had differentiated into specialities. Archaeology lends support to the assertion that the Goths became better craftsmen. Besides finer and more plentiful jewelry items, the Goths used better pottery, increasingly produced on the potter's wheel.

At the base of Gothic society the kindred remained strong. *Kuni* is variously used to translate Latin meaning kin, tribe, and generation. *Sibja* meant general relationship of kin and family including adopted sons. *Unsibja* meant lawless, impious, godless, or as a noun, a transgressor. In sum, the Gothic language although well developed for economic specification, betrays a very strong kindred focus, so much so that the notion of the tribe or Gothia as a territory was weak. The Romans on the other hand commonly referred to Gothia as a distinct territory in much the same manner as if it had been a legal jurisdiction similar to a province.[92]

Each development must be seen in the context of the frontier experience. A recent reconstruction of the brooches in the Pietroasa Treasure argued that the owners probably wore them in close imitation of Roman-style dress in which the Roman male's cloak was anchored by one clasp on the right shoulder and women wore one clasp on each shoulder.[93] The influence of the Roman bureaucracy on trade has been demonstrated by the analysis of loan words. Romans were several stages beyond the fourth-century Goths in the ability to territorialize ethnic groupings. The Romans thought of nations of barbarians; the barbarians rarely looked beyond small regions. The frontier was a two-way street. The chip-carved style was popular among soldiers: Goth, Roman, Frank, Burgundian it made little difference. If we can believe the old woman in Synesius of Cyrene's *de Providentia*, even the Constantinopolitans had adopted many barbarian customs by the turn of the century.[94]

Many of the actions of various Gothic leaders of the fifth century can be understood in terms of the actual power and influence they possessed rather than by ethnic or factional explanations. Alaric's timidity in pursuing an aggressive anti-Roman policy was attributable much more to the limits of his leadership than any pro-Roman policy he or

---

[92] Evangelos, K. Chrysos, "Gothia Romana. Zur Rechtslage des Föderatenlandes der Westgoten im 4. Jh.," *Dacoromania*, 1 (1973), pp. 52–64.

[93] Brown, *op. cit.*, p. 115.

[94] Synesius of Cyrene, II.2, *P.G.*, 66, 1263.

his dukes may have held. The Hun Uldis, a contemporary of Alaric, was abandoned by his dukes when he attempted to push his federation of tribes too hard in his invasion of Moesia.[95] Alaric's forces, ravaged by famine after the sieges of the cities of Liguria had failed, suffered mass desertions, especially among the infantry, which comprised the bulk of the army. The cavalry remained relatively intact, for its members were undoubtedly wealthy and could buy provisions.[96] Alaric made major decisions only after consulting with his council of warriors whose prowess or age had earned them a seat. When they spoke for retreat, Alaric had no choice but to heed their advice.[97] Royal authority did not command absolute allegiance, and in times of crisis royal power was insufficient to conduct extensive operations. One of Alaric's consistent goals was to be made *magister militum* and thus add the forces of the Empire to his own army. He took great pride in his office of *magister* of Illyricum, although the troops the office gave him did not figure in his campaigns.[98]

Alaric's use of Roman artisans deserves special consideration since it points to the continued employment of Romans as a solution to the more complex problems of the migrations, such as the possible use of Roman personnel to build siegecraft. Fritigern had summarized much of Gothic technical mastery when he lifted the siege of Adrianople saying that he "kept peace with walls."[99] Alaric revelled in forcing the

[95] Sozomen, ix, 5. The Sciri were members of this alliance and lost many members who were captured and sold into bondage. The leaders abandoned Uldis and went over to the Romans. On Uldis, the first Hun known by name, see E. A. Thompson, *History of Attila and the Huns* (Oxford, 1948), p. 25ff.

[96] Claudian, *vi cons. Hon.*, 242–55, 283–86. On Claudian, Alaric, and the court circle of Honorius see Alan Cameron, *Claudian. Poetry and Propaganda at the Court of Honorius* (Oxford, 1970). Alaric was never very successful in siege warfare (Zosimus, vi, 10, Alaric's siege of Bononia). His blockades of Rome have been studied by E. Demougeot, *De l'Unité à la divison de l'empire romain, 395–410. Essai sur le gouvernement impérial* (Paris, 1951), pp. 448–85.

[97] Claudian, *B.G.*, 482–85, 555, and generally the entire passage 480–555. The commentary of Helmut Schroff, *Claudians Gedicht vom Gotenkrieg* (Berlin, 1927), is quite helpful in following the movement of Alaric.

[98] Claudian, *B.G.*, 535. I cannot agree with E. A. Thompson, "The Visigoths from Fritigern to Euric, " p. 112, and H. St. L. B. Moss, *The Birth of the Middle Ages* (Oxford, 1935), p. p. 45 that Aleric's interests "were not wholly Visigothic (those of his people were limited to subsidies and land), but were concerned with achieving a definite place in the government of the Empire." For Alaric and Stilicho see Stewart I. Oost, *Galla Placidia Augusta* (Chicago, 1968), pp. 43–87, with references, and V. Grumel, "L'Illyricum de la mort de Valentinian Ier (375) à la mort de Stilicon (408)," *Revue des études byzantines*, 11 (1951) 5–46. On the magister militum see W. Ensslin, "Zum Heermeisteramt des spätrömischen Reiches," ii, iii, *Klio*, 24 (1931), pp. 102–46, 467–502; Alexander Demandt, "Magister militum," *R-E.*, Suppl. 12 (1970), cc. 572–73; and André Hoepffner, "Les 'Magistri militum praesentales' au IVe siècle," *Byzantion*, 11 (1936), pp. 483–98.

[99] Ammianus, xxxi, 6.4.

Thracians to forge his spears and swords, and Roman towns to contribute iron.[100] He boasted:

> Rome, whose territories I have laid waste year by year, has become my slave. She has supplied me with arms: her own metal has glowed in the furnaces, artfully molded and fashioned for her own undoing by reluctant smiths.[101]

Such bragging betrays a basic technological weakness in Gothic society. Weaponry was justly considered the most important product of the forge, and Alaric perhaps felt that Roman swords were better than those Gothic smiths could produce or that his own smiths could not turn them out in sufficient quantity for a lengthy campaign when many weapons would be lost or broken. As *magister militum per Illyricum* he controlled the rich mines of the area, yet he requisitioned iron from the cities.[102] The continued manufacture by local artisans under new masters accounts for the lack of a clear stylistic break in most areas. Alaric "compelled" the Roman smiths to forge for him, but they probably did so without much pressure. The facts are too striking to reject. The Goths had to employ Roman artisans in order to obtain the tools of conquest.[103]

When the Huns defeated the Ostrogoths, most of the Ostrogoths entered the Hunnic Empire. The average Goth found life difficult in the Hunnic federation, for the Huns requisitioned badly needed supplies.[104] Apart from forced requisitions and the occasional demand for military service, the routine of life continued. At several sites in the western Carpathian area, notably Botoşani-Cărămidărie, grave goods dating from the early fifth century appear Gothic — especially the fibulae, ear hangings, and belt buckles. Perhaps the survival of a Germanic cultural component of Ostrogothic origin,[105] the group was small and agrarian.

---

[100] Claudian, *B.G.* 537–9.

[101] *Ibid.*, 540–543. A comparative case is the use of Chinese artisans by the Hsiung-nu, Yü, *op. cit.*

[102] The mines of Noricum were praised by Rutilius Namatianus, 352, shortly after Alaric's sack of Rome. On the relative importance of smiths in early medieval society see Jacques Le Goff, "Travail, techniques et artisans dans les systèmes de valeur du haut moyen âge (V^e–Xe siècles)," *Settimane di Studio*, 18 (1971), pp. 239–66.

[103] In 376–78 the Goths had repeatedly armed themselves from fallen Romans, but this was because many arms had been seized when they crossed the Danube, T. Burns, *op. cit.*, p. 336.

[104] Priscus, frag. 39, ed. Dindorf, *Historici Graeci Minores*, p. 348, E. A. Thompson, *The History of Attila and the Huns*, p. 165. According to Priscus the plundering continued, and the Goths, who had no formal treaty with the Huns, pledged to escape the alliance. This passage of Priscus discusses the Ostrogothic revolt from Rome in 467 during which some sort of Gothic-Hunnic alliance was created.

[105] Emilia Zaharia, and N. Zaharia, "Contribuţii la cunvaşterea culturii materiale din secolul a V-lea e.n. din Moldava, în lumina săpăturilor de la Botoşari," *Arheologia Moldovei*, 6 (1969),

The site is little different from earlier ones east of the Dniester.

In spite of their daily hardships the yoke of bondage probably bore less heavily upon the Ostrogoths than upon others whose leaders (regnum diversarumque nationem ductores) trembled at a mere glance from Attila. Valamir their king, was a favorite.[106] In the early years of the federation the Hun king Balamber played one branch of the Amali against another, and after three campaigns the Ostrogoths acquiesced to membership in the Hun Empire with one Goth always holding the power over the tribe.[107] By favoring and backing the Amali kings the Huns strengthened the relative position of the Amali line, but did not destroy all resistance to the monarchy. Perhaps the Ostrogothic dukes and, in turn, the individual tribesmen realized that their pitiful lot would be even worse if their king fell from favor.

The Ostrogoths shared in the fortunes of the Hun Empire, but like the other allies they suffered more and received less than their overlords. Numerous Romans at the headquarters of Attila may have introduced some military and bureaucratic innovations. Roman advisors may have assisted Attila at Aquileia and Naissus where he manifested a better understanding of siege warfare than his predecessors.[108] Persumeably some Roman technology influenced the subject peoples, but in general they suffered. At the Battle of the Catalaunian Fields in 451, Hunnic allies lost heavily.[109]

While within the Hunnic federation and immediately thereafter the Ostrogoths continued to live in a Roman frontier context. Ostrogothic materials have been found at several Hungarian sites including Gáva,

pp. 167ff.; and Mircea Petrescu-Dîmbovita, "Die wichtigsten Ergebnisse der archäologischen Forschung über den Zeitraum vom 3.–10. Jh. östlich der Karpaten," *Dacoromania*, 1 (1973), pp. 162–73.

[106] *Getica*, 200. This is perhaps a case of political bias, but nevertheless the Ostrogoths were definitely a favored subject people.

[107] *Ibid.*, 249. The exact blood relationship between the various Ostrogothic princes has been subjected to a great deal of debate without any positive conclusions, see C. C. Mierow, *The Gothic History of Jordanes in English Version* (2nd ed., Princeton 1915, reprint Cambridge, New York, 1960), commentary to 248, p. 179.

[108] Romans such as Constantius served Attila freely, Priscus, frag. 8. For the siege or Aquileia see Jordanes, *Getica*, 219–21. At Naissus in 441 Attila broke through the circuit wall with battering rams and used towers and ladders to scale the remaining wall; Priscus, frag. 1b, ed. Dindorf, pp. 278–79.

[109] Although Hydatius' figure 300,000 dead (*MGH.AA*, 11, p. 26) at the battle cannot be accepted, the losses of each participant must have been large. The battle was certainly a watershed in Burgundian history. *Lex Burgundionum*, 17.1. Omnes omnino causae, quae inter Burgundiones habitae sunt et non sunt finitae usque ad pugnam Mauriacensum, habeantur abolitae. L. R. de Salis, ed. *MGH. Legum*, Sectio I,2 pars 1 (Hannover, 1892).

Kosino, Tiszalök, Gyulavári, and Kiskunfiligyhaza.[110] J. Werner tentatively dates the finds between 450 and 489, or shortly before Theodoric's march into Italy. At Kosino, Domolospuszta on the Drava, and elsewhere examples abound of fibulae and buckles in the late chip-carved style. Those at Domolospuszta cannot be dated earlier than 443 because of the presence of a solidus of Theodosius II. Roman or southern influences are also clear in the ornamental motifs and the use of nails in construction.[111] As J. Werner points out, many objects — particularly works in gold represent the stylistic antecedents of craft arts that developed in Italy in the early sixth century.[112] The Ostrogoths clung to the grasshopper motif particularly long. The style developed in the late fourth century and flourished in many forms under Theodoric.[113]

The first half of the fifth century was the period in which an "Ostrogothic style" developed out of the general Gothic motifs present in the artifacts of Sintana-de-Mures culture of western Rumania as well as several grave fields of the Gothic-Chernaiknov civilization of south Russia.[114] The intricate spiraled-tendril and braided patterns, which characterized sixth-century Ostrogothic fibulae, had not yet carried the field. An Ostrogothic style lay scarcely submerged in the frontier society so enamored of chip-carving, but the artifacts remained principally frontier and only secondarily Ostrogothic. A full Ostrogothic style, to the extent it ever existed, emerged along with operable tribal political and military structures under Theodoric. The chip-carved style was still visible in Ostrogothic materials until the end of the century but its popularity ebbed rapidly.[115] There is no point in inquiring into the

---

[110] J. Werner "Studien zu Grabfunden des V. Jahrhunderts aus der Slowakei und der Karpatenukraine," *Slovenská Archeologia*, 7 (1959), pp. 422–38.

[111] János Dombay, "Der gotische Grabfund von Domolospuszta. Der Fundort und die Umstände des Fundes," *Janus Pannonius Muzeum Evkonyne*, 1 (1956), pp. 126–28.

[112] In addition to Werner's article cited above see his introduction to M. Degani, *Il tesoro romano-barbarico di Reggio Emilia* (Firenze, 1959).

[113] Zdenko Vinskí, "Zikadenschmuck aus Jugoslawien," *Jahrbuch des Römisch-Germanischen Zentralmuseums Mainz*, 4 (1957), p. 157, and M. Degani, *op. cit.*, pp. 8–12. A new book by Volker Bierbrauer, *Die ostgotischen Grab- und Schatzfunde in Italien* (Spoleto, 1975) is a consumate study of Ostrogothic archaeology in Italy. His relative and absolute chronologies (pp. 108–113) essentially agree with those presented in this monograph and derived independently.

[114] See the excellent development by V. Bierbrauer, "Zu den Vorkommen ostrogotischer Bügelfibeln in Raetia II," *Bayerische Vorgeschichtsblätter*, 36 (1971), pp. 134–47.

[115] For examples of the late Gothic chip-carved fibuale see Herbert Kühn, *Die germanischen Bügelfibeln der Völkerwanderungszeit in der Rheinprovinz*, part 1 (Bonn, 1940, reprint Graz, 1965), pp. 101–6.

subtribal levels as seen in the archaeological record available, for the evidence is insufficient to support even crude speculation.

The strengthening of Ostrogothic kingship, attested in the literary record, was the most prominent result of the Ostrogothic captivity. When Thiudmir and his son Theodoric acted in the Balkans, they acted as powerful kings whose authority was noticeably more influential over their tribe than Fritigern's or Athanaric's had been in the fourth century.

CHAPTER THREE

THE OSTROGOTHS FIND A HOME

During the half century ca. 450–93 that the Ostrogoths searched for a home, their social structure continued the transformation to powerful tribal kingship. Theodoric, the son of Thiudmir, and later king of Italy, gradually brought more and more Gothic subtribal groups into his following. After a series of victories over the Byzantines and the rival Triarius line, Theodoric Thiudmir reached a new level of kingship under which the power of most of the nobility was held in check. When the Ostrogoths arrived in Italy in 489–90, the settlement territorialized noble power. As long as Theodoric lived he held local powers in check, but with his death the nobility reasserted its dominance.

The fifth century was a period of great anxiety and change in the western Empire. This was especially true for the last half of the century when the *limes* system of the previous era collapsed or fell into almost total neglect. The fifth-century Ostrogoths encountered a far different Empire when they settled in Pannonia than had the bands under Alatheus and Saphrax in 376. In the late fourth century the Roman army was basically well organized and well led, and even the *limitanei* functioned moderately well when handed the impossible task of supervising the Gothic crossing of the Danube. Although the strategic expertise of Valens must be severely questioned, the troops under his command fought hard and died honorably at Adrianople. No contemporary authority, not even the old soldier Ammianus Marcellinus, rebuked the Roman army for cowardice.

By 460 profound changes had transformed Romania along the entire length of the Danube. The first decisive change was signaled by Theodosius' decision to strip the fortifications in the Julian Alps in his effort to raise an army to fight the usurper Eugenius.[1] When Alaric passed

---

[1] Paulus Orosius, *Historiarum adversum paganos libri vii*, 35.3–4, ed. C. Zangemeister, *Corpus Scriptorum Ecclesiasticorum Latinorum*, 5 (Wien, 1882), pointed out in J. Šašel, *Claustra Alpium Iuliarum* (Ljubljana, 1971), p. 36. Šašel has collected the ancient sources and some of the archaeological data in this volume; however, the use of the material is largely left to the reader, especially concerning the abandonment of the defenses. On the battle against Eugenius see P. Hitzinger, "Der Kampf des Kaisers Theodosius gegen den Tyrannen Eugenius

through the area in 401 on his march to Italy, the Alpine defenses were very weak.[2] The Romans had built an elaborate crescent of walls and fortifications in the Julian Alps, which Diocletian stoutly garrisoned with legionary troops.[3] The strategic potential of the area was obvious since it commanded the easiest penetration route into Italy from the Balkans and the interior of the Germanic world. The Hungarian Plain acted as a funnel for southward migration to the Julian Alps and Italy well into the Middle Ages.[4] After Alaric the political and military situation in the Julian Alps, Noricum, Raetia, and the entire middle Danube was unstable at best.

The picture is confused, and only further archaeological research will draw it together. In the present state of research it seems that after Theodosius' withdrawal the Julian Alps corridor was periodically garrisoned but never again became a total fortification system. Aetius apparently garrisoned some areas in the crisis with Attila.[5] Some strongholds were never reoccupied after Theodosius while others were occupied by garrisons or outpost settlements of barbarians at least until the Avar incursions of the seventh century. For example, at Grandišče near Dolenji Lagatec approximately 250 coins have been found dating from the second half of the third century until the end of the fourth, whereas at Studeno the last datable find is a coin of Anastasius (491–518 A.D.), and at Ajdovscina (a castrum) the evidence points to an end of settlement in the seventh century.[6] The stone fixtures of the system remained and were used by the Ostrogoths and the Lombards in their attempts to prevent further Germanic penetration of Italy. However, between the Roman involvement and the restructuring of the

---

am Flusse Frigidus", *Mittheilungen des historischen Vereins für Krain*, 10 (1855), p. 81 ff., and O. Seeck and G. Veith, "Die Schlacht am Frigidus", *Klio*, 13 (1913), p. 451–467. For a discussion see my "The Alpine Frontiers and Early Medieval Italy to the Middle of the Seventh Century", in: The Frontier. Comparative Studies, Vol. 2 (Norman, Oklahoma, 1979), pp. 51–58.

[2] Claudian, *de Bello Gotico*, 562; Šašel, *op. cit.*, p. 41. Probably some forces were soon sent back into the area, Zosimus, v, 46.

[3] Šašel, *op. cit.*, p. 35. The legions are listed in the *Notitia Dignitatum*, occ., xxiv (ed. O. Seeck, 1876). That the *comes Italiae* originated under Diocletian see also E. Nischer, "The Army Reforms of Diocletian and Constantine and their Modifications up to the time of the Notitia Dignitatum", *JRS*, 13 (1923), pp. 1–55, especially p. 7.

[4] On the continuing importance of the Hungarian Plain see A. N. J. den Hollander, "The Great Hungarian Plain. A European Frontier Area", *Comparative Studies in Society and History*, 3 (1960), pp. 74–88, particularly 76–78 on the Magyars.

[5] Prosper Tiro, *Epitoma Chronicon, MGH.AA*, 9 (*Chronica Minora*, 1) 1367 (year 452); Šašel, *op. cit.*, p. 41.

[6] Šašel, *op. cit.*, pp. 90–91, 97, 99.

defenses by Theodoric and later the Lombards almost a century of local military and economic self-reliance intervened.

The abandoned garrison personnel had several alternatives. They could become brigands, as did a certain Coroticus and his men in western Britain.[7] They might remain as local garrisons, defending their homes and looking in vain to Rome for pay,[8] or they could join the following of a Germanic chief.[9] Finally, they might attempt to preserve their own customs and lands by serving their Germanic overlords along the frontier just as their ancestors had served the emperors.[10] Gradually the military structure, created over centuries, fell into disrepair as whole communities were abandoned. In Noricum the Rugian king Feletheus shifted whole populations to new locations in an attempt to maintain a taxable and manageable urban structure.[11] By redistributing the population he hoped to increase the tribute received from the towns along the river. Some towns were raided repeatedly by other Germans not under his control, and each raid decreased the amount of tribute the town could pay — tribute usually paid in grain, a commodity in short supply among the Rugians. Further south on the middle Danube Justinian had to rebuild forts, towns, and watch towers destroyed by Attila, the Ostrogoths, the Rugians, and various small tribes.[12] The towns of the interior suffered a fate similar to the river settlements. Gradually fortified villae in the interior, such as Fenekpuszta, became focal points for the romanized elements of the population to mix with the Germanic. In some cases the walled villae became islands for the survival of the ancient estate culture.[13] The Ostrogoths entered Pannonia seeking land and "peace" but discovered chaos and

[7] Saint Patrick's *Epistle to the Soldiers of Coroticus*, 2, 12, 19. Saint Patrick, *Confession et lettre à Coroticus*, 2ième rédaction, introduction, texte critique, traduction et notes, Richard P. C. Hanson, (Sources Chrétiennes, 249, Paris, 1978), pp. 136, 145, 151.

[8] Eugippius, *Vita Severini*, ed. T. Mommsen, *MGH, Scriptores rerum Germanicarum in usum scholarum* (Berlin, 1898), 20.1–2; the garrison at Batavis sent representatives to Augsburg for pay, but they were slain by brigands. Their bodies were found floating in the Inn River.

[9] Suggested by H. Zeiss, "Die Donaugermanen und ihr Verhältnis zur römischen Kultur nach der Vita Severini", *Ostbayerische Grenzmarken*, 17 (1928), pp. 9–13. *Vita Severini*, 44.2, in which a certain Avitianus appears in the following of the Rugian king.

[10] Some of the Rhine garrisons went over to the Franks and, according to Procopius, *B.G.*, VI, xii, 16–19, maintained their military traditions.

[11] *Vita Severini*, 31.1–6.

[12] Procopius, *de Aedif.*, IV, v–vi; V, v, 7–8; IV, iv, 32–34.

[13] B. Thomas, *Römische Villen in Pannonien* (Budapest, 1964), pp. 389–92, and András Mócsy, *Pannonia and Upper Moesia* (London, 1974), pp. 303–7, 353. In general see John Percival, *The Roman Villa. A Historical Introduction* (Berkeley, 1976).

uncertainty. Instead of stability they brought added unrest and new suffering.

In the confusion after the death of Attila, the Gepids, Ostrogoths, and others defeated his quarrelling sons in the battle of Nedao in 454 and broke free from Hun subjugation. The Ostrogoths under king Valamir and his brothers Thiudmir and Vidimer received "permission" to settle in Pannonia from the emperor Marcian.[14] Marcian had several choices, but none of them were foolproof solutions to the chaos about to engulf his northern and northeastern frontiers. If he wanted to maintain overland communication between Italy and the East, the strategic routes along the Drava and Sava had to be in friendly hands. Of course, he could have garrisoned the Julian *claustrae* as Aetius had against Attila, but Marcian made no such attempt. He surely realized that any military move would have to be a major undertaking to achieve lasting results. A full-scale expedition was out of the question, so in reality long-term solutions hinged upon alliances with strong Germanic groups. Two options were available – the Gepids or the Ostrogoths. If our portrayal of Marcian as a shrewd calculator is correct, he chose the Ostrogoths deliberately. The Gepids were contesting the transdanubian Hunnic lands with remnants of the Huns and other recently freed peoples. The Ostrogoths, on the other hand, sought admission into the Empire through their king whose position the Hunnic captivity had strengthened. Royal leadership could guarantee an alliance thereby making Marcian's decision much easier.[15]

The apparent cessation of Ostrogothic archaeological materials in Hungary by the third quarter of the fifth century suggests that almost all sizable groups of Ostrogoths fled soon after the dissolution of the Hun Empire. Those following Valamir and his brothers settled in Pannonia, an area already rent by invasion and previous settlement. Even if Marcian granted specific settlement areas, there was little hope of a peaceful Gothic penetration. From the beginning other Germanic groups opposed Gothic expansion and solidification, but opposition usually brought retaliation by restless Gothic bands raiding northward as far as Noricum. The Rugians were especially vulnerable to Gothic encroachment and quickly became deferential towards Goths.[16] Recent

---

[14] Jordanes, *Getica*, 264–65.

[15] Jordanes, *loc. cit.*; Friedrich Lotter, "Zur Rolle der Donausueben in der Völkerwanderungszeit", *Mitteilungen des Instituts für Österreichische Geschichtsforschung*, 76 (1968), pp. 286–89 and his *Severinus von Noricum, Legende und historische Wirklichkeit* (Stuttgart, 1976).

[16] Lotter, *op. cit.*, pp. 283–88.

attempts to fix particular settlement areas for Valamir and his brothers are highly conjectural but worthy of note: Thiudmir possibly consolidated his position in the north between the Danube and Lacus Pelso. Further south was Vidimer, and finally, the lands of Valamir himself.[17]

Not all the Ostrogoths migrating from the Hungarian plain did so under Amali leadership. Others under Theodoric, the son of Triarius and a member of a rival line to the Amali, entered the Empire as federates. As such they had a more favorable relationship with Constantinople than the Amali.[18] Friction occasionally led to open warfare between rival Gothic factions.

By the mid-fifth century various Germanic groups had peopled the entire Balkan area. Many Goths having entered the Empire in 376 and settled in Moesia, Illyria, and other provinces, had not followed Alaric westward. A large number were permanently settled in Moesia, where they continued their simple agrarian life based on herding and limited agriculture.[19] Some Ostrogoths following Alatheus and Saphrax may have permanently settled in Pannonia after the victory at Adrianople.[20] To these were now added the Ostrogoths of Valamir and Theodoric Triarius, Gepids, Sarmatians, Sciri, and Rugians. The new arrivals were essentially herdsmen. Cattle-rustling was rampant between communities.[21] Life was precarious for those towns still linked to the Roman Empire. Although St. Severinus spent most of his life in Noricum, his *Vita* reflects the general state of affairs for the area from Thrace west along the frontier zone. Noricum was perhaps unique in the number of small tribal units in the vicinity, but the Gothic raids into Noricum from the south indicate that elsewhere conditions were no better. The great variation in pottery and jewelry styles for the upper and middle Danubian area confirms the amorphous ethnic and political situation revealed in the *Vita*.

According to the *Vita* both Roman and German lived in small communities, although the Roman garrison towns along the Danube were more elaborate. The Rugians, the most powerful tribe in Noricum, had a permanent market place in at least one of their villages north of

[17] Miroslava Mirković, "Die Ostgoten in Pannonien nach dem Jahre 455", *Recueil de travaux de la faculté de philosophie,* 10.1 (Beograd, 1968), pp. 119–28.

[18] *Getica,* 270; Malchus Philadelphensis, frag. 11, C. Müller, *Fragmenta Historicorum Graecorum,* 4 (Paris, 1885), pp. 119–20.

[19] *Ibid.,* 267.

[20] *Ibid.,* 140; Zosimus, iv, 34.2; *C.I.L.* v, 1623, dated A.D. 413, O. Fiebiger, *Denkschriften der kaiserlichen Akademie der Wissenschaften in Wien. philosophisch-historische Klasse,* 70, Abh. 3 (1939), no. 34.

[21] *Getica,* 273–76; Procopius, *B.V.,* III, ii, 39.

the Danube where slaves and other commodities were ransomed or sold.[22] Goldsmiths occupied a high position in Rugian society and at least once acted as the self-appointed spokesmen for the tribe against the royal family.[23] Cattle and slaves were important items in the economy. Some captives were sold into slavery throughout the tribe, but others were quickly ransomed.[24] Some of the ransom, if paid in coin, may have been used to purchase food, for the Rugians were unable to produce sufficient grain and depended upon grain barges sent down the Inn from Raetia to the inhabitants of the river towns. The communities still carried on a limited agriculture within sight of the city walls.[25] The barbarians exacted tribute from Roman towns long ago thrown back on dwindling resources. Any foodstuffs surrendered to German hands were greatly welcomed by people not self-sufficient. Supplying the Roman towns with imports was hazardous. Oil was at a premium. But regardless of the restrictions, trade was still sought and conducted by Roman and Rugian alike.[26]

Urban settlements such as Comagenis, Cucullis, Quintanis, Tiburnia, and Batavis were the last survivals of a once elaborate Roman military, communication, and economic network. Should the term Roman even be used to label these communities? Eugippius and his exemplar Severinus drew a distinction between Arian-barbarian and Orthodox-Roman, but the superstitions surrounding illness, relics, and natural phenomena such as earthquakes influenced all. The barbarians respected the holy man Severinus no less than the townsmen. Except in the field of grain production, the economy of the Roman towns hardly appears superior to that of the Rugians. At Batavis the garrison lacked arms and hoped to collect some from the enemy.[27] Each community was forced to fend for itself. Local garrison commanders were inept and incapable of united action. Towns vied with each other in inviting the saintly protector to their community.[28] Romanism was a mental image that had lost a tangible quality, but a sense of being "Roman" did

---

[22] *Vita Severini*, 6.5, 9.1, and for a possible reference to similar Ostrogothic communities, 5.4.

[23] *Ibid.*, 8.3.

[24] *Ibid.*, 4.1, 19.5, 30.4.

[25] *Ibid.*, 3.3, 12.4, 22.4, 31.1.

[26] *Ibid.*, 22.2, 28.2.

[27] *Ibid.*, 4.2. The barbarians may have also "collected" rather than created their own weapons, but at Adrianople the collectors had been exclusively Gothic. Examples of Romans arming themselves from the Persian dead in the third century do not reflect technological shortcomings but battlefield necessity.

[28] *Ibid.*, 11.1.

remain in some of the towns. The townsmen were Romans because
they felt a vague attachment to the Empire. Sometimes this took the
form of sending a mission to Rome for garrison pay, but usually it was
associated with religion. Surely the grain traffic was an insufficient
material link to the Empire to inspire the citizens of Batavis to offer
such a tenacious defense of their homes. More often than not battles
between German and townsman were matters of self-preservation for
family and friends. Local well-being and communal pride worked to
preserve attachments to the Empire, although not even religion could
define in other than abstract dogmatic terms, the differences between
Roman and German.

When the Ostrogoths settled in Pannonia they added another dis-
rupting factor to the already complex life along the upper and middle
Danube as described in the *Vita*. Between 472 and 481 the Ostrogoths
under Theodoric loosely settled Illyria. Centered at Epidamnus, their
raiding parties struck north into Rugian territory and carried off captives and plunder. The unfortunate captives were taken back to the
Gothic settlements and undoubtedly sold as slaves.[29] The Goths tipped
what little balance of power existed in the area. Small raids of Germanic people, Rugians, Goths and others forced the towns along the
river to reach an accomodation with the local overlords, usually the
Rugian king Flaccitheus, to whom entire communities placed themselves in dependence. Eventually almost all the once autonomous towns
ceased to exist.[30] Walls were sometimes deliberately destroyed by the
barbarians, but in many places the walls simply crumbled. The process
was not complete when Eugippius wrote the *Vita Severini*, yet the signs
were obvious. Odovacar's supposed transporting of all Romans to Italy
from this exposed frontier must have applied only to the still independent aristocracy. It is very unlikely that the townsmen, dispersed among
the Germans or having surrendered the autonomy of their towns for
dependence and protection, could have left Noricum even after Odovacar's military successes in the area.[31]
left Noricum even after Odovacar's military successes in the area.[31]

The period after the initial settlement near Sirmium (455–465) was
characterized by local cattle raids, but soon the imperial penchant for

---

[29] Zeno offered Theodoric Pautalia, a province in Illyria, but he decided to settle further
west near Epidamnus, Malchus, frag. 18, Müller, pp. 125–30. For the Gothic raids see, *Vita
Severini*, 5.1, 5.4, 17.4. Even earlier the Goths and Rugians had raided each other's territory,
Getica, 277.

[30] *Vita Severini*, 24.1, 25.3, 27.1, 42.1.

[31] *Ibid.*, 42.4–5.

the Triarius line rather than the Amali ignited a bitter series of wars between Gothic factions. The Romans typically played one side against the other. Perhaps the most important result of the early phases of the struggle was that Theodoric, the son of Thiudmir and later king of Italy, was sent as a hostage to Constantinople at the age of seven.[32] Theodoric remained at the imperial court until he was eighteen.[33] During those years his father succeeded his uncle as king and waged a series of successful campaigns against the Rugians, Gepids, Sarmatians, and Sciri. That much is fact, but what happened to Theodoric? According to Ennodius he was impressed by the splendor and refinements of the court but was repelled by the tyranny.[34] He remained illiterate until death.[35] Although tyranny may have offended his Germanic sense of *libertas*, the systematic efficiency of the court must have deeply impressed the youth, who was to reveal great administrative talents years later in Italy.

When Theodoric returned to his father, he gathered a large personal following and crossed the Danube to wage war on the Sarmatians. He took the booty of slaves and other objects of value back to his father and proceeded to take the city of Singidunum from the Sarmatians. But rather than returning the prize to Roman jurisdiction he kept it for himself.[36] Any Germanic prince could have taken these actions, but perhaps Theodoric had learned the true weakness of the Empire, and hence he began to carve absolute spheres in the Balkans without even a semblance of deference to Rome. A man with such perspicacity was very dangerous to the Eastern Empire.

When the young Theodoric assembled a following to raid the Sarmatians, he began the slow process of increasing his power by recruiting other groups into his band. His father aided by giving Theodoric several of his personal attendants. Theodoric united his father's men with his own friends and retainers. According to Jordanes, the total was nearly 6000 men:

---

[32] *Getica*, 271; Ennodius, *Panegyricus Dictus Clementissimo Regi Theoderico ab Ennodio Dei Famulo*, iii, ed. Vogel, *MGH.AA*, 7 (Berlin, 1885, reprint 1961), p. 204.

[33] *Getica*, 282.

[34] Ennodius, *Pan.*, iii.

[35] Anonymous Valesianus, in J. C. Rolfe (Loeb edition, Cambridge, Mass., 1964 revision), 61, 79, (Theodoric used a stencil to sign edicts). He may well have participated in some of the general aspects of *iuvenes* education which included sports, horsemanship, the social graces, as well as literary, religious and legal training. On the *iuvenes* see S. L. Mohler, "The Iuvenes and Roman Education", *Transactions of the American Philological Association*, 68 (1937), pp. 442–79.

[36] *Getica*, 282.

ascites certis ex satellitibus patris et ex populo amatores sibi clientesque, paene sex milia viros, cum quibus inconscio patre emenso Danubio super Babai Sarmatarum rege discurrrit, . . .[37]

If we discount the figure 6000 (*paene* in Jordanes often indicates conjecture), the process seems a reasonable method for creating a new band: the father transfers some of his most trusted followers and the son adds these to his personal following thereby increasing the prestige of his band as well as its strength. The sources reveal two later instances in which Theodoric's following increased still further. In 471 the dying Thiudmir designated Theodoric king in the presence of the assembled Goths.[38] Finally, after the death of Odovacar in 493, the Goths again declared Theodoric king.[39] In each of the last two cases Theodoric may have been the subject of a special ceremony. But what probably was more important was the addition of first Thiudmir's followers and then the uniting of those who had crossed into Italy with the followers of Odovacar.[40]

The Byzantines now rightly regarded the Ostrogoths as a threat to the security of the entire Balkan area. Thiudmir led his people eastward soon after his son returned from the Sarmatian enterprise. The tribe suffered from a lack of foodstuffs.[41] Vidimer led his followers west into Italy and eventually joined the Visigoths in Gaul.[42] Just prior to Thiudmir's death his people received new lands in Macedonia and Thrace not far from Thessalonika.[43] The area had escaped heavy plundering and could support the new immigrants. Each settlement area was perhaps ruled by a *comes* such as Astat and Invilia, vigorous commanders in the expedition. The land around Pella was flat and suitable for agriculture. Unfortunately the Goths under Theodoric

---

[37] *Getica*, 282; Reinhard Wenskus, *Stammesbildung und Verfassung* (Köln, Graz, 1961), pp. 482–85.

[38] *Getica*, 288.

[39] Anonymous Valesianus, 57. There are many problems associated with this passage. Theodoric had been king for 22 years in 493; however, there probably was a special ceremony after the defeat of Odovacar.

[40] Odovacar's lieutenant Tufa and his men were readily accepted by Theodoric in the preceding year, Anonymous Valesianus, 51–52.

[41] *Ibid.*, 283.

[42] *Ibid.*, 284–87.

[43] *Ibid.*, 286–88; Nicholas G. L. Hammond, *A History of Macedonia*, vol. 1 (Oxford, 1972), pp. 108–9, has located this gift of land made by the patrician Hilarianus. Cerru = Cyrrus, Pellas = Pella, Europa = Europus (northeast of Pella), Mediana = Methone, Petina = Pydna, Bereu = Beroea, Sium = Dium. Hammond does not believe that Theodoric reached Thessaly.

Triarius already lived in Thrace as *foederati*.[44] Friction between the rival leaderships quickly led to open hostilities. The events of the next decade are illustrative of the actual power each leader possessed and emphasize some of the obligations accompaning that power.

The relative tribal position of the two Theodorics at this time remains confused because there are two separate traditions in our sources: the Amali-Ostrogothic tradition of Ennodius and Jordanes and the Byzantine tradition represented by Malchus, Joannes Antiochenus, Marcellinus Comes, Evagrius, and the Anonymous Valesianus. The Anonymous Valesianus covered the period 474—526 esssentially from a Catholic-exarchate point of view and was probably written near Ravenna ca. 540—550.[45] The Byzantine tradition referred to Theodoric Thiudmir as *dux Gothorum* or failed to give him a title at all.[46] On the other hand, Theodoric Triarius was called *rex Gothorum, archon,* or *autokrator*, until his death in 481.[47] According to the Anonymous, Theodoric Thiudmir was made king only after the death of Odovacar in 493 at Ravenna.[48] In the Amali tradition Theodoric became king immediately after Thiudmir's death in Thrace; the son of Triarius was merely a titleless Gothic leader favored by Constantinople.[49]

Each of the two Gothic leaders had his own personal following, but Theodoric Thiudmir had a claim to the kingship as a birthright, whereas Theodoric Triarius was a Byzantine creation. The latter was a king needing the support of the Emperor; the former a king whose personal reputation as a soldier was built at the Emperor's expense. After nearly

[44] Malchus, frag. 11, Müller, pp. 119—20. The Goths already settled in Thrace were φοιδέρατοι.

[45] L. M. Hartmann, "Anonymus Valesianus", *R—E*, I,2 (1894), cc. 2333—34, stated that the author had access to the so-called *Ravenna Fastes* and the *V i t a   S e v e r i n i*, and that the date of composition should be shortly after the fall of the Ostrogothic kingdom. However, I would prefer to date this ca. 540—50, when the bitterness of war heightened the importance of Theodoric's late anti-Catholic policy. Ravenna was never reoccupied by the Ostrogoths after Wittiges was sent back to Constantinople as a captive. The Anonymous was much more Byzantine in outlook than has been so far recognized by historians.

[46] Anonymus Valesianus, 42, Theodoricus dux Gothorum, filius Walamerici. Valamir was actually his uncle but this mistake was common, see Malchus, frag. 15. Joannes Antiochenus was correct when he pointed out that Thiudmir was Theodoric's father, Joannes Antiochenus, frag. 206 (2). The fragments of Joannes Antiochenus are found in Müller, *op. cit.*, iv, pp. 612—21, and v, pp. 27—28.

[47] Marcellinus Comes, 481, *MGH.AA*, 11 (*Chronica Minora*, 2), Theodoricus Triari filius rex Gothorum. For his death see Joannes Antiochenus, frag. 211.5.

[48] Anonymus, 57, also Evagrius, *Historia Ecclesiastica*, ed. J. Bidez and L. Parmentier (London, 1898), iii, 27.

[49] *Getica*, 288, 270.

a century of Hunnic support and domination the Amali line was clearly royal blood. The Anonymous conceded that this made a difference.

Vir enim bellicosissimus, fortis, cuius pater Walamir dictus rex Gothorum, naturalis tamen eius fuit. . .[50]

Theodoric Triarius and his war bands were quite disruptive early in the reign of Leo (457–74). Apparently Theodoric Triarius and a large following had broken out of the Hunnic Federation early, perhaps prior to Nedao, and had entered Thrace and Macedonia as raiders but were settled there as *foederati* by Leo. In a treaty Leo promised an annual tribute of 2000 pounds of gold to the Goths and that Theodoric would be their *magister militum praesentalis* and *autokrator*.[51] The new federates were settled in Thrace. Like Aspar before him, Theodoric Triarius sought to secure a place in his own nation through personal and military positions in the Empire.

Leo knew the Balkan situation first-hand, for he had served as a military tribune in Dacia and commanded the garrison of Selymbria on the southern coast of Thrace. He owed his proclamation as emperor in 457 in part to Aspar, whose inheritance Theodoric Triarius and his followers claimed from Leo.[52] Leo understood the pending crisis in the Balkans and decided to stabilize the situation by the creation of a new *foederati* system in Thrace as a buffer to Illyria, which he knew was effectively lost to the Empire. His plan required the effective control of both Ostrogothic groups — an impossible task. Ostrogothic federates, settled in Thrace by Leo, were happy with their leader Theodoric Triarius and took offense at the Byzantine overtures made later to Theodoric Thiudmir.[53]

For thirty years the Goths under the Amali were on the move in the Balkans. They came into the area later and settled (or were settled) in Pannonia but were not regarded as trustworthy until it became necessary to counter the power of the Gothic federates in Thrace. Thiudmir led his people south from the Sava to Macedonia settling them in and around several small communities near Pella. Along the way they took the city of Naissus, and Stobi opened its gates.[54] The literary sources

[50] Anonymus, 58.
[51] Malchus, frag. 2, Müller, pp. 113–4.
[52] Candidus, frag. 1, found in Photius, *Bibliotheka*, Codex 79, ed. L. Dindorf (Leipzig, 1870), and Malchus, frag. 2; see also Georg Ostrogorsky, *Geschichte des Byzantinischen Staates*, 3d. ed. (Handbuch der Altertumswissenschaft, Abt. 12, pt. 1, Bd. 2, München, 1963), pp. 51–53.
[53] Malchus, frag. 11, Müller, pp. 119–20.
[54] *Getica*, 285–88; James Wiseman, *Stobi* (Beograd, 1973), p. 18.

make sense if some Goths remained behind when the main body followed the king to a new settlement. The king still had a vague obligation to those remaining at the old sites.[55]

Shortly after the Goths settled around Pella, Theodoric was declared king and soon formed an alliance with the new Emperor, Zeno. Theodoric Triarius concurrently increased his power in Thrace and Macedonia — perhaps at the expense of both Zeno and Theodoric Thiudmir. In fulfillment of the new alliance, Theodoric Thiudmir encamped with some of his men near Marcianopolis. However, the majority of his followers remained near Pella, where some may have joined Theodoric Triarius' camp.[56] Since the alliance did not weaken Triarius, Zeno had the choice — wage war against him or abandon the federate system in Thrace. When war proved unavoidable, Theodoric Triarius assembled his peoples ($\check{\epsilon}\vartheta\nu\eta$) for the campaign. Once the step was taken he had either to feed them or lead them into battle.[57]

At this juncture Zeno clearly overplayed his hand and asked Theodoric Triarius to renounce the leadership of the Goths and send his son as hostage to Constantinople. In a show of generosity Zeno would allow him to keep his personal lands.[58] Although Theodoric Triarius lacked royal blood, he had cemented a strong following in over twenty years of providing successfully for the needs of his people. Zeno planned a combined attack on Theodoric Triarius by the *magister militum* of Thrace and Theodoric Thiudmir, who was to march south from Marcianopolis to meet the *magister* and 2000 cavalry in the Haemus range. Together they would then continue to Adrianople, where they would join the garrisons of the various Thracian cities numbering 20,000 foot and 6000 horse.[59] But Zeno overestimated the loyalty of his garrison troops. When the rival Theodorics met near Sondis in Thrace, Thiudmir was alone. Theodoric Triarius occupied the high ground. Initial skirmishes merely exchanged supplies, cattle, horses, and collected booty.

---

[55] *Getica*, 290. In 488 Theodoric responded to the discontent of his tribe living in Illyricum by starting west for Italy. Jordanes used Illyricum very loosely so that his passage cannot be used to point out the location of the Goths; however, other sources make it clear that they were concentrated in Dacia and Moesia inferior near Novae.

[56] The general nature of Gothic-Roman alliance in the ensuing years was for the Empire to grant land and supplies (or money for purchasing supplies) in return for the services of a stipulated number of warriors under the king. This same structure was probably true of the alliance between Zeno and Theodoric Thiudmir in 474—5.

[57] Malchus, frag. 14.

[58] *Ibid.*

[59] Malchus, frag. 15, Müller, pp. 121—3.

Then Triarius offered an alliance against the Romans, whom he saw playing Goth against Goth. He upbraided Theodoric Thiudmir.

> Why do you destroy my kin, you villain? Why have you widowed so many women? Where are their husbands? How has the wealth, which everyone had when they set out with you from home on this campaign, been wasted? Each of them had a pair or three horses, but now they advance horseless and on foot, following you through Thrace like slaves, though they are free men of no mean race. Since coming, have they shared a single medimus of gold? [60]

Theodoric Thiudmir's followers demanded compliance, or they would follow Triarius. The people had their way, and the leaders agreed to depart in peace. The tribe had, in effect, stated the limits of kingship. Like the followers of Triarius, Theodoric's people would accept his leadership and bear hardships only if he sought land, food, horses, and security. These goals were unobtainable in their eyes if Goth continued to fight Goth.

Sobered by the confrontation, Theodoric Thiudmir demanded new land to settle and grain sufficient to maintain his people until the first harvest. Wanting the grant to be legal and permanent, he asked Zeno to send officials to record the settlements.[61] Instead of granting the request, Zeno made preparations for war and eventually brought Triarius back to an alliance with the Empire by offering him Theodoric Thiudmir's command. In return Triarius agreed to lead a force of 13,000 men, paid and supplied by the Emperor, against his rival.[62]

The Goths under Theodoric Thiudmir retreated westward, plundering Thrace as they went. They sacked and burned Stobi.[63] At Thessalonika the inhabitants rebelled. The defense of the city was placed in the hands of the archbishop. Although an agreement was reached with Theodoric, he could not prevent foraging for food. Many of the Goths settled near Pella and Beroea probably joined Theodoric as he marched west towards Epirus Nova. At Heraclea he obtained some supplies from the archbishop, and consequently could control plundering.[64] At last Zeno offered land — Pautalia, a province in nearby Illyricum. In addition, he promised that "since you have no time to sow

---

[60] *Ibid.*, trans. C. D. Gordon, *The Age of Attila* (Ann Arbor, Mich., 1966), pp. 165–66.

[61] Malchus, frag. 16, Müller, pp. 123–4.

[62] *Ibid.*, frag. 15, Müller, p. 121–123.

[63] *Ibid.*, frag. 18, Müller, p. 125. Stobi was on an important cross roads linking the Danube and the Via Ignatia to the south. Its walls were apparently destroyed at this time, but they were rebuilt and the city continued to grow, flowering during the reign of Justinian. E. Kitzinger, "A Survey of the Early Christian Town of Stobi", *Dumbarton Oaks Papers*, 3 (1946), pp. 81–182.

[64] Malchus, frag. 18, Müller, p. 125.

and have no hope of obtaining natural products in Pautalia," he would issue 200 pounds of gold to the prefect of the province to buy necessities.[65] Theodoric refused knowing that better land lay farther west along the coast.

West of Heraclea the Via Egnatia snaked from river valley to river valley, often passing over precipitous mountain passes. Byzantine garrisons in the passes threatened to slow or stop the hungry Goths, but only the town of Lychnidus held out when Gothic troops appeared. The inhabitants of other towns like Scampa ran at the first sight of the Ostrogoths and sought refuge in mountain strongholds.[66] Theodoric sent a certain barbarian Sidimundus, a former resident of Epidamnus, to convince the inhabitants there to flee and thus leave their city open for the Ostrogoths who "wished to stop wandering and settle in a walled city." Obviously they did not seek domination as overlords but rather land, food, and security. As Zeno perceived when he offered land and supplies until the harvest could be reaped, these men were driven by hunger and sought to return permanently to an agrarian life although they had no mystical fear of cities. A certain amount of raiding, especially cattle-rustling, was an intrinsic part of life. Needless bloodshed and slaughter were exceptional. Indeed, when Theodoric Thiudmir was still angry over his betrayal by the Byzantines and the confrontation concerning his authority over his people, he raided the lands near the Rhodope Range, carried of the cattle, and killed and despoiled whomever and whatever he could not carry off. Theodoric Triarius criticized his policy, declaring that the Roman farmers were already sorely abused by the Emperor.[67] Both leaders recognized that a co-operative peasantry was essential to the well-being of their people while on the march. In the long run their own positions depended on the welfare of their tribe.

Towns along the route to Epirus either barred their gates or took their supplies into the mountains. Foraging was difficult, delay inevitable. To facilitate supply, Theodoric divided the Goths into three units. He commanded the lead element. His next in command, *dux* Soas, led the main body, leaving his brother Theodimundus in charge of the rear guard and much of the baggage.[68] When Sidimundus succeeded in

[65] *Ibid.*, Müller, p. 126.

[66] Malchus, frag. 18, Müller, pp. 125–30. The inhabitants of Heraclea too retreated to a nearby fortress when Theodoric stepped up his demands for supplies.

[67] Malchus, frag. 17, Müller, p. 124.

[68] Malchus, frag. 18, Müller, p. 127–8. I have translated Σόαν τε τὸν αὐτοῦ στρατηγὸν as "Soas, his *dux*." Soas was clearly a man of great military authority in this campaign, and as such would be called *dux* in Latin.

frightening the citizens of Epidamnus out of their city, Theodoric rushed ahead with his cavalry to seize the town. He had every reason to believe that his people were safe from attack, for Zeno was busily negotiating a settlement in the "fertile and uninhabited land" of Dardania in the interior of Illyria, land much more extensive than Epirus Nova, where they could farm and easily feed themselves.[69] Zeno feared that Theodoric would capture boats and cross to Italy, but the Ostrogoths had no intention of traveling so far.[70] Theodoric agreed to settle in Dardania provided the Emperor would establish wintering quarters for his men and women near Epidamnus. In addition he offered Zeno 6000 men who could be used against the Goths in Thrace (Triarius was again in revolt) or to restore Nepos in the West, and he agreed to surrender his mother and sister as hostages. In return he wanted to be made commander (*strategos*) in Triarius' place and be received in Constantinople as a Roman citizen.[71] Theodoric must have felt a need to be at the center of imperial power in order to influence the Emperor. When this round of negotiations broke off, Theodoric was unaware that Zeno had decided once again on war instead of peace.

While negotiations were going on between Theodoric and the Byzantine envoy Adamantius, Roman troops assembled at Lychnidus and prepared to attack the sluggish caravan of Gothic wagons from the rear. The Byzantine *magister militum* for Thrace, Sabinianus, managed to raise an army by stripping the garrisons from the towns and apparently received some aid from Onoulph, the brother of Odovacar and an important commander in Illyricum. He attacked at Candavia, taking "nearly 2000 wagons, more than 5000 captives and no little booty."[72] Indeed, he cancelled his requisition for supply wagons from the cities, for he now had more than he could use. He chose to burn many rather than to allow them to fall back into Gothic hands. Theodimundus and his mother only escaped by burning a vital bridge behind them, thereby trapping many fellow Goths.[73]

---

[69] Malchus, frag. 18, Müller, p. 129.

[70] *Ibid.*, p. 127.

[71] *Ibid.*, p. 129. These negotiations may have been concluded, for in A.D. 486 Zeno returned Theodoric's sister, Joannes Antiochenus, frag. 214.8. She was not apparently captured in any battle which followed these negotiations, and Theodoric did not again offer hostages, at least not according to the extant sources. Perhaps she was given as security when the tribe moved into Moesia, but again the sources are silent.

[72] Malchus, p. 130.

[73] *Ibid.*, Adamantius, even while negotiating, kept Sabinianus alerted to the Ostrogothic movement. Zeno had little intention of concluding a peaceful settlement.

If the above figures are even approximate, the catastrophe at Candavia severely crippled Theodoric's ability to muster his people to arms. 2000 wagons and 5000 captives are not outlandish numbers, for Theodorc offered the service of 6000 men as an article of the proposed settlement — the figure might well have been recorded somewhere in the diplomatic archives of Constantinople. Theodimundus commanded only the rear guard and the slowest baggage wagons, whereas the bulk of the tribe was under Soas in the middle assemblage somewhere farther west along the road. Soas never entered the battle at Candavia. In order to approximate the total number of Ostrogoths under Theodoric, it is reasonable to postulate that his division of forces was in a ratio of 1:2:1 and that the entire rear detachment was captured. This would yield a figure of approximately 20,000 Goths on the move through southern Illyricum.[74] The captives were presumably sold as slaves throughout the East.

The negotiations for the settlement in Dardania naturally broke off, and until Zeno had Sabinianus eliminated in 482 Theodoric and his followers were content to stay in Epirus Nova.[75] During these years (ca. 477–482) Zeno struggled against the usurpers Illus and Marcian. Theodoric Triarius left the quiet of his estates in Thrace to rescue Zeno during the rebellion of Marcian.[76] Triarius died in battle in Greece in 481, but prior to his death he allied himself with Theodoric Thiudmir still in Epirus. In 482 Theodoric Thiudmir (henceforth simply Theodoric) moved out of Epirus Nova, raided Greece, and sacked Larissa, Macedonia, and perhaps Thessaly.[77] Theodoric may have added many Goths in Macedonia and Thrace to his following after the death of their own leader, Triarius. By 483, Zeno's position was precarious, and he made a pact with Theodoric making him *magister praesentis militiae*, consul designate for 484, and commander of a large area along the Danube including Ripensia Dacia and part of Moesia inferior "with its satellites, for a time."[78] While Byzantium pursued a consistent policy

[74] By the migration to Italy in 488–89 this figure had doubled through the addition of Triarius' followers and others.

[75] Joannes Antiochenus, frag. 213.

[76] Malchus, frag. 19, Müller, pp. 130–31, and frags. 20 and 21 concerning the activities of Pamprepicus and Illus and the careers of Zeno's brothers Longinus and Conon. In general see J. B. Bury, *The Later Roman Empire* (London, 1889, reprint New York, 1958), pp. 389–400.

[77] Joannes Antiochenus, frag. 213; Marcellinus Comes, 482. N. Hammond denies that Theodoric reached Thessaly, *op. cit.*, pp. 108–9. The evidence is inconclusive against Marcellinus who states that Thessaly was raided at this time.

[78] Marcellinus Comes, 483. This peculiar spelling of the title is found only in Marcellinus Comes, the more common form is *magister militum praesentalis*. See A. H. M. Jones, *The Later Roman Empire*, vol. 1 (Norman, Okla., 1964), p. 181.

aimed at the reestablishment of a federate system, Theodoric remained restless. In 486 he pillaged Thrace.[79] The next year he sacked Melentia and burned Novae in Moesia.[80] Meanwhile Zeno faced a rebellion at home led by Illus and threats of invasion from the west by Odovacar. As the war clouds gathered Zeno made a last attempt to secure federate support. The Emperor sought to calm Theodoric by returning his sister and paying a tribute. He simultaneously allied himself with the Rugians.[81] Unfortunately for the Byzantines, the Rugians were not quite up to challenging Odovacar. Their king was easily defeated and fled with his followers to Theodoric at Novae.[82]

Regardless of whose idea it was to leave Moesia for Italy in 488, the political, military and perhaps economic situation in the Balkans was rapidly becoming untenable for Goth and Byzantine alike.[83] The pressures for a permanent home, already expressed during the trek to Epirus Nova, were probably stronger by 488. Theodoric himself was unsatisfied with their position in Moesia. Moesia was geographically isolated from the rest of the Balkans by the Haemus Range (now the Balkan Mountains). The Dobruja to the east offered the only area open to easy expansion, but the desolate and monotonous land remained sparsely populated. By this time the entire Balkan area showed the effects of a century of brigandage, looting, burning and servere economic disruption.

Zeno too had problems, which the Ostrogothic exodus would have lessened. Perhaps the most pressing demand was to provide some semblance of security for Thrace, including the immediate vicinity of Constantinople — the famous long wall across the isthmus from Selymbria northward was not built until 497. Thrace was raided by Theodoric in 486, but the Byzantines never gave up trying to establish an inner defense system in the Rhodope Mountains on the west and the Haemus Range along the northern border of Thrace. The garrisons of the Haemus and the cities of Thrace were expected to join Theodoric Thiudmir in his campaign against Triarius (475–76). The *magister militum* for Thrace continued to be a "loyal Roman" and was clearly the most

---

[79] Joannes Antiochenus, frag. 214.7.

[80] Marcellinus Comes, 487. For Novae see the new study of Bulgaria by R. F. Hoddinott, *Bulgaria in Antiquity* (New York, 1975).

[81] Joannes Antiochenus, frag. 214.8. On Theodoric's sister see note 71.

[82] *Vita Severini*, 42.4.

[83] The evidence supports both Zeno and Theodoric as initiating the march to Italy. For Theodoric: Malchus, frag. 18, Müller, p. 129; *Getica*, 290–1. For Zeno: Anonymus Valesianus, 49; Procopius, *B.G.*, V, i, 10. Finally, Evagrius, *Historica Ecclesiastica*, iii, 27, gives both sides of the issue but favors the idea that Theodoric first devised the migration.

powerful imperial commander in the Balkans until the reforms of Justinian reorganized the entire area.[84] Odovacar had supported Illus and had routed the Rugians, who were in alliance with the Empire. The Byzantines finally abandoned any hope of anchoring Balkan stability on the Ostrogoths. The federate system could not harness a people strong enough to challenge the Empire and with leaders owing nothing to imperial intervention.

Neither side acted blindly. Theodoric and his people were veterans of migration. The elders could recall the initial settlement near Sirmium and were well aware of the obstacles en route to Italy. The Rugian king Fredericus and his followers in the Ostrogothic train knew that Odovacar would not be a weak-kneed opponent. Zeno's decision was easier, but no one could have predicted the new balance of power after the Ostrogoths departed. The migration to Italy, like other long marches in more recent history, tested leadership, endurance, and cohesiveness.

The composite nature of his following taxed Theodoric's leadership more than ever before. In addition to those faithful who had loyally entrusted their welfare to him throughout his Balkan campaigns, his forces included groups of Rugians, having followed their king to Novae, and Goths from Thrace and Pannonia. Many Gothic settlers apparently decided to follow Theodoric to Italy although they had previously remained behind when Theodoric and his band moved to successive homes in the Balkan area. Now they put their families and possessions into wagons and set out for the West.[85] Most but not all Ostrogoths followed Theodoric. At least one noble refused to leave his homeland. This was Bessas, who later allied with Belisarius and led his followers against Wittigis.[86] Unfortunately the evidence does not reveal the pressure other nobles, perhaps only slightly less independent, placed on Theodoric's leadership in the course of the migration.

By the time the Ostrogoths reached the Ulca River, a tributary of the Danube near Cibalae, famine had taken a toll.[87] Such cities as Sirmium

---

[84] The *magistri militi* for Thrace in the late fifth century were Sabinianus (killed in 482), Joannes the Scythian, and Moschianus. Joannes Antiochenus, frag. 213.

[85] *Chronicorum Caesaraugustanorum Reliquiae*, 490, *MGH.AA*, 11 (*Chronica Minora*, 2), p. 222. Hoc cos. Theudericus Ostrogothorum rex a Thracia et Pannonia Italiam venit. For possible references to the federate nature of the Ostrogothic forces of 488–89 see *Getica*, 292, and Anonymus Valesianus, 49, both of whom refer to the entire tribe setting out for Italy. The Rogi, a Gothic people, were encorporated by Theodoric into the "Gothic nation", but they maintained their own customs and bloodlines, Procopius, *B.G.*, VII, ii, 1–3; VI, xiv, 24.

[86] Procopius, *B.G.*, V, xvi, 2.

[87] Ennodius, *Pan.*, 29 (ch. vii), p. 206. The Goths must have decided to take the northern route to Aquileia, following the Drava upstream. That the Ulca should be located just north of Cibalae see the *Tabula Imperii Romani*, Foglio L 34, (Aquincum-Sarmizegetusa-Sirmium,

neither opened their gates nor established a sufficient market. Sirmium, perhaps inside the Gepid sphere, dared not supply the Goths. The news of such a host of hungry people inspired hoarding to protect already impoverished larders.[88] Sirmium undoubtedly shared in the economic decline of the area now too poor to support a siege. Apparently, the harvests were in from the area close to the city, and the farms far distant were abandoned long ago. Wild sources and the gleanings from the fields were sparse sustenance for the Gothic people — they had to move on or starve.

The Gepids met them at the Ulca, which formed a natural defense against invaders going northeast. They had stored their crops in wagons behind their lines and defied the Goths to cross the river. Theodoric sent legates to the Gepids in a fruitless attempt to avoid battle, but the envoys were rebuked by "the long unconquered Gepids," who could hardly have failed to realize their commanding position. The Goths had no alternatives since retreat or deadlock meant starvation. They attacked, but the first assault was quickly repulsed as the attackers became mired in the mud. Their wicker shields were no protection against the Gepid spearmen. Disaster was averted when Theodoric rallied his men declaring that he himself would show the way for "the army's plight has been gauged by me and in the way which I show, the people shall triumph." Then with great personal courage Theodoric led his forces to victory. Ennodius did not record Theodoric's strategy, but perhaps he discovered a safe passage through the mud. The battle raged until nightfall when the Goths broke through to the Gepid wagons.[89] The captured supplies meant survival, and with them the Ostrogoths continued to push slowly west through the fall and winter of 488—489. In the spring of 489, they descended the Julian Alps into Italy. Although the daily hardships and problems of command even at the top level are lost, Theodoric, soon to become king of Italy over both Goths and Romans, was a much more powerful ruler than when he headed the

Amsterdam, 1968). The important reference in Ennodius, *Pan.*, 29 (ch. vii.1), p. 206 is included among the sources in the *Tabula*. But see Miroslava Mirkovic, "Sirmium. Its History from the First Century A.D. to 582 A.D.", *Sirmium I* (Beograd, 1961), pp. 50—51, who places the Ulca east of Sirmium.

[88] To date no circuit walls have been excavated at Sirmium but the site was clearly inhabited at this time, and the walls were probably still defensible. The Gepids had also been expanding from their mid-fifth-century settlements north of the Danube. When the Ostrogoths under Valamir were in the area, the Gepids were north of the river, *Getica*, 262—65. There can be no doubt that the Goths took the most direct route to Italy, passing through Sirmium, *Getica*, 292.

[89] The sole source for the entire discussion of the march is Ennodius, *Pan.*, vii, pp. 206—7.

Ostrogothic raiding parties in the Balkans. The events of the march further strengthened his leadership.

At the Isonzo River, north of Aquileia, the future met the past — Theodoric and Odovacar clashed for the first time. In September of that year Theodoric drove Odovacar from Verona; in 490 on the Addua River near Como the story was repeated; and in 491 Odovacar met defeat again while attempting to break Theodoric's siege of Ravenna. Finally in 493, after a short-lived co-rulership, Theodoric slew his "spineless" adversary and purged Odovacar's troops.[90] Little need be said about the actual military campaigns except that the three year siege of Ravenna was never very effective because Theodoric could not prevent supplies from entering the city by sea. More important, however, is the early policy of Theodoric towards the native Italians, his tribe, and the legacies of Odovacar, which were incorporated into the Ostrogothic state.

Odovacar was never a true king in the sense that he had a tribal following largely drawn from one group. Rather he was in the direct line of the last *magister militum praesentalis*. As a youth he had served steadfastly under Ricimer, and when he moved into the power vacuum after the assassination of Nepos, Odovacar acted as *magister militum.*[91] He was a Sciri, son of Edeco, and the brother of Onoulph, a powerful military figure in Pannonia and a nominal ally of the Eastern Empire. By 489, Odovacar was king of those soldiers and their families serving with him, but each group of soldiers had its own leader who owed allegiance to Odovacar as a friend and comrade rather than to any "royal prerogative."[92] Under Odovacar the imperial bureaucracy continued to function, and the upper classes were rewarded with office in the traditional manner.[93] Before Theodoric's invasion, Italy had enjoyed several decades of long sought peace. Odovacar concentrated his military adventures outside Italy, particularly in Noricum, Raetia, and upper Pannonia. As far as the Ostrogothic kingdom was concerned,

[90] Joannes Antiochenus, frag. 214a; Anonymus Valesianus, 50–57; Cassiodorus, *Chronica*, 1319–26; *Getica*, 293–95; *Chronicorum Caesaraugustanorum Reliquiae*, 492; Marius Episcopus Aventicensis, *MGH.AA*, 11 (*Chronica Minora*, 2), 489, 493; Marcellinus Comes, *Chronicon*, 488–89; and Procopius, *B.G.*, V, i, 18–22.

[91] Candidus, frag. 1, Photius codex, 79; Joannes Antiochenus, frag. 209 (1); G. Ostrogorsky, *op. cit.*, p. 53.

[92] Ennodius, *Pan.*, viii, concerning Odovacar's call to arms: tot reges tecum ad bella convenerant, quot sustinere generalitas milites vix valeret. Ennodius may well echo the sense of comradeship upon which Odovacar depended when he referred in this passage to "all the kings allied with you for war." That Odovacar was called *rex* see further, Anonymus Valesianus, 46–48.

[93] Taxes were collected under the direction of the Praetorian Prefect, and abuses as well as

Odovacar's most precedent-setting action was the decision to grant a third of the lands of Italy to his Germanic followers.[94]

After defeating Odovacar at Verona in 489, the Ostrogoths continued west through Milan and south to Pavia, where they camped for the winter in family groups within the town — some of the abandoned buildings were demolished to make room. Quickly work began to rebuild the walls of the city.[95] Theodoric dealt with the native inhabitants through the bishop, Epiphanius. Epiphanius naturally served as the town's spokesman, for as bishop of Pavia he supervised many of the "secular" functions of local government, including the operation of the formerly imperial brick factory.[96] Pavians were long accustomed to billeting troops: the *Notitia Dignitatum* reveals Sarmatians there in the late fourth century. Other signs of barbarian influence at Pavia include zoomorphic patterns found on metal workings and jewelry.[97]

Theodoric's initial policy was severe towards the "Roman inhabitants," for he allowed testamentary rights and the free sale of property only to active supporters.[98] Some friction existed between the Goths and the Pavians, but whatever its nature Theodoric and Epiphanius combined to calm the unrest. Shortly thereafter Theodoric changed his attitude towards the Romans. The church was hardly a disinterested party in matters of testament, and Epiphanius prevailed on Theodoric to bar only the open supporters of Odovacar from testamentary rights and full legal privileges. The change was promulgated in a edict by Urbicus, a man of senatorial rank and already high in the palace officialdom.[99] One hallmark of Ostrogothic rule was already clear:

---

beneficial exemptions also continued, Ennodius, *Vita Epiphanius*, 106–7, ed., Vogel, *MGH.AA*, 7 (Berlin, 1885, reprint 1961). I cannot hope to give an exhaustive bibliography for Odovacar; however, A. Chastagnol, *Le Sénat romain sous le règne d'Odovacre* (Bonn, 1966), provides a good bibliography for problems related to Odovacar on a wider basis than the title suggests.

[94] Procopius, *B.G.*, V, i, 7–8.

[95] Ennodius, *Vita Epiphani*, 111. Only a small section of the southeast wall has so far been excavated. The reconstruction there has been tentatively dated to the initial Ostrogothic occupation, D. A. Bullough, "Urban Change in Early Medieval Italy. The example of Pavia", *Papers of the British School at Rome*, 34 (1966), pp. 88–90.

[96] The name of the bishop Crispin II, successor to Ennodius, has been found on molded, kiln-fired tiles in the city, Bullough, *op. cit.*, p. 94.

[97] N. Degrassi, "Rinvenimento di un tesoretto. La oreficerie tardo-romane di Pavia", *Notizie degli scavi di antichità* (Roma, 1941), pp. 307–8. Degrassi believes that northern Italian jewelry, especially around Pavia, reveals a Gernanic style (zoomorphic but not yet recognizable animals) which he suggests reflects the Sarmatian presence in the area at the time of Theodosius (Notitia Dignitatum, occ., 9, 28).

[98] *Vita Epiphanius*, 122.

[99] *Ibid.*, 135.

working through the established ecclesiastical and secular structures and using indigenous personnel for routine administration.

With Odovacar eliminated, the Ostrogoths abandoned their migration-oriented life centered around warfare, marching, and the wagon. Believing Italy to be their new homeland, the leaders began settling the people. After the settlement, the problem of governing an urban society was approached slowly by those with a real concern for government. The majority of the Goths undoubtedly came to Italy in search of the farmland and the security unobtainable in the chaotic Balkans. Their goals realized, these people happily abandoned the tasks of government to their nobility.

There are three problems associated with the Ostrogothic settlement in Italy which, when answered, help clarify the next fifty years in Ostrogothic history and explain subsequent stratification and the devolution of kingship. First, what system for settlement was used by the Ostrogoths, and what were its antecedents? Second, what were the effects of the settlement on the Roman population and what were the ramifications for the Ostrogoths themselves? Finally, where did they settle and in what concentration?

The settlement was conducted along well established principles for the billeting of troops. Odovacar granted a third of the lands in Italy to his followers, and Theodoric "simply" took over these units.[100] The quartering procedures, as spelled out in the Theodosian Code, guided the actual mechanism for distribution. According to the Code (vii, 8, 1.5) the quartered soldier had the right to one third of the house where he received *hospitalitas.* The proprietor divided his domain into three parts, keeping one and offering the soldier his choice of one of the two remaining shares. The same legislation also made special provision for men of illustrious rank, who had a right to half of the estate.[101] The senator Liberius, a loyal follower of Odovacar and praetorian prefect under Theodoric, supervised the division and maintained the continuity between Odovacar and Theodoric. By employing his discretionary power Liberius could benefit his friends and, presumably, penalize his enemies.[102]

[100] Procopius, *B.G.*, V, i, 28.

[101] The legislation of Arcadius and Honorius is in *Codex Theodosianus*, ed. T. Mommsen, *Theodosiani libri XVI cum constitutionibus Sirmondianus et leges novellae ad Theodosianum pertinentes*, ed. T. Mommsen and P. M. Meyer, 2nd. ed. (Berlin, 1954), I, pt. II, vii, 8, 1.5. The best study of hospitality remains F. Lot, "Du Régime de l'hospitalité", *Revue belge de philologie et d'histoire*, 7 (1928), pp. 975–1011.

[102] Ennodius, *Epistolae*, ed. F. Vogel, *MGH.AA*, 7 (Berlin, 1885, reprint 1961), xxiii, in which Ennodius asked Liberius to be as kind to his property (or his family's) in Gaul as he had been in Italy.

The estate system in Italy continued throughout the Ostrogothic period, and, in fact, recent archaeological data indicate that the trend towards larger estates accelerated during the fifth and sixth centuries. In the area north of Veii in Etruria of 310 estates in the second century only 85 remained by the end of the third century. Much of the decline was made up by the increased size of individual units. In the fourth century the number of estates remained about 90, but in the fifth and sixth centuries the rapid growth of large estates shattered the stability. By the sixth century only 45 estates survived. Most of them were sizable centers of diverse activity.[103]

The piecemeal absorption of small farms by wealthy holders, which clearly created some of the larger estates, received a powerful stimulus from the breakdown of order during the third century. Between the mid-fifth and late-sixth centuries settlement in general slowly retreated from the more exposed areas. The few new small farms in this period may have been squatter occupations on vacant land. The late estates were large enough to warrant the term *latifundia*. In general the late ancient settlement pattern survived intact in the area of Veii until the tenth century.[104]

Liberius need not have concerned himself with the details of land distribution, for he undoubtedly paired Roman proprietor and Gothic nobleman. The latter would subdivide his grant among his followers. There were many Gothic and Rugian nobles subordinate to Theodoric. For the early phase of the settlement their names have been lost, but some of these men (*comites*) were taken prisoner by Odovacar.[105] The same class of men became territorial leaders after the settlement.

The settlement of the Burgundians in southeastern Gaul, better documented than the Ostrogothic settlement in Italy, provides analogies, which while not completely applicable to the Ostrogoths, nonetheless suggest problems relating to the settlement in Italy. The Burgundian guests were not commoners but the heads of families, *faramanni*, similar

---

[103] Anne Kahane, Leslie M. Threipland, and John Ward-Perkins, "The Ager Veientianus, North and East of Rome", *Papers of the British School at Rome*, 36 (1968), p. 53, notice particularly estates no. 105, 118, 128, 185, 210, 212, 214, 219, 232, 268, 270, 429, 434, 435, 447, 521, 522, and 525.

[104] L. Ruggini, *Economia e società nell' "Italia annonaria." Rapporti fra agricoltura e commercio del IV al VI secolo d.c.* (Milano, 1961), and A. Kahane, L. M. Threipland, and J. Ward-Perkins, *op. cit.*, pp. 151–57, 161–65. The evidence for the late classical period is almost exclusively the late red polished pottery still being imported from north Africa.

[105] Anonymus Valesianus, 52. et exiit Odocar de Ravenna, et venit Faventiam, et Tufa tradidit Odoacri comites patricii Theoderici, et missi sunt in ferro, et adducti Ravennam.

the *fara* of the Lombards. The *fara* was comprised of blood kin, servants, and personal followers, and was not only a line of kinship but also a military unit. The leader of the *fara* represented his people in the division of land with the senators of Gaul.[106] The *fara* as such may not have existed among the Ostrogoths, yet the suffix "fara" associated with personal names in two inscriptions is potential evidence for an Ostrogothic *fara*. The name Sendefara appears in an inscription from Dertona dated A.D. 541, and Wilifara appears similarly at Centum Cellae (now Città Vecchia) dated A.D. 557.[107] The *fara* or its equivalent was probably a basic social unit among all Germanic peoples. Perhaps *fara* was the Germanic equivalent of $\varphi v \lambda \dot{\eta}$. If so then the names containing *fara* are proof of the survival of the Gothic subunits first mentioned by Eunapius. J. Werner has concluded that the Lombards settled in Pannonia by *fara* und further that the term and concept must be assumed for the Gepidae, a tribe of quite similar background to the Ostrogoths.[108] At the very least the suffix *fara* was an indicator of personal prestige.[109] It seems reasonable to equate such prestige with leadership over subunits similar if not identical to Burgundian units with the same name.

Theoretically, Liberius paired the landowners of Italy and the noble Goths, who would select their third (*tertia*) and apportion it to their followers. In reality the Ostrogoths were numerically insufficient to take physical possession of a third of the land of Italy. Scattering Goths over Italy would have irreparably weakened Gothic tribal structure, destroyed the power base of the Amali kings, and further eroded whatever peculiarities of Germanic community and liberty survived the ongoing hierarchization of Gothic society.[110] Instead, Gothic social organi-

---

[106] Paulus Diaconus, *Pauli Historia Langobardorum*, ed., L. Bethmann and G. Waitz, *MGH. Scriptores rerum Langobardicarum et Italicarum*, sec. *vi-ix* (Hannover, 1878), ii, 9; *Edictus Rothari*, ch. 177, ed. F. Walter, *Corpus Juris Germanici Antiqui*, 1 (Berlin, 1824), pp. 683–753; and Marius of Avenches, 456, who states: eo anno Burgundiones partem Galliae occupaverunt terrasque cum Gallis senatoribus diviserunt. See further, F. Lot, *op. cit.*, pp. 983–96, and G. Waitz, *Deutsche Rechtsgeschichte*, 1, 2nd. ed., p. 118, note 37 on the *fara*. *Faramanni* long puzzled translators, but du Cange, *Glossarium Mediae et Infirmae Latinitatis*, 3, pp. 204–5, suggested *fara* meant *generatio*, and man was *homo*, hence head of the family. This translation has been widely accepted.

[107] *C.I.L.*, v, 7417 (Fiebiger, 1917, no. 230); *C.I.L.*, xi, 3567 (Fiebiger, 1917, no. 231).

[108] J. Werner, *Die Langobarden in Pannonien. Beiträge zur Kenntnis der langobardischen Bodenfunde vor 568* (Bayerische Akad. d. Wissenschaften, phil.-hist. Klasse, Abh., Neue Folge, Heft 55A, München, 1962), pp. 119–20.

[109] Ferdinand Wrede, *Über die Sprache der Ostgoten in Italien* (Strassburg, 1891), pp. 134, 153, 155.

[110] The potential dichotomy between Germanic community and liberty and Roman urban structure and slavery has been discussed by Z.V. Udalcova and E. V. Goutnova, "La Genèse du

zation continued to preserve a sense of Germanic liberty in which each warrior and his family had a right to special treatment and freedom of choice even in the final stages of the Justinianic Wars. Major decisions by Theodoric's successors were made with the advice of the council — advice necessarily heeded because Ostrogothic kingship never mastered the power of local leadership. Three major areas were settled: Liguria (around Tortona, Pavia, Milan, and Como); the area around Ravenna; and a large settlement area in eastern Tuscany, Picenum, and Samnium.[111] Agricultural and strategic interests combined with political necessity and the natural desire to live among friends to yield the final settlement pattern.

The road system clearly held the key to controlling Italy. The major settlement areas effectively controlled traffic northeast of Rome and in the vital Po valley.[112] Official documents manifest the desire for effective communication and the proper use of the post system. For heavy transport, barges continued to operate on the Po and Tiber. But no matter how strategic the settlements appear, the agricultural demands were equally responsible for the settlement system. If the Ostrogoths were concerned only with strategic realities they would have settled much more heavily in the area of Trent and Aquileia, for the threat to their rule came from the north, not from Italy itself. In the areas where the Ostrogoths did not settle, the payment of the *tertia* (the pecuniary equivalent of the barbarian share) merged with the *tributum* as a general tax.[113]

The physical problems associated with any division of land for occupation rather than revenue-sharing cannot be overestimated. Although some large open fields could be surveyed and divided,[114] most large landowners held a complex of small farms. Each farm needed partureland, meadow, wood, and arable to function as a unit. Simply

féodalisme dans les pays d'Europe", *XIII Congrès international des sciences historiques* (1970). The topic of *libertas* is cloudy for Ostrogothic studies because of the scant legal information available, but, judged by their actions during the wars of Justinian and the payment of donatives to the Gothic soldiers by Theodoric, the individual did retain a considerable amount of personal liberty at least in the initial period after the settlement.

[111] L. M. Hartmann, *Geschichte Italiens im Mittelalter* (Gotha, 1903), 1, pp. 93—96, 127—28.

[112] Cassiodorus made frequent reference to road maintenance and the post system; for example, *Variae*, ii, 31; xii, 18.

[113] Fabien Thibault, "L'Impôt direct dans les royaumes des Ostrogoths, des Wisigoths, et des Burgundes," *Nouvelle revue historique de droit français et étranger*, 25 (1901), pp. 715—25.

[114] Signs of centuriation have been detected around Pavia. See *Tabula Imperii Romani, Mediolanum* (Roma, 1966).

surveying and granting a third to a Gothic chief without regard for the various types of land needed to supply an active agricultural settlement would have destroyed the system. If the Roman possessor owned farms in a multiple of three, the division into thirds was simplified. The unfortunate landowner unable to divide his total farm units evenly may have divided an odd farm into smaller units giving a third part of each type of land to the guest, but more likely a division of revenue settled the matter. The division of revenue was commonly employed in matters of testament, probably because of the awkwardness of physical division of the land. For example, Papyrus no. 13 in the Tjäder collection, dated 553, recording the gift by the woman Ranilo to the church of Ravenna, made explicit a previous grant of revenue by her father Aderit:

> ... my deceased father, Aderit, formerly vir gloriosus, has left a previous gift namely 50 lbs. of silver; in income 100 solidi divided from the following massae (land with dwelling houses): 6/12 Firmidiana in the vicinity of Urbino, and of the massa ... liana in the vicinity of Lucca 6/12. . .[115]

If for any reason a division of revenue was unsatisfactory, Roman law assumed the property would be sold and the proceeds divided according to proportions recorded in the will. Each particular settlement arrangement negotiated between a senator and a Gothic noble probably involved some revenue-sharing and/or sale. However, around Pavia, Ravenna, and in Picenum the goal was the physical occupation of the soil. The economic prosperity of the Ostrogothic Kingdom is inexplicable with the agrarian units destroyed.[116]

Once the division into viable agrarian units was accomplished, the Ostrogothic noble faced the problem of further division among his followers. But what about the labor force already working some or all of the land in question? Two titles of the Burgundian *Liber Constitutionum sive Lex Gundobada* are helpful in conceptualizing the general problems associated with barbarian settlement. One such problem was the division of the labor force; another was taking into account the nature of the land.

[115] Tjäder, *op. cit.*, p. 304, line 1–5: [. . .22. . . . Aderit, glor] i [o] se recordationis patris mei, argenti libras quinquaginta; in reditibus solidos centum, idest massae (:) Firmidianae (:) territoria Urbinate (:) et (:) [. . .] lianae (:) territorio Lucense constitutarum uncias senas, . . . The twelfth was an arbitrary division used for testament. According to *Institutiones* (ii, 14.5) the custom derived from the unit *As* which had twelve divisions. Since no one could be partially intestate in Roman Law, if the units of an estate added up to less than 12 *unciae*, then the stipulated heirs divided the remainder according to their share of the assigned portion. If the units totalled more than 12 *unciae*, the *As* was doubled or tripled and the estate divided according to the percentage of the *As* units, now 24 or 36 *unciae* per *As*.

[116] Knud Hannestad, *L'Évolution des ressources agricoles de l'Italie du IVe au VIe siècle de notre ère* (Hist.-filos. Medd. Dan. Vid. Selsk., 40, 1, København, 1962).

LIV

Of those who presume to take a third of the slaves and two parts of the land (of their host) contrary to public prohibition.

1. It was commanded at the time the order was issued whereby our people should receive one-third of the slaves, and two thirds of the land, that whoever had received land together with slaves either by the gift of our predecessors or of ourselves, should not require a third of the slaves nor two parts of the land from that place in which hospitality had been assigned him; nevertheless inasmuch as we find many unmindful of their danger because they have taken in excess of those things which we have ordered, it is necessary that the present authority issued in the image of eternal law coerce the presumptuous and provide a remedy of due security against these acts of contempt. We order then that whatever lands have been taken contrary to our official prohibition from their hosts by those who already have possession of fields and slaves through our gift shall be restored without delay.

2. Also concerning clearings, we order that the new and unjust strife and trickery of the *faramanni* which causes anxiety and disquiet to the possessors be suppressed by this law, with the result that just as concerning forests, so also concerning clearings made either heretofore or at present time, the Roman possessors shall have a share with the Burgundians, for, as was established previously, we order half of the forests in general to belong to the Romans; likewise concerning courtyards and orchards, let this condition be followed among the *faramanni*, that is, that the Romans may lay claim to take half the property.

3. But if anyone exceeds the established provisions of this law and is not reprimanded and punished by you, do not doubt that the fervor of our wrath will be aroused to your peril.

LV

Of excluding barbarians whenever contention arises between two Romans concerning the boundaries of their fields.

1. Inasmuch as it has been established under certain penalty that no barbarian should dare to involve himself in a suit which a Roman has brought against another Roman, we advocate a stricter handling of these cases, and command that the law remain just as we ordered it established in earlier times.

2. As often as cases arise between two Romans concerning the boundaries of fields which are possessed by barbarians through the law of hospitality, let the guests of the contestants not be involved in the quarrel, but let them await the outcome between the Romans contending in judgment. And the guest of the victor shall have a share of the property obtained as a result of his success.

3. But if any barbarian involves himself in a litigation of this kind and is defeated, let him pay a fine of twelve solidi for holding this law in contempt.

4. But if a Roman presumes to engage him who is his guest in litigation, we order both to pay twelve solidi, and the case to be settled by Roman law.

5. But if a contention has been raised concerning the boundaries of a field which a barbarian has received intact with slaves by public gift, it is permitted him to settle the case by Roman law whether it is brought against him or he himself has instigated it.

6. Further, if a native freeman presumes to remove or destroy a boundary marker, let him be condemned to the loss of a hand. If a slave has done this, let him be killed.

7. If indeed a native freeman wishes to avert this mutilating punishment, let him pay half his wergeld.[117]

---

[117] Translated by Katherine Fischer Drew, *The Burgundian Code* (Philadelphia, Penn., 1972), pp. 62–4, from L. R. de Salis, *Leges Burgundionum, MGH. Legum*, Sec. I, II, i (Hannover, 1892).

Except for the fact that the Burgundians claimed two thirds of the land rather than one third, these titles probably represent an accurate assessment of the general problems of the Ostrogothic settlement in Italy. The code has greatly simplified the division by assuming that all estates were identical. The explanation of the peculiar division of two thirds of the land but only a third of the labor force may be that the Roman proprietors kept two-thirds of the reserve (*indominicatum*) and thus two thirds of the laborers who worked the reserve.[118] In short, that the Burgundian two thirds of the total was made up of the half of the estate operated by coloni as tenant farmers plus one third of the reserve which was operated by slaves (3/6 + 1/6 = 2/3 total). It has been suggested that the division of any newly cleared land was equal to the portion of the original share of the arable (one half).[119]

If these suggestions are correct, then the original division was extremely complex, since the barbarian two thirds somehow encompassed half of the arable divided between the tenants (now presumably under Burgundian control) and the reserve. Another possible explanation would be that the Burgundian *faramanni* had a labor force already partially adequate to farm the land, for as heads of families and leaders of military, followers, they had kin, friends, and slaves. Title LIV acknowledges that some had received land and slaves prior to the *hospitalitas* system, and slave owning was certainly not uncommon among the Germans. The question of field boundaries in title LV strongly suggests an actual division of land rather than revenue. An equal share in the fruits of *défrichement* probably reflects an equal investment in the undertaking, which members of the senatorial class could well afford regardless of their particular landed wealth in the area settled by the Burgundians.

Rather than link the settlement to complex divisions of the reserve, which would effectively destroy the agrarian economy, it seems reasonable to accept the alternative of actual Burgundian exploitation of at least part of their share. This rests on an assumption that the barbarians were essentially farmers. The Burgundian nobility probably did not actually plow, nor did their Ostrogothic counterparts. The legislation of Gundobad demonstrates that the barbarians were well aware of the importance of the various types of land, especially forest, needed to support a balanced agriculture. The continuity of the agarian

---

[118] F. Lot, *op. cit.*, p. 983.

[119] *Ibid.*, p. 996. For the Roman legal precedents see Sextus Julius Frontinus, *Strategemata libri quattuor*, i, 15, 18, ed., G. Gundermann, Teubner edition (Leipzig 1888).

economy suggests that the Ostrogoths were also concerned with different types of land.[120]

The same principles of land distribution may have been followed in the Ostrogothic settlement, maintaining the integrity of the *fundus* (villa-estate) both as an agricultural unit as well as a fiscal unit. The importance of laborers and different types of land was also recognized by the Ostrogoths. Concern for land and labor was common to almost all Germanic invaders. For example, the *Edictum* of Theodoric II, the Visigothic king at Toulouse (ca. 458–59), recognized the right of the landlord, who possessed "rustica utriusque sexus mancipia, etiamsi originaria" bodily and legally, to transfer them from one estate to another or to sell or give them away from the land of their birth.[121] The same legislation provided that parents could buy back any children sold in hard times.[122] The transfer of labor also applied to urban lords with domestics. This probably was intended to create a sufficient labor force on at least some of the estates. The heavy fines established in the *Edictum* for overworking another's slave or ox reveal that labor was occasionally pooled by landlords.[123] Careful distinction was made between cornland (*seges*) and woodland (*arbor*).[124] Similar comparative material can be found readily for other settlements.

Coloni and slaves were vital to the operation of Italian agriculture.[125] During warfare the slaves typically escaped their bondage. An example of rural labor mobility is found in a gift made to the church of Ravenna by *sublimis femina* Ranilo in 553. Part of the gift was property near Lucca including "the slaves, who are actually on the properties in question, and specifically those who can still be found there, since they have been able to run away during this barbarous time."[126] Throughout the last phase of the war against Justinian, both sides used runaway slaves to sabotage their masters and occasionally to fight in the front lines.[127]

---

[120] Lellia C. Ruggini, *Economia e società nell' "Italia annoraria". Rapporti fra agricultura e commercio dal IV al VI secolo d.c.* (Milano, 1961); K. Hannestad, *L'Évolution des ressources agricoles de l'Italie du IVe au VIe siècle de notre ère* (København, 1962).

[121] *Edictum Theodorici Regis*, 142, ed., Frederic Bluhme, *MGH. Legum*, 5 (Hannover, 1875–89).

[122] *Ibid.*, 94.

[123] *Ibid.*, 150.

[124] *Ibid.*, 151. Tjäder, *op. cit.*, P. 3.

[125] Tjäder, *op. cit.*, P. 3 (mid sixth century); *Edictum*, 56, 70, 142.

[126] Tjäder, *op. cit.*, P. 13, dated April 4, 553, from Ravenna. si qua tempore hoc barbarici ex eisdem lapsa repperiri potuerint, p. 304, lines 11–12. Tjäder suggests (p. 305) that this refers to the unrest caused by the final actions of the Justinianic Wars.

[127] For example, Procopius, *B.G.*, VII, xvi, 15; VII, xxii, 4–6; and VII, xxii, 20 which states

Cassiodorus left a short and grossly simplified statement of Liberius' division in a letter from Theodoric to the Roman Senate elevating Venantius, the son of Liberius. In the following passage the Senate was reminded of the deeds of Liberius.

> We especially like to remember how in the assigment of the Thirds he joined both the possessions and the hearts of Goths and Romans alike. For whereas men desire to come into collision on account of their being neighbors, with these men the common holding of their farms proved in practice a reason for concord. Thus it has happened that while the two nations have been living in common they have concurred in the same desires. A new fact, and one wholly laudable. The friendship of the lords (gratia dominorum) has been joined with the division of the soil; amity has grown out of the loss of the Provincials, and by the land a defender has been gained whose occupation of part guarantees the quiet enjoyment of the whole. One law includes them: one equal administration rules them: for it is necessary that sweet affection should grow between those who always keep the boundaries which have been allotted them.[128]

The division of revenue or actual property was not a universally welcomed event among the Roman aristocracy as some historians, following Cassiodorus, have claimed.[129] The letters of Ennodius are very instructive on the attitudes of the Roman aristocracy, although he rarely directly involved Goths in the correspondence. A kinsman of Ennodius, Asturius by name, had retired permanently to his villa in the Alps where even his writing style suffered the barbarities of the age.[130] Men like Asturius sought solitude and security in remote mountain villas at least as early as the opening of the fifth century. Therefore, he is an example of continued insecurity rather than a fugitive from the Ostrogoths. Most aristocrats endured the unrest and diminution of their estates. If they had enough influence at court, the decisions could be reversed.

Lupicinus, a nephew of Ennodius, had received a certain Torisa and others as a guest, but as host he found the grant unbearable and asked Ennodius, the deacon at Pavia, to intercede in his behalf. Ennodius first appealed to the local count Tancila, who informed him that only

---

that Totila offered the peasants fighting with John (a Byzantine commander then operating in Calabria) their masters' lands if they would return to the soil.

[128] T. Hodgkin, trans., *The Letters of Cassiodorus* (London, 1886), p. 179–80. Latin text in *MGH.AA, 12, Variarum*, ii, 16.5, pp. 55–56.

[129] For example, Maurice Dumoulin, "Le Gouvernement de Théodoric et la domination des Ostrogoths en Italie d'après les oeuvres d'Ennodius", *Revue historique*, 78 (1902), pp. 1–7, 241–65, and 79 (1902), pp. 1–22, especially p. 3, who believed that the division was made by granting vacant public lands which were part of the fisc, thus hurting no one. Abuse of neighbors was common and called for special legislation and appointments, for example, *Variae*, vii, 3.

[130] Ennodius, *Epist.*, i, 24.

Theodoric could act on such a request. Following up Tancila's advice, Ennodius wrote a letter to his friend Faustus, then probably praetorian prefect, seeking his aid at court.[131] Unfortunately, the final resolution of the case remains a mystery. Another Roman nobleman, Aurelianus, also requested Ennodius' aid at court for a similar petition. Once again Ennodius consented, but this time he cautioned his friend that the loss of property might have to be accepted. However, Ennodius went on to say, the loss might become a boon if his appeal afforded him an opportunity to ingratiate himself with the King, the ultimate controller of all the wealth in Italy.[132]

These letters support the contention that the division of lands concerned senatorial lands rather than vacant land or the possessions of the small owners and *curiales*, who continued to struggle for self-preservation as they had for centuries. Unfortunately, the letters do not discuss the nature of divisions-settlement, or a division of produce and rent. Any additional burden placed on the small *possessores* would have crushed them out of existence. They were vital elements of late Roman society and were "protected" for practical not philanthropic reasons. The *curiales* too were protected from further hardships. Nevertheless, their oppressive roles in urban government continued. By basing the settlement of the Goths on senatorial property, Theodoric simultaneously brought the upper classes of Roman society into working contact with the new state and helped preserve the lower classes and the elements of classical civilization dependent upon the existing social structure, particularly the tax system and municipal government.

In addition to the settlement in Italy, Theodoric had to make provision for the security of his new land against further barbarian invasion. Other tribes, such as the Gepids and Thuringians, were eager for new wealth. New people constantly wandered into the vacuums left by the departing tribes. The Lombards were the most famous and successful second generation invaders, but others such as the the Bulgars and the Sclaveni, whose social structure was quite egalitarian,[133] were also on the move. The Ostrogoths took over many of the old imperial defenses along the northern and northeastern frontiers. In the Julian Alps Theodoric manned most of the defensive works, forming a protective crescent for Italy. Forum Julii north of Aquileia was a key headquarters for the northwest section of the defenses. Numerous archaeological artifacts found in the crescent area attest to a continuation

---

[131] *Ibid.*, ii, 23. The division had been made, a Torisa vel aliis.
[132] *Ibid.*, vi, 5.
[133] Procopius, *B. G.*, VII, xiv, 21–31.

of the defensive system there by the Lombards.[134] Elsewhere in Illyria the Ostrogoths maintained their control by settlement or garrisions established in key towns. Gothic place-names survived longer in the Balkans than anywhere else in Europe, perhaps indicating that in scattered areas a sizable number of Goths remained and did not migrate all the way to Italy. The names occurred along the Dalmatian coast where philological evidence reveals that initially perhaps two regions existed under the semi-independent leadership of Goduscaner and Neretljaner.[135]

In spite of the extreme complexity of the archaeological material introduced by generations of participants in the Völkerwanderungszeit, a pattern is emerging for the Ostrogothic settlements in Illyria. Several sites in the upper Drava-Sava area have revealed further proof of Ostrogothic presence. At Kranj on the Sava belt buckles and bow fibulae of Ostrogothic provenance were found dating from the early sixth century, probably prior to the death of Theodoric.

Down stream at Dravlje two Ostrogothic female graves (no. 1 and 15) contain bow fibulae characteristic of the early sixth century. Similar materials were discovered at nearby Rifnik.[136] A few Gothic burials have turned up in Bosnia and Herzegovina with evidence of Gothic wall construction as far south as Dubrovnik. Farther south scattered coins imply trade connections but certainly cannot prove settlement.[137]

Considering the half century of Gothic dominion, the physical remains to date are unimpressive. Other sites[138] could be added to the few

---

[134] Šašel, *op. cit.*, pp. 85–86. The archaeological data for the Julian Alps is to form a second volume which has yet to be published.

[135] J. Kelemina, "Goti na Balkanu", *Casopis za zgodovino in Narodopisje*, 27 (1932), pp. 121–36, German summary, pp. 135–36. Such conclusions are based on the twelfth-century, *Presbyteri Diocleatis Regnum Slavorum*, ii–iv (Scriptores rerum Hungaricarum veteres . . . Cura et Studio Ioannis Georgi Schwandtheri . . . Vinobonae, 3, 1748), pp. 476–78, usually called the *Libellus Gothorum*. Others have been skeptical of Kelemina's views, for example, Ludmil Hauptmann, "Kroaten, Goten and Sarmaten", *Germanoslavica*, 3 (1935), pp. 95–127, 315–53, particularly pp. 110–12.

[136] Zdenko Vinskí, "Die völkerwanderungszeitliche Nekropole in Kranj und der Reihengräberfelder Horizont des 6. Jahrhunderts im westlichen Jugoslawien", *Actes de VIIe congrès international des sciences préhistoriques et protohistoriques*, 1 (Beograd, 1971), pp. 259–65; and Lojze Bolta, "Spätantikes Gräberfeld auf Rifnik bei Sentzur", *Acta Archaeologica. Arheološki Vestnik* (Ljubljana), 21–22 (1970–71), pp. 138–40. Ostrogothic materials were found in grave no. 9; and Marijan Slabe, "La Nécropole de la période de la migration des peuples à Dravlje", *Acta Archaeologica. Arheološki Vestnik*, 21–22 (1970–71), p. 150.

[137] Jovan Kovačević, *Varvarska Kolonizacija Južnoslovenskih Oblasti od IV do početka VII veka* (Musée de Voivodina Monographie 2, Novi Sad, 1960), pp. 64–65.

[138] The diamond-style belt buckles found in Savia are very similar to those found at Pavia,

chosen as examples but the overall picture would remain. The Goths did not settle in strength in Illyria. They chose instead to garrison a few strongpoints along the main penetration routes to Italy. Only rarely did they even establish a sizable garrison population. One such place was Salona, another possibly Fenekpuszta.

Several innovative studies focus on Fenekpuszta, an extraordinary site by any standard. Originally Fenekpuszta seems to have been an imperial latifundia and was inhabited until the ninth century. In the course of the fourth century the urban complex was surrounded by a rectangular wall and tower system characteristic of late Roman military architecture. Recent excavations have demonstrated the presence of two extramural cemeteries of different periods. The exact relationship between the two remains unclear, but it seems that the burial sites were used in the late Roman period and again in the ninth century. In addition, the 1959 excavations of the basilica unearthed 16 graves of another cemetery within the city. Diggings in 1966 raised the number of graves to 31. These graves, the Fenekpuszta-*Horreum* burials, raise a great many questions about the sixth and seventh centuries; e.g. the survival of the Roman population, the establishment of various barbarian groups, and their precise identity.[139]

The *Horreum* burial is clearly Germanic. To be sure there are late Roman precedents for disk fibulae and the other jewelry found in the *Horreum*, but the aggregate grave goods are very similar to fifth-century burials in Hungary and elsewhere where there is no question of Roman survivals.[140] Several graves contain curious reminders of the Roman-Christian background shared by the barbarians. For example, grave 9, the final resting place of a rich woman, besides numerous earrings of gold and silver, a gold head band, hair-net ornaments, and assorted glass beads of various colors, contains a silver ring with a gilded Byzantine cross and a circular shield.[141] The otherwise poor and simple grave no. 31 contains a small bronze coin of Valens.[142]

The *Horreum* is divided according to wealth along a north-south axis. The rich graves, such as no. 9, are located in the north, the poorer in

Aquileia, and Acquasanta. On stylistic similarities between Italy and Savia see further Giovanni Annibaldi and Joachim Werner, "Ostrogotische Grabfunde aus Acquasanta, Prov. Ascoli Piceno (Marche)", *Germania*, 41 (1963), pp. 356–73.

[139] L. Barkóczi, "A 6th Century Cemetery from Keszthely-Fenekpuszta", *Acta Archaeologica*, 20 (1968), pp. 275–86.

[140] For example, M. Parducz, "Der gotische Fund von Csongrád", *Dolgozatok*, 14 (1938), pp. 124–38.

[141] Barkóczi, *op. cit.*, p. 281.

[142] *Ibid.*, p. 286.

the south. Since the indigenous population was buried outside the wall in the late Roman cemetery and even the poor graves in the *horreum* are undoubtedly Germanic, the evidence of grave goods demonstrates some stratification of the ruling group based upon wealth. The rich were buried close to the basilica or within it, perhaps implying a belief that eternal prestige followed in accordance with earthly success. The poor intererments were not survivals of the autochthonous population, buried elsewhere, but were subordinate members of the ruling group.

It is possible to offer more than random guesswork regarding the ethnic identity of the group buried in the *horreum.* I. Lengyel has compared the chemical composition of human bones from 15 sixth-century sites in the Pannonian area using the fully excavated Lombard site of Szentendre as a standard. His tables establish certain norms in blood type ratios, decomposition rates, and sex/mortality functions. According to these tables Fenekpuszta-*horreum* dates from 500–525 and is clearly neither Lombardic nor Avaric.[143] Almost all the Germanic grave goods from the *horreum* can be connected to similar styles and developments in Ostrogothic Italy: gold earrings with small basket-pendants, disc-brooches, the Bellerophon portrayal, and others.[144] How-ever, excavation has yet to unearth any purely Ostrogothic materials, such as characteristic fibulae. The nature of the *horreum* material does not suggest a uniform ethnic group, but rather a group essentially different from either Lombard or Avar, yet heterogeneous. The early sixth century date, the distinctive bone-analysis patterns, and the geographic location of Fenekpuszta along the road network connecting Italy and the central Balkans, all point to a strong Ostrogothic interest and presence. Yet if the scattered Ostrogothic materials from such sites as Kranj and Rifnik are any indication, the Ostrogothic domination of the Sava-Drava area was an ethnically diffuse hegemony incorporating other Germanic groups as well as elements of the surviving Roman population.

Salona was the principal city of Dalmatia, and it definitely held a Gothic garrison as well as other Goths not directly in the garrison. A letter from Theodoric to Assium, *vir illustris* and *comes* at Salona, instructed the latter to arm the inhabitants of the city and to instruct

---

[143] I. Lengyel, "Chemico-analytical Aspects of Human Bone Finds from the 6th Century 'Pannonian' Cemeteries", *Acta Archaeologica*, 23 (1971), p. 158 table iv, and p. 160 figure 2.

[144] L. Barkóczi and A. Salamon, "Remarks on the 6th Century History of 'Pannonia'," *Acta Archaeologica*, 23 (1971), pp. 139–43.

them in the use of arms.[145] The order to train and equip the inhabitants may have applied only to the Goths, but surely the garrison was already armed. Therefore, the instruction of the inhabitants must have referred to the non-garrison personnel. The exposed situation of Dalmatia probably demanded a militia reserve of all able-bodied males including the native population.

Salona was the scene of the first battles in the Justinianic War, when the Goths under Asinarius, Gripas, and others engaged the Roman forces under Mundus while negotiations were conducted between Theodatus and Justinian. At this time the walls of Salona fell into disrepair and had to be rebuilt by the Byzantine general Constantianus after he had driven Gripas out for the last time.[146] The actions of Gripas and the other Gothic leaders were in accord with the independent command of marcher-lords of a later date. The border areas were commanded by those closest to the throne[147] – a policy that recognized the value of their loyalty as well as the need for proven commanders along the frontier. The Roman legal structure continued to exist alongside the Gothic military command in Dalmatia. The *princeps* of Dalmatia maintained the legal framework intact and must have worked closely with the Gothic comes of the province. Apparently, the office of *princeps* was held by several men at one time under the direction of the *comes*; moreover, they may have been assigned to each major city.[148] The provincial governor (*praeses*) maintained some civil authority and had some responsibility for tax collection.[149]

The Sava and Drava basins formed a similar Gothic area, but the details are even more sketchy than for Salona. The majority of the population remained "Pannonian."[150] What little can be said about the Gothic administration in the area derives from a brief passage in Ennodius' *Panegyric*, a few notices in the *Variae* of Cassiodorus, and scattered references in Procopius.

The Ostrogoths called this territory Savia and occasionally linked it administratively to Dalmatia by appointing the same man as count for

---

[145] *C.I.L.*, iii, 9563 = 12867 (Fiebiger, 1944, Ostgoten, no. 12), and Cassiodorus, *Variae*, i, 40 to Assuin.

[146] Procopius, *B.G.*, V, ii, 2–10; V, vii, 32–36. Wittiges later attempted to retake Salona with a combined land and sea blockade; V, xvi, 9–11.

[147] *Ibid.*, V, ii, 21–22; see also, Cassiodorus, *Variae*, ii, 35 and 36.

[148] *Variae*, vii, 24 and 25. For a discussion of the problems which these formulae create see T. Hodgkin, *op. cit.*, p. 335. Other references to the Romans living in Dalmatia are *Variae*, viii, 4; ix, 9.

[149] *Ibid.*, v, 24. See also John Wilkes, *Dalmatia* (London, 1969), p. 427.

[150] Procopius, *B.G.*, V, xv, 27–28.

both. However, the appointment of Osuin, *vir illustris comes*,[151] as ruler of both provinces indicates a new policy, for previously Savia had received its own governor.[152] Before the Sirmium War (504–05), Savia was a separate territory ruled from Sirmium in a loose allegiance to Theodoric. Sirmium was the boundary of Theodoric's Italian-based kingdom and was guarded by an alliance of senior lords (large owners) under a *regentium (dux* would be a more correct title) charged with the defense of the city or that portion still inhabited. The *regentium* so neglected the city's defenses that the Gepids, (under *ductor* Gundeuth, a pugnacious member of their royal line), moved in and sent daily insults to the Goths living in the countryside. Theodoric, angered that his commander (this time Ennodius used the term *retenator*) could not expel the Gepids, appointed Pitzia, a noble Goth, to take charge of the campaigns and either to make peace or to drive them out once for all.[153]

The control of the middle Danube area was uneasily balanced among Ostrogoth, Gepid and Byzantine. At the opening of the Sirmium War a new factor upset the entire area. Mundo, a Hun of noble ancestry, broke out of an alliance with the Gepids and recruited a following from the brigands and barbarous peoples beyond the Danube.[154] Against the new threat the Byzantines sent Sabinianus, *magister militum* for Illyria, and their new allies the Bulgars, who made their first historical appearance just prior to the Sirmium War. Pitzia won the war in two campaigns. Pitzia's task was to subdue the Gepids and reestablish Ostrogothic control at Sirmium. He left Italy and had little trouble driving

---

[151] *Variae*, ix, 8. Clearly two provinces, not one, were to be administered. atque ideo illustrem magnitudinem tuam deo iuvante ad Delmatiarum atque Saviae provincias iterum credidimus destinandum, . . .

[152] *Variae*, iv, 49. Fridibad was appointed governor and announced to the people of Savia. Although the epistle appointing Fridibad was written ca. 507–11 (*MGH.AA*, p. 136) and that concerning Osiun ca. 526 (*MGH.AA*, p. 275), it remains unknown why the shift to one man over both provinces occurred. The Gepids may have been active during this period after their temporary reversal at the hands of Pitzia. Theodoric was the only Ostrogothic king to mint coins at Sirmium, and the latest coin was a half-siliqua piece with Theodoric and Justinus I (518–27), F. K. Kraus, *Die Münzen Odovacars und des Ostrogotenreiches in Italien* (Halle, 1928), pp. 6, 94–95.

[153] Ennodius, *Pan.*, xii (60–62), p. 210, lines 23–32; *Getica*, 300, p. 135.

[154] A descendant of Attila, *Getica*, 301, nam hic Mundo de Attilanis quondam origine descendens; but a Getae in Marcellinus Comes, *Chronicon*, c.a. 505. When Procopius wrote the *Vandalic War* he stated that the Gepids had gained control of the country around Singidunum and Sirmium and remained settled there until the time of his writing (Procopius, III, ii, 1), but the Gepid expansion must have been checked as a result of the Sirmium War. Thus the period of expansion would have been ca. 510–550. Procopius (*B.G.*, VII, xxxiii, 7–8) states that Sirmium and Dacia were taken by the Gepids when Justinian took them from the Goths.

the Gepids from Sirmium. He was given a great deal of freedom of command by Theodoric, being "free to choose his own council." Appropriating what he regarded as wasteland, he returned it to cultivation as a compensation for his losses.[155] Regardless of his original goals, Pitzia quickly realized that the stability of the area required his intervention in the struggle against Sabinianus, and at an abandoned watch tower called Herta along the Danube Pitzia joined forces with Mundo, recoiling from a recent defeat. According to Jordanes, Pitzia's forces numbered 2000 infantry and 500 cavalry.[156] Ennodius reported that prior to the battle Pitzia addressed his men in the traditional manner: he asked his followers (*socii*) to remember that they had marched to the ends of the Empire for Theodoric whose fame fought with them, and whatever they owed to Theodoric was now owed to his appointee, Pitzia.[157] The battle can be only inaccurately reconstructed from Ennodius. The Ostrogoths faced the Bulgars and were victorious, but the cost in life was too high for either side to celebrate a true victory. The status quo was maintained. Sabinianus could no longer pursue an expansionistic policy in the Sirmium area. Pitzia reestablished the ancient customs (*praecepta*) among the Sirmians, which they traditionally held from the Ostrogoths.[158]Pitzia himself probably remained on his new lands, where he lived on without notice in history, but some soldiers returned to Italy.[159] By the spring of 535 Sirmium was again nominally under Byzantine control.[160]

The Sirmium War illustrates the type of control Theodoric exerted over the outlying Gothic territories. Until the situation threatened the stability of the entire area, he was quite content to allow the local lords to operate alone. When outside intervention and the general turmoil became critical he acted by sending in an able commander with a great

---

[155] Ennodius, *Pan.*, xxi (62), p. 210, line 37–39. continuo Patzia, qui et de te eventus utiles sumpserat et consiliorum momenta librabat, non adquisitam esse terram credidit sed refusam, nec rapinis ut lucrative populatus est, sed dispensationibus servavit ut propria. The Bulgarians had invaded the Balkans as early as 499; Marcellinus Comes, 499 and 502.

[156] *Getica*, 300.

[157] Ennodius, *Pan.*, xxi (65), p. 211, lines 5–13.

[158] *Ibid.*, lines 25–30.

[159] Cassiodorus, *Chronica*, s.a. 504. "In this year Theodoric defeated the Bulgars at Sirmium and returned to Italy." Theodoric himself never left Italy but appointed Pitzia. Pitzia may have returned and governed his new holdings as an absentee landlord but no positive conclusions can be reached concerning his remaining career.

[160] *Novellae*, xi (April 14, 535), *Codex Iustinianus*, ed. P. Krüger, *Corpus Iuris Civilis*, II (Berlin, 1915, 12th ed., 1959), creating a new metropolitan see, including Sirmium. See also J. Wilkes, *op. cit.*, p. 425. However, the real powers were the Gepids, Erulians, and Sclaveni, Procopius, *B.G.*, VII, xxxiii, 7–13 ;*Aedif.*, III, ii, 1.

reservoir of power. At Sirmium, at least, the Goths did not live in the city itself, although a garrison was maintained. The nobles lived instead on nearby estates easily created from the good farm land then untilled and vacant. The citizens lived under their own laws as elaborated by the *curiales.*[161] As usual, the bulk of the population suffered during the wars.[162] The campaign itself would seem insignificant except that many Goths who later became important leaders served as youths in the war, including the future king Wittigis.[163]

The administration of Savia closely paralleled that of Italy with similar abuses. Rich proprietors profited by tax-farming their poorer neighbors. Barbarians married rich Roman wives and had to be forced to pay taxes on their new lands. Judges abused their right to three days maintenance at any town per year. Other Goths forced provincials to sell their land.[164] As these abuses reveal the system of administration and justice, they will be discussed in the following chapter. What stands out is the influence of the central government in maintaining a semblance of regular administration in its distant dominions by appointing ministers and judges just as for Italy. Unfortunately, we cannot know how effective the royal officials were in the field; however, all the abuses mentioned for redress were equally prevalent in Italy itself and do not indicate that the authority of the king was weaker in Savia than elsewhere. The royal authority was everywhere too intrinsically weak to prevent personal disputes over land and private abuses of power granted to one man or group over others.

The Ostrogoths were also concerned with the Alpine Passes and with the flow of people and trade north and south. The defense of the northern frontier was twofold. First, Theodoric and his successors

---

[161] *Variae*, iv, 49. Addressed to all the Provincial and Capillates (longhaired men, i.e. nobles), the *defensores* and *curiales* residing in Savia. Fridibad the new governor was charged with maintaining peace and especially with the punishment of cattle rustlers. *Capillates* was used by Jordanes to mean Gothic noblemen, *Getica*, 72. There can be no doubt concerning the Gothic presence in Savia, although they were certainly not the only Germanic people in the vicinity.

[162] Procopius, *B.G.*, V, iii, 15 and 17. Similar circumstances followed the Visigoths in southeastern Gaul for which Paulinus Pellaeus has left a marvellous description of shared estates, forces requisition, and occasionally a welcomed purchase by the Goths, *Eucharisticus* , Loeb edition, trans., Hugh G. White (Cambridge, Mass., 1921).

[163] For Wittigis, Procopius, *B.G.*, V, xi, 5. Others included Tulus, who eventually became a senator after being commander in Gaul, ambassador to the Byzantines, and a close personal advisor to Theodoric in matters of war (*Variae*, viii, 9, 19, 11). Cyprianus, the son of Opilio (Count of the Sacred Largess under Odovacar), also fought in the war and took part in the break-through against the Bulgars. Eventually he followed his father's precedent and became Count of the Sacred Largess and finally senator (*Variae*, viii, 22).

[164] *Variae*, v, 14 and 15 to Severinus, *vir illustris.*

attempted to create a system of buffer kingdoms along the northern flank to provide protection against the Franks. The keystone of the system was the Raetians, whose leader received a special recognition as *ducatus Raetiarum* each indiction. The Raetians were to entangle "the wild and cruel nations beyond" until they could be effectively dealt with by the Ostrogoths.[165] Ostrogothic materials arrived in Raetia and the transalpine lands soon after Theodoric's conquest. Raetia in particular had a prolonged trade relationship with Ostrogothic Italy as seen in numerous examples of the tendril (early sixth century) fibulae, scattered coins, and assorted grave goods.[166] Numerous examples of Ostrogothic fibulae have been found along the Rhine as far north as Brabant.[167] In all the lands north of the Alps Ostrogothic influence competed with strong Frankish and local traditions dating back to the early fifth century and before. Theodoric extended his jurisdiction to Raetia I, but the advance was not destined to survive his death.[168] The Thuringians, Burgundians, and Alemanni also figured in the buffer zone.[169] Second, garrisons were established in the north to monitor the Alpine passes. The Ostrogoths garrisoned the strategic area between the upper Drava and the Danube with small settlements along the Glan, Gorschita, and Gurk Rivers north of Klagenfurt in Kärnten.[170]

Theodoric anchored the northeastern flank at Trent and ordered a new fortress constructed and all the inhabitants to share in the effort, including the servants of the royal estates and slaves of the fisc. The free inhabitants were suitably paid. Theodahad later opened the granaries at Trent and sold a third of the stores at a fixed price to relieve a famine.[171] By the Justinianic Wars, if not originally, the Gothic garrisons in the Alps were small settlements of families guarding the passes,

---

[165] *Variae*, vii, Formula 4. See also R. Heuberger, "Das ostgotische Rätien", *Klio*, 30 (1937), pp. 77–109.

[166] Volker Bierbrauer, "Zu den Vorkommen ostgotischer Bügelfibeln in Raetia II:", *Bayerische Vorgeschichtsblätter*, 26 (1961), pp. 68–75.

[167] *Ibid.*, pp. 156–57, figures 8 and 9; see also Herbert Kühn, *Die germanischen Bügelfibeln der Völkerwanderungszeit* part 1. *Die germanischen Bügelfibeln in der Rheinprovinz* (Bonn, 1940, rev. reprint Graz, 1965), pp. 95–100. On Ostrogothic archaeology in Italy and elsewhere see now Volker Bierbrauer, *Die ostgotischen Grab- und Schatzfunde in Italien* (Spoleto, 1975).

[168] H. Zeiss, "Die Nordgrenze des Ostgotenreiches", *Germania*, 12 (1928), pp. 25–34.

[169] For the Thuringians see, *Variae*, iii, 3, and for the marriage alliance, iv, 1. The Burgundians were more concerned with Provence and will be discussed in that regard. For Alemmanni see *Variae*, iii, 3 and 50.

[170] Emmerich Schaffran, "Zur Nordgrenze des ostgotischen Reiches in Kärnten", *Österreichisches archäologisches Institut in Wien, Jahreshefte* (Beiblatt), 42 (1955), pp. 111–30.

[171] *Variae*, v, 9; x, 27.

and when Belisarius' lieutenant John raided these settlements the Goths deserted Urais' army in Liguria to protect their families.[172]

Provence was by far the most important frontier for the Ostrogoths, for the Burgundians posed a threat to all northwestern Italy. They had to be bought off as early as 489—90 when Theodoric was at Pavia.[173] But the rise of the Franks, particularly under Clovis, made some sort of an alliance mutually advantageous. Until 534, when the kingdom of the Burgundians was taken over by the Franks, the Ostrogothic kings eagerly sought Burgundian friendship. The invasion of Provence by the Gothic duke Mammo in 509 marks the earliest reliable date for Ostrogothic activity in the area.[174] The letters of Ennodius in behalf of his friends and relatives still living around Arles attest that a land division accompanied the Gothic occupation of Provence. The occupation and garrisoning occurred only as a result of a war against Clovis, for the Ostrogoths, ever mindful of spreading themselves too thinly, were reluctant to expand beyond Italy.

The new garrisons did not always get along well with the native inhabitants. The commander at Avignon had to be told to discipline his troops more strictly and assure the people that the troops were there to protect, not to plunder.[175] Ostrogoths manning forts along the Durance River were supplied by boat from Marseilles, and the Roman Governor, Gemellus, was charged with supervising their supply.[176] The periodic ravaging of the countryside by Frankish raiding parties exacerbated the supply problem. In 510—11 the destruction was so widespread that tax relief was granted to the whole province not, as usual, to only those individuals proving damage.[177] At principial cities such as Arles the defenses were built and grain stored. Grain was shipped to Arles when

---

[172] Procopius, *B.G.*, VI, xxviii, 33—35.

[173] Ennodius, *Vita Epiphani*, 155—57. The contest at this time was over captives taken by the Burgundians in a recent raid. Liguria was already desolate and could ill afford to lose more workers (*Vita*, 138—39). A letter of Gelasius (dated 494) sanctioning the elevation of laymen to the priesthood, since so many had died of war and famine, may point toward the depopulation of Liguria; Andreas Thiel, *Epistolae Romanorum Pontificum a S. Hilario usque ad F. Hormisdam* (Braunsberg, 1868). See also G. M. Cook, *The Life of Saint Epiphanius by Ennodius* (Washington D.C., 1942), p. 210. Depopulation must have facilitated the settlement in this area, but it cannot account for the entire settlement. The redemption of captives is also recorded in the *Liber Pontificalis* as accomplished by Pope Symmachus. I disagree with editor Loomis who believes that the capitives were held by the Ostrogoths.

[174] Marius Aventicensis, 509; *Variae*, I, 24 probably also refers to this campaign.

[175] *Variae*, iii, 38.

[176] *Variae*, iii, 41.

[177] *Variae*, iii, 40 and 42.

Clovis had destroyed the crops.[178] Sometime around 530 the Ostrogoths may have abandoned much of Provence as a condition for a new
alliance with the Burgundians against the Franks, but in 534 the
Frankish conquest of the kingdom of Burgundy destroyed the alliance.[179] During the early phases of Wittiges' war with Belisarius, the
frontier troops from both Gaul and Venetia were recalled to fight in
Italy.[180]

Life along the frontiers was difficult and monotonous. The central
government knew that regular pay (usually in kind) and proper supplies
were essential elements of morale. The garrisons themselves were small,
sixty men at Aosta,[181] and were outposts where families were reared
while the men kept alert for invasion. In most places Goths occupied the
deserted late Roman fortifications, but occasionally a new location,
such as Verruca, was fortified.[182] In all outposts the Goths literally set
up house, much as the *limitanei* had done in the fifth century.[183] The
frontier commands were not intended to check a full-fledged invasion
but to supervise passes and road crossings as well as act as provosts
against brigands and small raiding parties. Even when confronted by an
all out invasion, the garrisons could hold out and disrupt supplies and
discourage small foraging parties while the main Gothic army assembled.

The presence of semi-autonomous Gothic commands along the
borders of the kingdom was a factor in preventing the crown from
consolidating its rule regardless of the size and skill of the Roman
bureaucracy. Although the number of examples is admittedly few, men
such as Tulum, Cyprianus, and Wittigis prove that at least one path to
power was military success on the frontier. The frontier commanders
were selected because of their proven capability and loyalty, for once in
command they were virtually commanders-in-chief. Communications
were never fast enough to allow tactical or even many strategic decisions to be made at court. As a result, men like Pitzia had the full
power of peace and war in their territory. The power and independence of garrison and provincial commanders grew when they were

---

[178] *Variae*, iii, 44. Another attempt to supply grain by ship failed when a storm sank most
of the ships (*Variae*, iv, 5 and 7). Other decrees concerning Provence include iii, 17; iii, 18; iv,
19; v, 10; viii, 7; xi, 1.

[179] *Variae*, xi,1 and the comments of T. Hodgkins, *op. cit.*, p. 456.

[180] Procopius, *B.G.*, V, xiii, 17–20.

[181] *Variae*, ii, 5.

[182] *Variae*, iii, 48; Thomas Hodgkin, *Letters*, p. 224, believes that Verruca cannot be
identified in the *Notitia*.

[183] Procopius, *B.G.*, VI, xxvii, 28–29.

recalled to Italy during the Justinianic War, but the individual soldier was never totally eclipsed by his superiors on the battle field, as was proved by the unopposed desertion of the Alpine garrisons from Urais. The lonely garrisons, the settlements in Provence, and the complex diplomacy sought to guarantee peace for Italy. The arts of peace not those of war stand as milestones of the short-lived Ostrogothic Kingdom of Italy.

CHAPTER FOUR

THE KINGDOM

The Ostrogothic Kingdom of Italy endured for but half a century (494–553), yet in spite of its brevity important social changes occurred during the period. Once settled in Italy, tensions appeared between the ordinary Ostrogoths and the military aristocracy whose positions were strengthened by the settlement. The conflict increasingly produced divisions within Ostrogothic society very similar to the *honestiores-humiliores* dichotomy among the Roman population. The process was incomplete when Narses defeated the last Ostrogothic belligerents at Campsas in 553. But even in the final days of the kingdom it was clear that the ducal nobility profited most from the Italian experience, not the Amali whose blood now flowed in Byzantine veins, not the humble Ostrogoth who once again saw his home plundered. After the death of Teias, the last king, dukes Aligernus and Ragnaris took over command of the Goths still under arms. Aligernus joined Narses against the Franks ravaging northern Italy. Ragnaris, a leader of perhaps 7000 Goths, refused to join Narsus and was besieged at Campsas.[1] The explanation for the eventual triumph of the nobility over the central government lies at the heart of Ostrogothic society — in the solidification of class structure, the mechanics of government, the law, and the army. The established Roman culture influenced every aspect of Ostrogothic society. The breakdown of central authority demonstrates the incomplete transformation to central structures. Where the evidence permits inquiry, Ostrogoths can be seen adopting Roman ways; however, only rarely did they totally abandon their own customs.

At each stage in Ostrogothic history the nobles were vital members of society. Theodoric won their loyalty slowly by effective leadership. Yet even within his lifetime local rulers, perhaps the descendants of sub-group leaders and the military commanders of the migrations, began to reassert their autonomy. One such leader was Theodoric's nephew and future king, Theodahad, but others such as *dux* Gudui,

---

[1] Agathias, *Historiarum Libri Quinque*, CFHB, 2, ed., Rudolf Keydell (Berlin, 1967). Aligernus, ii, 9 (Keydell, p. 53, line 11), Ragnaris, ii, 13 (Keydell, p. 57, line 17).

charged with enslaving his fellow free Goths, were restless.[2] But instances of abuse of power and disregard for royal authority were atypical of Theodoric's reign. In general, the administration of law and government was well executed under him. His men, *saiones*, sent out from the court, were obeyed (except in Theodahad's lands in Liguria) and were usually unoppressive. The noblest men in the realm attended the *comitatus* as advisers and were selected for important missions and frontier commands. However, when *comes* Odoin plotted against Theodoric, he was summarily beheaded.[3] Obviously Amali blood and sound government alone did not always inspire loyalty. There were still occasions when naked power was needed.

After the death of Theodoric in 526, the power of local leaders acted to weaken royal government and destroy the administrative accomplishments of the early years. Even the *saiones* were feckless. Athalaric issued (ca. 527) a general edict to the *comes patrimoni* to protect the *curiales* from oppression by the *saiones* and other officials.[4] By the deposition and slaying of Theodahad in 536, the administrative personnel often were neither willing nor able to carry out royal orders. In 535–36 Cassiodorus, the praetorian prefect, characterized *saiones* as violent and boastful men.[5] Simultaneously, general unrest permeated Liguria, the center of Theodahad's power.[6] The northern alliance system of Theodoric broke down.[7] Athalaric was overwhelmed with appeals from provincial *iudices*, who too often lacked the power to settle disputes between powerful nobles.[8] The edict of Athalaric published in 533–34 is an outline of disintegration. He decried the general return to lawlessness, the appropriation of land by the powerful, the usurpation of the royal right to fix titles to land, forced donations to the rich, the personal abuse of those under special royal protection (*tuitio*), the local editing of royal decrees, and a variety of moral abuses.[9] In almost every case the root of the problem was local power, particularly that of the nobility, integrated into the government. The essential aspects of government remained as they had been under Theodoric, but administrative effectiveness rapidly declined. To some

---

[2] For Theodahad see Procopius, *B.G.*, V, iii, 2–4; V, iii, 29; and *Variae*, iv, 39; v, 12. For Gudui see *Variae*, v, 30.

[3] Anonymus Valesianus, 68 and 69.

[4] *Variae*, ix, 2.

[5] *Variae*, xii, 3.

[6] *Variae*, viii, 16.

[7] Agathias, i, 5, Keydell, pp. 15–17.

[8] *Variae*, ix, 20.

[9] *Variae*, ix, 18.

extent the pressures of the wars of Justinian compelled local leadership to cooperate with the central authority, yet success in war simultaneously entrenched the nobility, for at all times during the wars local leaders and local recruitment and supply were the keys of survival. Belisarius realized this and sent John and Bessas into Liguria, Picenum, and to the vicinity of Ravenna to destroy the Gothic regional power centers. Byzantine inability to garrison enough strategic towns led to a war of attrition and years of marching and counter-marching. When Byzantine troops left, the Goths simply came out of hiding.

Theoretically, free-born Goths were not to be forced into personally degrading positions, especially slavery. But the example of duke Gudui enslaving his subordinates is proof that theory and practice were not always synonymous. An old Gothic warrior, gone blind, had to petition (ca. 523–26) Theodoric to protect him from enslavement by two fellow Goths, Gudila and Oppas. The old soldier had brought his case before the *comes* of his area, Pythius, but the count could not force Gudila and Oppas to free him.[10] In Verona, Theodoric encountered a poor Gothic woman lying in the streets.[11] When Theodoric sent administrators to Spain during his regency there, they reported that free-born Visigoths, especially those in the cities, were being downtrodden.[12] Apparently the poor Visigoths of Spain, like their Ostrogothic counterparts, paid the price of a reassertive nobility, and they did so with but few murmurs of discontent. In general, social divisions of noble and poor carried over into the army in which careful distinction was made between the leaders and the private soldiers.

Theodoric's sister, Amalafila, brought to the Vandal Trasmundus as a wedding gift a bodyguard of 1000 "well-provided Goths" and 5000 lesser fighting men.[13] Totila sought to conceal his presence in the army by changing his golden armor for that of a private soldier. He died standing with the rank and file.[14] Near the end Aligernus, forsaking Ostrogothic independence for an alliance with Narses, inveighed to the Franks that the supportive wealth of the monarchy was no more. Future claimants to the throne could only "don the garb of a common soldier and a private citizen."[15] The cavalry was mainly composed of

---

[10] *Variae*, v, 29.
[11] Anonymus, 84, mulier pauper de gente Gothica.
[12] *Variae*, v, 39.
[13] Procopius, *B.V.*, III, viii, 12–13.
[14] Procopius, *B.G.*, VIII, xxxii, 2 and 34.
[15] Agathias, A, 20.10.

nobles.[16] There were undoubtedly a great many variations in wealth, power, and prestige among the common Ostrogoths, but it remains impossible to specify any such gradations. Even the role of the ordinary Ostrogoth in the economy remains difficult to discern.

Some evidence suggests that the majority of the Ostrogoths lived as farmer-soldiers in small settlements in Liguria, Picenum-Samnium, and the Romagna. After Wittiges surrendered at Ravenna, Belisarius urged the barbarians living south of the Po to "go home and tend their lands" unmolested by Roman soliders.[17] Theodahad earlier raised a garrison for Rome from soldiers who had "left their families and homes" to defend the ungrateful citizens of the city who barred the gates.[18] In Picenum and Samnium, if not everywhere, the settlers were divided into groups under noble leadership; one such leader was Pitzia, who later surrendered to Belisarius. Belisarius': lieutenant, John had little difficulty in capturing the tiny Gothic fortified settlements in Picenum, as many were deserted. Only at Aterna did the Goths offer any resistance. There *dux* Tremonus, the local commander, led the resistance but to no avail.[19]

In a highly rhetorical letter dated ca. 526, Athalaric addressed all the inhabitants of Reate (now Rieti) and Nursia announcing that he had appointed Quidila, the son of Sibia, *prior* over them as they desired.[20] From the remainder of the letter it seems that the *prior* had some sort of legal and military function, but Cassiodorus couched his responsibilities in vague references, exhorting the people to obey the law and the *iudices* and reminding them of their victories and the donatives awarded to them. Felix Dahn and Thomas Hodgkin believed that the *prior* corresponded to the "Gothic" hundafath.[21] Ludwig Schmidt thought that the *prior* was similar to, if not identical with, the *tribunatus provinciarum* of *Variae* vii, 30 and was the ruler of a small region within a province.[22] The evidence is insufficient to draw positive conclusions beyond what is stated in this one letter. The letter is addressed to all the inhabitants (*universis*) of both towns and only one *prior* is appointed. The choice may have been influenced by popular pressure from

[16] Procopius, *B.G.*, VI, xxiii, 17–21; V, xxvii, 27–29; VII, iv, 21–29.

[17] *Ibid.*, VI, xxix, 36–37.

[18] *Variae*, x, 14.

[19] Procopius, *B.G.*, VI, vii, 28–34; V, xv, 1–3; and Marcellinus Comes, 538.

[20] *Variae*, viii, 26.

[21] Felix Dahn, *Die Könige der Germanen*, 4 (Würzburg, 1866), p. 173; T. Hodgkin, *The Letters of Cassiodorus* (London, 1886), p. 375.

[22] L. Schmidt, "Die Comites Gothorum", *Mitteilungen des österreichischen Instituts für Geschichtsforschung*, 40 (1925), p. 132.

the communities. Unless the Roman population had fled, and this seems doubtful, the *prior* was appointed over both groups. Indeed both are mentioned. The Romans paid tribute, which was eventually given to the Goths as donatives. *Prior* Quidila may be the same man as *saio* Quidila sent to Syracuse by Athalaric at about the same time, but there is no way of being certain.[23] There is no doubt that Quidila and his father were Goths. Dukes such as Tremonus, the defender of Aterna, may have commanded several *priores* in their region.

In northern Italy, at least, the rural population lived in *condomae*, small agrarian units probably family farms. Late in his reign (523/526) Theodoric transferred some allied Gepids from his northeastern flank to bolster the defense of Gaul and ordered his *saio* Veranus supervising the move to requisition supplies from the *condomae*.[24] These single-family farms in northern Italy survived the Ostrogothic demise and existed in Lombard Italy. Unlike urban units they were apparently outside intermediate levels of bureaucratic control such as the *priores*. Never swallowed by the villa economy, such free-farms endured and, as the villa system dwindled, especially in Gaul, merged with shattered pieces of once great estates to flourish after the seventh century as the *mansus*.[25] Although it is tempting to attribute the *condoma* to the Goths, known to have based agriculture on family units even before Adrianople, they probably antedated the *adventus Ostrogothorum*.[26]

Until the 1950's it was customary for historians studying the Ostrogothic Kingdom to draw upon the *Edictum Theodorici* to point out the continued distinctions regarding *honestiores-humiliores* in sixth-century Italy.[27] Recent scholarship has demonstrated that the *Edictum* is Visigothic rather than Ostrogothic and was issued under Theodoric II at Toulouse ca. 458–59.[28] An origin in southern Gaul is

---

[23] *Variae*, ix, 10.

[24] Cassiodorus, *Variae*, V, 10 and 11.

[25] David Herlihy, "The Carolingian Mansus", *Economic History Review*, 13 (1961), p. 83 n. 4, and A. R. Korsunskij, "Small Landed Property in the Western Provinces of the Late Roman Empire" [in Russian with an English summary], *Vestnik Drevnej Istorii*, 112 (1970), pp. 167–74.

[26] Alexander Souter, *A Glossary of Later Latin* (Oxford, 1964), p. 69, thought that the *condoma* was a Gothic measure of land.

[27] For example, A. Gaudenzi, "Die Entstehungszeit des Edictum Theodorici", *Zeitschrift der Savigny-Stiftung für Rechtsgeschichte, Germ. Abt.*, 7 (1887), pp. 29–52; Thomas Hodgkin, *Italy and her Invaders*, 306–814, Vol. 3 (New York, 1880–89).

[28] Guilio Vismara, "El 'Edictum Theodorici'," in: *Estudios visigóthicos* (Roma, Madrid, 1956), pt. 1, pp. 49–89 (Cuadernos del Instituto Juridico Español, 5); Alvaro d'Ors, *Estudios visigóticos*, pt. 2: *El Código de Eurico* (Cuadernos del Instituto Juridico Español, 12, Roma, Madrid, 1960), p. 8; P. Rasi, "Sulla paternità de c. d. Edictum Theodorici regis," *Archivio*

clear.[29] The applicability of the *Edictum* to the Ostrogoths was always problematic even before recent studies totally removed it from Italy. Nevertheless, several of the conclusions drawn by earlier scholars regarding the continued presence of the estate system, the importance of social class, and Theodoric's legal activities nonetheless are valid. In each of these areas there remains ample evidence in the papyri, inscriptions, and in various literary sources to draw conclusions very similar to those previously based largely on the *Edictum*.

Perhaps the most obvious aspect of the papyri fragments is the survival of the Roman estates system, in which the Ostrogoths were deeply involved because of the settlement.[30] The estates system and the economy in general are by far the most discussed aspects of Ostrogothic Italy and need not be greatly elucidated.[31] But the economic importance of illegal selling and transporting of merchandise by officials and coloni should probably receive more attention than is customary. The *Variae* reveal that legislation barring such enterprises, common to rich and poor alike, was ineffective.[32] Cattle rustling was just as prevalent in Italy as it had been in the Balkans.[33]

In spite of the fact that the *Edictum* is no longer attributable to Theodoric the Ostrogoth, there remain clear indications that he was deeply involved in the legal structure and, furthermore, that he issued edicts applicable to the Ostrogoths. According to the Anonymous Valesianus, the Goths remembered him because of his edict.

Giuridico, 145, sesta serie, 14 (1953), p. 105 ff.; P. Rasi, "Ancora sulla paternità del c. d. 'Edictum Theodorici'," *Annali de Storia del Diritto*, 5–6 (1961–2), pp. 113–36; and G. Vismara, *Edictum Theodorici* (Ius Romanum Medii Aevi, pars 1, 2b, aa, *a*, Milano, 1967).

[29] So concludes Ernst Levy in his review of Alvaro d'Ors' *El Código de Eurico* in *Zeitschrift der Savigny-Stiftung für Rechtsgeschichte, Rom. Abt.*, 79 (1962), pp. 479–88.

[30] Tjäder, particularly papyri No. 3 dated mid-sixth-century from Padua.

[31] On the survival of the villa system see Lellia C. Ruggini, *Economia e società nell' "Italia annoraria," Rapporti fra agricultura e commercio dal IV al VI secolo d. c.* (Milano, 1961). Also L. Ruggini, "Vicende rurali dell' Italia antica dall' età tetrarchia ai Langobardi," *Rivista Storica Italiana*, 76 (1964), pp. 261–86. On the economy in general see H. Geiss, *Geld- und naturalwirtschaftliche Erscheinungsformen im staatlichen Aufbau Italiens während der Gothenzeit* (Beiheft 27 zur Vierteljahresschrift für Sozial- und Wirtschaftsgeschichte, Stuttgart, 1931); K. Hannestad, *L'Évolution des ressources agricoles de l.Italie du IVe au VIe siècle de notre ère* (Kφbenhavn, 1962); M. Lecce, "La vita economica dell' Italia durante la dominazione dei Goti nelle "Variae di Cassidoro," *Economia e Storia, Rivista Italiana di Storia Economica e Sociale*, III, 4 (1956), pp. 354–408; John Percival, "Seigneurial Aspects of the Late Roman Estate Management," *English Historical Review*, 84 (1969), pp. 449–73; and M. A. Wes, *Das Ende des Kaisertums im Westen des römischen Reiches*, (Archeologische Studien van het Nederlands Historisch Instituut te Roma, 3, 's-Gravenhage, 1967).

[32] *Variae*, iv, 47; v, 5.

[33] *Variae*, v, 27.

So that even by the Romans he Theodoric was called a Trajan or a Valentinian, whose times he took as a model; and by the Goths, because of his edict, in which he established justice he was judged to be in all respects their best king.[34]

Theodoric ordered the *comites Gothorum*[35] to decide disputes between two Goths according to his edicts. If the dispute involved a Goth and a Roman, the *comes* associated with himself a Roman knowledgable in the law and decided the matter according to fair reason. If between two Romans, the Roman examiners handled the case.[36] Unfortunately, none of Theodoric's edicts has survived.

The complete silence of the edict of Athalaric on Ostrogothic family relations indicates that other legal customs existed.[37] On the Roman side, the law of the *Code* applied to every case not covered by royal legislation.[38] Although proof of the widespread use of Roman Law is weak, the argument is reasonable, since Roman society scarcely could have operated under the limited legal system promulgated by Athalaric. The lost edicts of Theodoric were perhaps more detailed than those of his successor, but if the early edicts formed an elaborate basis for future legislation, the silence of the sources on this point is very difficult to explain.

Theodoric's instructions to the *comites Gothorum* indicate a concern for the personality of the law. If an absolute division of the legal system according to personality existed behind these instructions, legal process was quite cumbersome — especially in those cases in which the issue of personality itself was in question. In many cases, such as merchant transactions, there was little point in the Ostrogoths' duplicating Roman Law, and there is no evidence that they did, although the nobility dealt with merchants.

The non-legal sources are particularly helpful in reconstructing the activities of the Ostrogothic nobility, and occasionally they offer a rare view of the non-noble population. Social distinctions similar in many

---

[34] Trans., J.C. Rolfe, *Ammianus Marcellinus*, p. 545.

[35] On this important office see below pages 114–116.

[36] *Variae*, vii, 3. Cum deo iuvante sciamus Gothos vobiscum habitare permixtos, ne qua inter consortes, ut assolet, indisciplinatio nasceretur, necessarium duximus illum sublimem virum, bonis nobis moribus hactenus comprobatum, ad vos comitem destinare, qui secundum edicta nostra inter duos Gothos litem debeat amputare, si quod etiam inter Gothum et Romanum natum fuerit fortasse negotium, adhibitio sibi prudente Romano certamen possit aequabili ratione discingere. inter duos autem Romanos Romani audiant quos per provincias dirigimus cognitores, ut uncuique sua iura serventur et sub diversitate iudicum una iustitia complectatur universos.

[37] The Edict of Athalaric is genuine and is preserved in *Variae*, ix, 18.

[38] Francesco Calasso, *Medio evo del diritto* (Milano, 1954), pp. 74–77.

respects to those of the Roman social hierarchy enhanced the positions of the Gothic nobility.

There can be no doubt that the Roman *honestiores-humiliores* distinction continued into the sixth century.[39] However, it is incorrect to regard this division as directly applicable to the Goths. The terms themselves are Roman labels disguising a great range of diversity.[40] It is significant that Ostrogothic society approached the same division. Ordinary Ostrogoths never became *humiliores*, but nobles were very similar to *honestiores*. They occupied favored positions in the administration and the army, they dressed differently, and they lived differently than the ordinary Goths. Just as there were various gradations within the *honestiores* so were there among the Ostrogothic nobility. In fact, many of the titular expressions of degrees of rank were shared. For the most part the complicated hierarchy of interrelated titles and ranks inherited from the Empire was maintained under the Ostrogoths. The evidence does not indicate whether fine titular distinctions were actually important in the day-to-day operation of government, but they clearly had social significance.

The *comes primi* was one of the highest honors in the Ostrogothic hierarchy as it had been in the Empire. Cassiodorus preserved the formula by which the title was awarded:

> The rank of Comes is one which is reached by Governors (Rectores) of Provinces after a year's tenure in office, and by the Counsellors of the Praefect, whose functions are so important that we look upon them as almost Quaestors.
>
> Their rank gives the holder of it, though only a Spectabilis, admission to our Consistory, where he sits side by side with all the Illustres.
>
> We bestow it upon you, and name you a Comes Primi Ordinis, thereby indicating that you are to take your place at the head of all the other Spectabiles and next after the Illustres. See that you are not surpassed in excellence of character by any of those below you.[41]

The formula is somewhat misleading, since it implies that admission to the consistory was part of the elevation. In fact, only the *comites* serving in the provinces and the counselors of the praetorian prefect were automatically members of the consistory.[42] At least one important Ostrogoth was a count of the first order. A certain Gudila set up an

---

[39] Pointed out by G. Cardascia, "L'Apparition dans le droit des classes d'"honestiores' et d'"humiliores'," *Revue historique de droit français et étranger*, 28 (1950), pp. 478–85.

[40] Peter Garnsey, *Social Status and Legal Privilege in the Roman Empire* (Oxford, 1970), pp. 221–33.

[41] This difficult formula is translated by T. Hodgkin, *Letters*, p. 308.

[42] William Sinnigen, "Comites Consistoriani in Ostrogothic Italy," *Classica et Mediaevalia*, 24 (1963), pp. 158–65, and T. Mommsen, "Ostgothische Studien," p. 419, n. 6.

inscription bearing his full title to honor the citizens of Faventina. The same name appears in the list of signatories at the Synod of Rome in 501.[43] Unfortunately, the narrative sources did not distinguish the various grades of *comites*, and inscriptions are rare.

A humorous example of Gothic concern for rank and its outward manifestations is the dispute between the wives of Uraias and Hildibadus. *Dux* Hildibadus, commander of Verona, became king shortly after Wittiges surrendered to Belisarius outside Ravenna in 540. His closest comrade was *dux* Uraias, the nephew of Wittiges and successful commander of the Gothic army in Liguria.[44] Their wives met at a bath — the wife of Uraias in splendid attire but the wife of the king in plain clothes. Uraias' wife was so disrespectful as to ignore her social superior's presence. That was too much for Hildibadus' wife, and she went storming back to her husband complaining of the insult. Supposedly this resulted in the denunciation of Uraias, his assassination, and retaliation in kind by Uraias' followers against Hildibadus.[45] The ducal rivals had better reasons than a squabble between wives to eliminate each other. Indeed, the story of the wives' encounter may be apocryphal, but the emphasis on dress among the nobility is well documented.[46] To dress in the manner appropriate to one's class was just as important to the Ostrogoths as to citizens of the Roman Empire. When Hildibaldus was made king he was "clad in the purple", at least according to Procopius,[47] and the "soldier-king" Wittiges was raised on a shield in the center of a circle of swords.[48]

Dress and titles aside, the Ostrogothic nobility exerted its power in the central government by membership in the *comitatus* where the king brought legal questions beyond the power of provincial *iudices*. Theodoric used the council as a law court and a reservoir of potential leadership. Pitzia was chosen "from the chief men of the kingdom" and departed the court for the campaigns of the Sirmium War.[49] Even Theodohad was asked to bring his case to the *comitatus* after reported-

---

[43] O. Fiebiger, and L. Schmidt, "Inschriftensammlung zur Geschichte der Ostgermanen," *Denkschriften der kaiserlichen Akademie der Wissenschaften in Wien, philosophisch-historische Klasse*, 60 Abh. 3 (1917), continued by Fiebiger alone in 70, Abh. 3 (1939) and 72 (1944), no. 182 (1917); *C.I.L.*, xi, 268. vir sub(limis) Gudila com(es) [ord(inis) pr(imi) et cura]tor r(ei) p(u)b(licae)hane sta[tuam terrae m]oto ... See commentary by Fiebiger, p. 94.

[44] Marcellinus Comes, 539, *MGH.AA*, 11 (*Chronica Minora*, 2).

[45] Procopius, *B.G.*, VII, i, 37–47.

[46] *Ibid.*, VI, xxiii, 37; VI, xxx, 7; VI, xxx, 17; VIII, xxxii, 2; Agathias, A. 20.10.

[47] *Ibid.*, VI, xxx, 17.

[48] *Variae*, x, 31.

[49] *Getica*, 300.

ly seizing the lands of *spectabilis* Domitius and refusing to obey
Theodoric's *saio*, Duda. He was ordered to cease or bring his case before
Theodoric and the *comitatus*.[50] The relationship between Theodoric
and his *comitatus* was advisory. There is no record of the council op-
posing him or being indispensable.

Later kings were not able to dominate so firmly the nobility.
Wittiges asked their consent to surrender Gaul to the Franks in an
attempt to achieve peace on that front.[51] Totila appointed the most
notable Goths commanders of the army he sent to Picenum, including
dukes Scipuar, Gibal, and Gundulf, who had been a bodyguard to
Belisarius.[52] He was strongly opposed by the council when he sought to
imprison one of his own bodyguards.[53] He suffered further rebuke for
not totally levelling Rome.[54] After Totila's death in battle the nobles
had no trouble continuing and negotiating a surrender the following
day.[55] The transition from duke and/or member of the council to king
was easy for Wittiges, Hildibadus, and Eraric. The dukes owed their
thrones to the necessity for coordinated command and the tradition of
Ostrogothic monarchy. Prior to the war of Justinian the Amali could
claim the kingship by inheritance without sprecial ceremonies. Only
now did Ostrogothic dukes grasp the royal cloak.[56] But regardless of
their title or the ceremony of kingship each underwent, later Ostrogothic kings never matched the power and authority of Theodoric,
especially over their noble counterparts. But unlike the Lombards, the
Ostrogoths never questioned the idea of monarchy. There was no
attempt to return to acephalous ducal leadership, and as a result the
idea of central structures endured.

Differences between rich and poor Goth occasionally produced friction, but no bitter cleavage existed within Ostrogothic society. The
common soldier served his commanders loyally. Only the Alpine garrisons serving in Liguria deserted, and then no one branded them as
traitors, for they left to protect their families from Byzantine attack.
The monopoly of power by the nobility failed to disturb the rest of the
nation, nor for that matter, was there any hostility over the fact that

---

[50] *Variae*, iv, 39.
[51] Procopius, *B. G.*, V, xiii, 17–25.
[52] *Ibid.*, VIII, xxiii, 1.
[53] *Ibid.*, VII, viii, 12–25.
[54] *Ibid.*, VII, xxiv, 27.
[55] *Ibid.*, VIII, xxxv, 31–33.
[56] Wallace-Hadrill has shown that this was usually an easy task for other Germanic dukes
who did not face the strong Amali tradition, *Early Germanic Kingship in England and on the
Continent* (Oxford, 1971), pp. 15–19.

the nobles had better armor and rode more than they walked in battle. Why should such differences have shocked Ostrogothic society when both their own and Roman history was a tableau of ranking? Every Goth had access to the legal system and could take his case beyond the local level where ducal authority was paramount. He received an annual donative from the king paid through his commander.[57] Perhaps the greatest obstacle to be overcome by a Roman *humilior* was his lack of access to the courts, especially if he had little or no money. The donative provided the Goth with money for travel, counsel, even, if need be, bribery. By serving in local garrisons the ordinary Ostrogoth could coerce favors from civilians. Such abuse of the soldier's cloak was common to both the humble and noble soldier.[58]

By chance a papyrus fragment from Ravenna dated July 17, 564 has survived almost intact. The document is from the Exarchate, but it reveals relative material differences between rich and poor probably applicable to the Ostrogothic period. Several of the names are clearly Germanic, perhaps Ostrogothic. Germana, the widow of Collictus, had employed the priest Gratianus as the legal guardian of her son Stephen. His fee was a third of the son's inheritance including cash, revenue from land, a house, several slaves, and the property of a freedman, Guderit, whose possessions had reverted to his former master when he died intestate. Gratianus received 36 gold solidi as his share of the monetary wealth, the proceeds from the sale of slaves (*mercedes*), and the value of the domestic slave (*ancilla*) Ranihilda and the oxen, neither of which was apparently sold. The household items of one manor house and the possessions of the deceased Guderit were sold and their prices listed. The total amount received from the sale of property and paid to Gratianus was 45 gold solidi, 23 gold siliquae, and 60 gold nummi.[59] The household items for the domus as listed represent the total articles in the house. Gratianus then received a third of their sale value. He also received a percentage of the revenues from the various other estates throughout the Romagna. His total income was a third of Stephen's inheritance, but he did not receive a third of the revenue from each estate. In several cases he did receive 4/12 of the revenue but in others 2/12, 3/12 and even 1/2 an uncia. One explanation of the fractions is

---

[57] *Variae*, v, 27.
[58] *Edictum*, 89.
[59] See Franz F. Kraus, *Die Münzen Odovacars und des Ostgotenreiches in Italien* (Halle, 1928) on the value of sixth-century coinage; however, the list itself is probably a better indicator.

that Stephen himself had not inherited the entire estate in which less than a third was given to Gratianus.

The Domus in Ravenna

No. of Items	Description	Value (when recorded)
7	spoons (*cocliares*) soup ladels?	
1	large bow (*scotella*)	
1	clasp (*fibula*) for an apron	2 pounds silver
1	clasp for a garter	
12	molds	
2	woven colored tapestries	1 solidus and 1 tremissis
1	embroidered cover	1 solidus
1	old basket [pliction?]	4 gold siliquae
1	shirt of silk and cotton in scarlet and leek (*camisia tramosirica in cocci et prasino*) – green	3 1/2 solidi
1	varigate leek-green garment	1 1/2 solidi
1	locked trunk with key	2 siliquae
1	mixed silk shirt (short sleeves)	2 gold siliquae
1	linen pair of trousers	1 gold siliqua
1	pillow	1/2 solidus
1	large copper barrel (?)	
1	small cooking pot	
1	small copper pitcher	12 pounds iron scrap
1	copper lamp with attached chain	
1	vat for vinegar	1 tremissis
1	small vat	2 1/2 siliquae 40 nummi
1	barrel for grain	2 1/2 gold siliquae 40 nummi
1	small grain box with iron binding	2 gold siliquae
1	harvesting sickle	1 gold siliqua
4	1 barrel, 1 hoe, 2 oil barrels	1 1/2 silver siliquae
1	cabinet	4 gold sliquae
2	twisted ropes	6 gold siliquae
1	chair with a seat of woven iron	1 semis
1	chair with woven wooden seat	40 gold nummi
1	table and flat (cuttingboard?)	1 gold siliqua
2	stone mortars	1 gold siliqua
1	wooden trough	40 gold nummi
1	pack saddle	1 gold asprio
1	lambskin blanket	2 gold siliquae
1	slave named Proiectus	

The possessions of Guderit

No. of Items	Description	Value
1	closed trunk (iron binding, key)	2 gold siliquae
1	other trunk in poor condition	1 siliquae and 1/2 asprio

1 used wine vat	1 asprio-siliquae
1 old cooking pot with iron handle (weighing 1 1/2 lbs.)	
1 broken kettle (1 lb.)	
1 iron cooking chain (2 1/2 lbs.)	
1 seeding tool (*satario*)	1 asprio-siliquae
1 sharpening stone (whetstone) with the oil to mosten it	2 asprio-siliquae
1 kneading-trough, broken	
1 small box	80 nummi
1 small earthen jug	80 nummi
1 broken earthen pot (*olla = estea*)	
1 bar (*talea*)	1 asprio
1 tub (*albio*)	80 nummi
1 grain basket (*rapo*)	1 asprio
1 measure (*modio*)	1 asprio
1 grain jug (*butticella granaria*)	1 siliqua-asprio
1 old colored (dyed) shirt (*sareca*)	3 gold siliquae
1 decorated shirt (*camisia ornata*)	6 gold siliquae
1 cloth (*mappa* in Souter = linen book)	1 asprio-siliquae
1 old coat	
1 old *sagello* – a short thick cloak worn by the Germans (Tac. *G.* 17) (*sagum*) usually a military cloak in Cic., now Tjäder suggests a travelling cloak, a *Reisemantel* in German, p. 243.	

The similarities are striking. The domus had finer kitchen utensils, two colored tapestries, a green and red shirt made of silk and cotton, two chairs, and a few other items of exceptional value. Guderit too owned a dyed shirt, and one with ornate decorations, but his dyed shirt was old and the decorated one only bought 6 gold siliquae, whereas the best shirt in the domus was valued at 3 1/2 solidi. The domus was not Stephen's only holding, but the list gives a detailed account of what wealth entailed – more and slightly better items, but generally the same as those of a freedman. Other estates had other houses but they were probably similar. Historians tend to overemphasize material differences between rich and poor. The case of Stephen and Guderit suggests that the real differences were not so much material as social. Stephen was neither very rich nor very important, but even if he were a high official, his domestic surroundings may not have differed greatly. To be sure some exceptional senatorial estates continued to have private baths and elaborate plumbing.

Guderit was a German as his name and *sagello* (short thick cloak) indicate. Perhaps captured in battle or sold into slavery for any number of reasons, he was poor but not necessarily discontent. The ordinary Ostrogoth had much more in common with Guderit than Stephen. Guderit must remain isolated, but he may be the clearest example for the bulk of early medieval society regardless of their nationality. Stephen's wealth is representative of the wealth of the lesser nobility in the exarchate. Most noble Goths did not have the wealth of Uraias. Clearly Hildibadus did not. None rivalled Theodoric, who drew upon the wealth of the state to build his palaces, fortifications, and, indeed, his mausoleum. Noble Goths probably lived much as Stephen.

The evidence for Ostrogothic nobles living on estates similar to Stephen's dates from after the fall of the Kingdom and is therefore inconclusive although highly suggestive. A papyrus fragment dated December 6, 557,[60] from the *Acta* of the city of Rieti located along the via *Salaria*, an area of heavy Ostrogothic settlement, is revealing. Gundihild, the widow of Gudahals, asked the curia of Rieti to appoint a special guardian for her two sons Lendarit and Landerit in order to pursue legal action against Aderid, *vir inluster*, Rosemund, also called Taffo, and Gunderit, *vir magnificus*. These men had seized property belonging to Gundihild's sons who, as minors, could not defend themselves in court and were incapable of physically expelling the accused. Every participant has a very Germanic (Ostrogothic?) name. Aderid and Gundirit were nobles bearing important titles. Rieti was in an area of known Ostrogothic settlement. The probability is high that the case was the result of the breakdown of order within Ostrogothic society after the victories of Narses. Less than five years had elapsed since Ragnaris surrendered. Narses sent many of the recalcitrant rebels at Campsas to Constantinople but did not drive all the Ostrogoths out of Italy but instead, following Belisarius' precedent, he returned them to their homes in peace. It seems likely that Aderit, the highest in rank, expanded his control in alliance with Gundirit, a lesser noble, and that Taffo was a member of Aderid's following.[61]

In response to Gundihild's appeal, the council of Rieti appointed a certain Flavianus so that "right can be established and the boundaries can be correctly determined."[62] Gundihild was an *inlustris femina* and knew how to use Roman legal processes to protect her rights. Since the record is dated after the fall of the kingdom, perhaps Felix Dahn was correct in his belief that two bodies of law co-existed in Italy. However, it should be emphasized that less than five years after the defeat of Totila, people of obvious Germanic descent eagerly and effectively sought Roman justice. The precedents may have dated far into the

---

[60] Tjäder, Papyrus no. 7, pp. 228–34.

[61] A Gunderit (perhaps the same as Gundirit) owned the estate Savilianus, papyrus no. 8, dated 17 July 564.

[62] Tjäder, Papyrus no. 7, 45–52, p. 230.

Kingdom. The degree of usage of Roman Law by Goths surely varied from region to region depending upon the power structure in each area.

There is no direct evidence that local power struggles existed among the Ostrogoths before the defeat: they were quite occupied with a foreign aggressor. However, such struggles may have existed as early as the reign of Theodoric. A reference in the *Variae* to *pignoratio*, the illegal seizure of property as security in a law suit, in Campania and Samnium (ca. 507–11) is a case in point.[63] Thomas Hodgkin suggested that in this case Theodoric attempted to combat the creation of a hierarchy of *pignus* in which the most powerful man controlled others by granting or denying protection from illegal seizure.[64] Campania, never settled by Ostrogoths, contained a few garrisons. Hence the letter of Theodoric probably applied to the local south Italian nobility. But the creation of legal patronage typified a weak central authority in the Eastern Empire and during the Middle Ages in the West.[65] Theodahad perhaps attempted to create such a system in Liguria. Local power struggles were doubtless commonplace in Ostrogothic Italy.

The struggles between nobles for power and prestige, the social differences within Ostrogothic society, and the fundamental weakness of the central government (particularly after the death of Theodoric) form the background for all events of the Kingdom. It is against this background that the government, the legal system, the army, and fiscal policy must be evaluated. In each case, Goth and Roman frequently found themselves working together for the common good. The traditional historiographic distinction, first drawn by Cassiodorus, of workers and soldiers, Roman and Goth, was never absolute. Theodoric and his successors attempted to expand the limits of centralization imposed by Gothic tribal organization by continuing the operation of the old imperial bureaucracy, especially the praetorian prefecture and the fiscal system. Roman officials were influential councillors in areas beyond their titular functions: Senarius', *comes privat.* and *patri.*, influence in peace, war, and the making of treaties was praised in his epitaph.[66] Most of the great magistracies of the Roman Empire continued. The *magister officiorum*, once the head of the civil bureaucracy, was eclipsed by the praetorian prefect and various regional Gothic military

---

[63] *Variae*, iv, 10.
[64] T. Hodgkin, *Letters*, pp. 240–1.
[65] See the references to legal patronage in Peter Brown, "The Rise and Function of the Holy Man in Late Antiquity," *JRS*, 61 (1971), pp. 80–101, particularly the examples drawn from Libanius.
[66] Fiebiger, no. 8 (1944), P. Pithou, *Epigrammata vetera* (Paris, 1590), 108 ff.

commands.[67] If the situation demanded extraordinary action, standard procedure dispatched a special royal agent to handle the problem. In a few instances Roman bureaucrats such as Gemellas, the Roman Governor in Provence, and Cassiodorus, while praetorian prefect, ventured beyond their traditional functions to aid in a military crisis.[68] In short, the government of Ostrogothic Italy was *ad hoc*. The only entirely new officers were the *comes Gothorum* and the *saiones*.

Many Gothic nobles assimilated much of the Roman aristocratic life style once in office in the cities and towns across Italy, while adding flexibility and efficiency to government. Many *saiones* are known by name and with but two possible exceptions they had no other title.[69] Of the dozen known *saiones*, none ever became a *comes* or a *dux*. They were the king's men and that was enough. They had no specific functions other than to enforce the king's will over local officials, both Roman and Goth. The institution, if the *saiones* can be so classified, existed as early as 508 when Theodoric instructed *saio* Nandus to assemble troops for the invasion of Gaul.[70] In ca. 507−11 Theodoric sent a *saio* to assist in tax collection − a function they were still involved in as late as 533−37.[71] Fruirarith was asked by Theodoric to judge a case involving a Roman court official. Unigilis directed the provisionment for Theodoric's roving court on one of his visits to Liguria.[72] *Saio* Grenoda along with a special military aide investigated charges against ex-praetorian prefect, Faustus.[73] Leodifrid supervised the building of the new fortifications at Verruca although theoretically the palace architect was in charge of the construction of fortifications.[74] Gesila, in a controversial letter, was sent to Picenum and Tuscany to force certain Goths to pay taxes.[75] Duda, a *saio* of exceptional talents, unsuccessfully brought a case against Theodahad, then *dux* in Liguria. Duda also channeled a troublesome legal case to the proper court and supervised grave robbing to ensure that the treasure went to the crown![76] Veranus supervised the movement of the Gepids

[67] See Further William G. Sinnigen, "Administrative Shifts of Competence under Theodoric," *Traditio*, 21 (1965), pp. 456−67.

[68] *Variae*, ix, 24−25.

[69] One exception may be Quidila. Saio Tezutzat definitely became a *defensor*.

[70] *Variae*, i, 24.

[71] *Variae*, ii, 4; xii, 3.

[72] *Variae*, ii, 20.

[73] *Variae*, iii, 20.

[74] *Variae*, iii, 48; vii, 15.

[75] *Variae*, iv, 14.

[76] *Variae*, iv, 32, 34, and 39.

across Venetia and Liguria when Theodoric (ca. 523–26) sought to strengthen his Frankish frontier.[77] Dumerit was sent to Faventia to punish the plunderers of small farmers "whether the culprits were Goth or Roman."[78] The last datable reference to *saiones* is under Athalaric when he sent a *saio* to correct *comes* Gildila at Syracuse (ca. 533).[79] Although this is among the last references to *saiones*, Cassiodorus, our only source, left very few letters for the later kings and none after Wittiges. The number of examples could be expanded, but there is no need to belabor the point that the *saiones* were a very versatile group with authority unlimited by institutional or ethnic boundaries. The absence of *saiones* after 533 is symptomatic of the general breakdown of effective central government within a decade of Theodoric's death.

Less is known about the *comes Gothorum* than about the *saiones*. There were three types of Gothic counts: provincial, special city, and, occasionally, special royal agents. Provincial counts were primarily legal officers responsible for Gothic cases beyond the authority of the *iudex* of the province. The count also heard cases involving disputes between Goth and Roman and in general promoted mutual respect. Cassiodorus preserved the formula for the *Comes*.

> As we know that, by God's help, Goths are dwelling intermingled among you, in order to prevent the trouble (*indisciplinatio*) which is wont to arise among partners (*consortes*) we have thought it right to send to you as Count, A B, a sublime person, a man already proved to be of high character, in order that he may terminate (*amputare*) any contests arising between two Goths according to our edicts; but that, if any matter should arise between a Goth and a born Roman, he may, after associating with himself a Roman jurisconsult, decide the strife by fair reason. As between two Romans let the decision rest with the Roman examiners (*cognitores*), whom we appoint in the various Provinces; that thus each may keep his own laws, and with various Judges one Justice may embrace the whole realm. Thus, sharing one common peace, may both nations, if God favour us, enjoy the sweets of tranquility.
>
> Let both nations hear what we have at heart. You oh Goths! have the Romans as neighbours to your lands; even so let them be joined to you in affection. You too, oh Romans! ought dearly to love the Goths, who in peace swell the numbers of your people and in war defend the whole Republic. It is fitting therefore that you obey the Judge whom we have appointed for you, that you may ordain for the preservation of the laws; and thus you will be found to have promoted your own interests while obeying our command.[80]

In Dalmatia the *comes* was superior to the *principes* and the Roman governor, who was increasingly a fiscal officer.[81] In Provence the

[77] *Variae*, v, 10.
[78] *Variae*, v, 27.
[79] *Variae*, ix, 10.
[80] *Variae*, vii, 3, trans., Hodgkin, pp. 321–22.
[81] *Variae*, iii, 25.

Gothic *comes*, Marabad, worked closely with the Roman governor
Gemellus in special legal cases and cooperated during famine and
invasions by the Franks. The *comes* was the superior official.[82] Ludwig
Schmidt believed that such provincial counts also existed in Sicily,
Istria, Pannonia II (Sirmium), Savia (Siscia), and perhaps Noricum and
Switzerland.[83] However, it must be pointed out that there are no direct
references to *comes* in any of these areas.

Naples, Pavia, and Syracuse had urban *comites* who were primarily
legal officials, but other towns may have shared the distinction.[84] The
comes of Syracuse, far removed from the center of government, was a
special case. He was not only a legal official but also the commander of
the Gothic garrison there. The troops at Syracuse were especially
troublesome (perhaps this too was the result of isolation), and the
comes was given special instructions to keep them under control by
promptly provisioning his men lest they plunder the farmers.[85] Ostrogothic administration, of necessity, had to grant more power and
autonomy to distant outposts.

The majority of references to counts are to special enterprises under-
taken in the king's behalf. In each case the count may have been an
urban count sent on an extra errand. When they acted as special agents
the *comites* were just as versatile as the *saiones*. Generally, they undertook more complex operations than the *saiones* but not necessarily.
When Liberius' son faced accusations of gross misconduct, *comes*
Arigern looked into the matter.[86] Liberius oversaw the settlement and
his son became a member of the senate. Anabilis coordinated shipping
along the entire western coast in Theodoric's effort to relieve famine in
Gaul.[87] Julian conducted military field exercises for which praetorian
prefect Abundantius was ordered to provide rations and sea transport.[88]
Similarly, Luvirit and Ampelius investigated and fined grain merchants
for failing to deliver grain taken on in Spain.[89] Counts did not always

---

[82] *Variae*, iv, 12 and 46.

[83] L. Schmidt, *op. cit.*, p. 127.

[84] *Variae*, ix, 4 (Gildias of Syracuse); x, 29 (Winusiad of Pavia). Also *Variae*, vi, 22–25.
Erduic and later Trasemund may have been *comites* of Milan, but Ennodius did not call them
either *dux* or *comes*. Erduic was, however, *vir inlustris*. Ennodius, *Epistolae*, ii, 3; iii, 20.

[85] *Variae*, vi, 22.

[86] *Variae*, iii, 36.

[87] *Variae*, iv, 5.

[88] *Variae*, v, 23. See further on Ostrogothic maritime commerce, J. Rougé, "Quelques
aspects de la navigation en Mediterranée au Ve siècle et dans la première moitié du VIe siècle,"
Cahiers d'histoire, 6 (1961), pp. 129–54, particularly pp. 139–47.

[89] *Variae*, v, 35.

have enough power to enforce their decisions as the case of Pythias and
the blind soldier attests, but in most cases they were respected, if not
feared, members of Gothic society.[90]

Unlike *comites* and *saiones*, Gothic *duces* were primarily military
leaders. *Dux* Gudui was notorious for his enslavement of other Goths;
his command is unknown, but he owed his appointment to Theodoric.[91] Tremonus commanded the Goths at Aterna in Samnium. A few
other dukes are known. Uraias and Hildibadus were dukes. Hildibadus
was the commander of the garrison at Verona, one of the key cities in
the defense of Venetia. Theodoric had a palace at Verona from which
he personally commanded the defense of Venetia during the northern
barbarian unrest early in his reign.[92]*Dux* Wilitancus was asked to judge
a case of adultery.[93] It seems clear from the context of the letter that
Wilitancus was *dux* in southern Gaul. This letter was written ca.
523–26 after several expeditions against the Franks; one campaign is
mentioned in the text. A provincial count (Marabad, *var.* iv, 12)
initially administered the frontier area in Gaul, but after repeated
Frankish incursions Theodoric committed stronger forces under ducal
command. During the early phases of the war of Justinian, Wittiges sent
a force to Perusia under *dux* Hunila.[94]

Tulum is the only duke whose career can be reconstructed from his
youth. As a young noble he accompanied Pitzia in the Sirmium War
(504 A.D.). He was one of several dukes participating in the initial
conquests of southern Gaul against Clovis, during which he distinguished himself in a battle over a key bridge on the Rhone at Arles. In 523
Theodoric again sent him to Gaul where he successfully organized the
defenses during the Burgundian-Frankish war. After the defeat of their
Burgundian allies, the Ostrogoths had little choice but to increase their
military power in the area. One manifestation of their new policy was
the maintenance of a large force under permanent ducal leadership.
Although Wilitancus was appointed to the command, Tulum also
profited by the new military demands in that he was rewarded with large
tracts of land, probably in southern Gaul. He later became a personal

---

[90] See further J. Declareuil, "Des Comtes de cites à la fin du Ve siècle," *Revue historique de
droit*, 34 (1910), pp. 794–836, especially pp. 814–28; and R. Sprandel, "Dux und Comes in
der Merovingerzeit," *Zeitschrift der Savigny-Stiftung für Rechtsgeschichte, Germ. Abt.*, 74
(1957), pp. 41–84, especially pp. 56–65 on the Ostrogoths.
[91] *Variae*, v, 30. Quos duces eligimus, simul et aequitatis iura delegamus, quia non tantum
armis quantum iudiciis vos effici.
[92] Anonymus Valesianus, 81–83.
[93] *Variae*, v, 33.
[94] *Getica*, 312.

adviser to Theodoric and was instrumental in raising several men to the Senate, an honor he himself later received.[95]

Several attributes of sixth-centruy Ostrogothic dukes stand out. Under Theodoric, at least, they were appointed. Although their primary responsibility was military command, they also were important figures in the legal system. Prior to the war of Justinian, dukes generally exercised their commands along the frontiers where constant military danger necessitated a strong military presence. In peaceful Italy garrisons were typically police forces administered by the *comites* as part of their urban office. If the career of Tulum is any indication of general practice, dukes were chosen from tested soldiers of noble ancestry. Whenever a *dux* was assigned to a region he automatically became the paramount Ostrogothic leader.

Unfortunately, there is very little evidence about the relationship of dukes to subunits of the Ostrogoths in Italy. What little evidence there is derives exclusively from Procopius, and he seldom employed the Latin terminology for leadership. Procopius reports that Sisigis commanded the Gothic garrisons in the Cottian Alps, so fearful for their families that they deserted.[96] He was probably a *dux*, but there is no proof that the families in his charge constituted a true subgroup. The case of Eraric, leader of the Rogi, is more informative. The Rogi refused to intermarry with other Goths and preserved their own customs long after Theodoric incorporated them into the tribe.[97] Eraric was clearly the *dux* of the Rogi when they declared him king. It seems likely that the appointment of dukes, like the appointment of Quidila as *prior* of Raete and Nursia, reflected the individual's previous position at the local level. There is nothing in the sources contradicting the assumption that personal followings comprised the kernels of ducal armies. By officially appointing such a leader as duke, the kings elevated, perhaps only temporarily, a local leader to the tribal level and simultaneously augmented his forces with troops drawn from the whole tribe. This was in keeping with the limits of centralization created by the long process of tribe building and regularized by the settlement.

The Rogi clung with extraordinary tenacity to their group autonomy, but they were not necessarily peculiar. Jordanes' narrative of the early migrations, without question the most troublesome section of the

---

[95] *Variae*, viii, 9, 10, 11.

[96] Procopius, *B.G.*, VI, xxviii, 30–33. He is considered a *dux* by L. Schmidt, *op. cit.*, p. 133.

[97] Procopius, *B.G.*, VII, ii, 1–4; VI, xiv, 24.

Getica, contained numerous names of participating peoples of which scholars have linked 28 to various areas in Scandinavia.[98] Why did Jordanes include their names? Perhaps he did so for purely antiquarian reasons, but it is quite possible that groups of sixth-century Ostrogoths still conceived of themselves as members of prestigious lineages stretching back to the earliest times — as far back as the Amali, or farther. Whether a direct line actually connected his readers with remote and legendary times and places was germane only if some groups, perhaps zealous of their association with shadowy ancestors, still harkened to the magic of these names.

The office of *defensor civitatis* is illustrative of the Ostrogothic response to the problems of urban government. The office was originally created by Valentinian in 364 to defend the citizens of the communities from the incursions of imperial officials. But over the next century the office slipped into disuse until reestablished by Majorian in 458. The *defensor civitatis* continued to exist in most early Germanic kingdoms as well as in the Eastern Empire, but each area witnessed a different evolution. In Gaul where the institution lasted the longest in the West, the *defensor* merely enrolled acts in the municipal registers with the aid of the local curia.[99] In Italy the Ostrogoths continued the office as a local "protector". *Defensores* were supposed to protect the community from oppression just as Valentinian had planned, but their protection included the seasonal fixing of prices and often the forced requisition of military supplies.[100] In small towns the *defensor* and the curia were the government; the *defensor* represented the central government, the curia, of course, was drawn from the locality.[101] Roman senators also were accorded the honor of having a *defensor*. In the only case in which a *defensor* is known by name, *saio* Tezutzat replaced Amara as *defensor* for senator Petrus. Amara had "protected" his ward by occasionally beating him![102] Since only Amara and Tezutzat are known (the *saio* was clearly an Ostrogoth), it is perhaps unwarranted to assume that all *defensores* were Goths. However, Theodoric and his

---

[98] *Getica*, 19–24. Some of the voluminous debate surrounding the early Goths is contained in the bibliography. Joseph G. A. Svennung's *Jordanes and Scandia* (Stockholm, 1967) is one of the most recent attempts to vindicate Jordanes, an impossible task if archaeological supports are sought. See also my "Pursuing the Early Gothic Migrations," *Acta Archaeologica*, 31 (1979), pp. 189–199.

[99] Émile Chénon, "Étude historique sur le *defensor civitatis*," *Revue historique de droit*, 13 (1889), pp. 515–37.

[100] *Variae*, iv, 43; vii, 11.

[101] *Variae*, vii, 12.

[102] *Variae*, iv, 27–28.

successors could not allow men of questionable loyalty to hold the office, for the *defensor* alone represented the central government in many towns. In times of famine the town probably sought tax reductions through its *defensor*. However, the decision whether to grant a reduction for a given indiction rested exclusively with the central government and its representatives the counts, provincial judges, and the Roman governors.[103]

The tax structure and military obligation are the most obvious areas to survey in order to discover the division of Italian society into Ostrogothic and Roman spheres. Cassiodorus stated as much in *Variae* vii, 3 (quoted above, p. 115). But he rhetorically simplified fiscal and military structure just as he distorted the settlement problem by failing to mention the great diversity among farms throughout Italy. In fact, Goth and Roman shared responsibilities even in the fields of tax and defense.

The main tax fell on land and was collected through the communities where the *curiales* continued to be responsible for the payment just as under the emperors. The pressure on the *curiales* forced some to seek slavery with the church while others had to mortgage heavily to meet the payments. Some were even allowed to remove their names from the lists of councillors, but they then faced the *compulsores*. Instead of farming the tax they would pay themselves. The small *possessores* paid heavily as they had always done. In a partial tax list from Patavino (Padua) dating from the mid-sixth century the *possessores* paid the tax in kind: a set figure in pounds of lard and honey, chickens and geese. In the swampy areas of Micauri and Pampiliana the tax was paid in milk (100 lbs.). *Possessores* bringing wastelands into cultivation were given tax exemptions. In the area of Patavino the coloniae Candidiana and Simpliciaca, which had been lying in weeds, were returned to production by coloni Repartus and Justinius in return for a five year remission of taxes.[104] Similar land clearance incentives were common under the Ostrogoths, but the terms are not so specific.[105] Tax exemptions were commonly given to areas damaged in war or by the passage of the army.[106] Whole provinces were frequently ordered to pay in kind. Most of the produce so raised was stored in urban supply centers, where

[103] *Variae*, i, 16; iv, 19; ix, 10; xii, 2. On the tax system in general see Fabian Thibault, "L'Impôt direct dans les royaumes des Ostrogoths, des Wisigoths et des Burgundes," *Nouvelle Revue historique de droit français et étranger*, 25 (1901), pp. 698–728, 26 (1902), pp. 32–48.

[104] Tjäder, P. 3, II, 1, 5 and 6; II, 3, 1–10.

[105] *Variae*, ii, 21; ii, 32; vii, 44.

[106] *Variae*, i, 16; ii, 38; iv, 39; iv, 36; ix, 10.

provisions were needed for the garrisons.[107] Merchants continued to pay the *chrysargyon* on each transaction.[108] Even the senators, traditionally immune from taxation, paid a tax specifically assessed on members of the Senate.[109]

The *Variae* contains two statements concerning Goths paying taxes.

> If any of the Goths has failed to pay the fisc after the *curiales* have posted the list of taxable property, let them have their property confiscated.[110] *(Variae, I, 19)*

> It is a great offence to put off the burden of one's own debts upon other people. That man ought to pay the "tributum" for a property who receives the income of it. But some of the Goths in Picenum and the two Tuscanies are evading the payment of their proper taxes.[111] *(Variae, iv, 14)*

Fabien Thibault studied the tax systems of the Ostrogoths, Visigoths, and Burgundians, and believed that it was "absurd to think they the Ostrogoths paid taxes like the Roman possessores," yet he admitted that at least some Ostrogoths paid taxes. He concluded that the original *sortes* (shares given in the settlement) were non-taxable but that anything acquired after the settlement was taxable. He adduced as further evidence the letter to the *comes* of Savia dated ca. 514—5.

> Men who were formerly barbarians, who have married Roman wives and acquired property in land, are to be compelled to pay their indictional and other taxes to the fisc ...[112]

Thibault partially destroyed his own argument by claiming that "the barbarians" in Savia were not Goths but other Germans. If true, then the document is worthless in explaining the tax system of Italy. That the "barbari" were not Goths is not beyond question. The document is important for substantiating the difference between settlement grants and recent acquisitions. But the point is lost in the debate, for by the end of the kingdom the original settlement grants had changed. The

---

[107] *Variae*, xi, 16; xi, 39; xii, 24, 26.

[108] *Variae*, ii, 26; from *Cod. Theod.*, xiii, 1.

[109] *Variae*, ii, 24.

[110] *Variae*, i, 19 addressed to Saturninus and Verbusius, viri sublimes, concerning the collection of taxes by the *curiales* of Adriana. quicumque Gothorum fiscum detrectat implere, eum ad aequitatem redhibitionis artetis, ne tenuis de proprio cogatur exsolvere, quid constat idoneos indebite detinere.

[111] *Variae*, iv, 14, trans., T. Hodgkin, *Letters*, pp. 242—43. Magni peccati genus est alienus debitis alterum praegravare, ut qui potest exigi non mereatur audiri. Sua quemque damna respiciant et is solvat tributum, qui possessionis noscitur habere compendium. Atque ideo praesenti tibi auctoritate delegamus, ut Gothi per Picenum sive Tuscias utrasque residentes te imminente cogantur exsolvere debitas functiones.

[112] Thibault, *op. cit.*, pp. 707—9; *Variae*, v, 14.

sources reveal numerous instances of Goths "liberating" Roman land.[113] As the case of Gundihild versus Aderid, Taffo, and Gunderit at Rieti demonstrates, the Goths did not long respect ethnic divisions and grabbed other Gothic properties as well as Roman. Within a generation after the settlement every noble Goth, in particular, owed taxes on newly acquired land. The problem for the central government was not whom to tax but from whom they could collect. In that regard, powerful Gothic nobles may indeed have escaped payment, but the ordinary Goth, even if not a tiller, could not resist the power of the bureaucracy. This was especially important as long as Theodoric with his immense power and prestige reigned and thwarted the local nobility in their struggle to carve absolute domains and thereby redirect revenues bound for Ravenna.

The principal expenditures in Ostrogothic Italy were for the army. Because of the military's demands on the fiscal system and because of Procopius' lengthy narrative on the war of Justinian, there is much more information about the army than for any other aspect of Ostrogothic Italy. It would be pointless to attempt a narrative of the long war against the Byzantines so well detailed by Procopius, but the military obligations and remunerations bear directly on the problem of ethnic divisions.

At all times the army was predominantly Ostrogothic. Every Goth had an obligation to serve in the army whenever summoned. Gothic manhood was equated with soldierung, and the prowess of a soldier was the basis for exercising his rights.[114] If a soldier was released from service before he was too old to fight, he lost his annual donative, and his rivals regarded him as a traitor.[115]

Apparently, each Goth had the right to go to Ravenna himself and collect his donative, and many did; but the customary procedure was payment through the *millenarii*.[116] The *millenarii* are otherwise unknown. The identification of *millenarius* as an Ostrogothic equivalent to the Visigothic *thiufadus* or the Vandalic *chiliarchus* is probably correct, but such comparison is of little help since the Visigothic and Vandalic institutions are equally obscure. Christian Courtois has offered the most convincing suggestion to date. He claims that the *chiliarchi* were the leaders of subunits whose members included women and

---

[113] For example *Variae*, i, 18; iv, 39; ix, 18; and Procopius, *B.G.*, V, iii, 2; V, iv, 1–2.

[114] *Variae*, i, 24; i, 38.

[115] The case of Starcedius, *Variae*, v, 36.

[116] *Variae*, v, 27; and v, 26 in which special measures were spelled out to reduce the need to forage for supplies enroute to Ravenna. See also Procopius, *B.G.*, V, xii, 46–48.

children and totalled approximately one thousand.[117] E. A. Thompson
has shown that by the seventh century *thiufadus* was an official of low
or middle rank, not sharing the privileges of the *duces* and *comites*. He
had both legal and military functions.[118] The absolute silence of the
copious military sources suggests that the *millenarii* were of minor military importance and were paymasters with military functions limited to
supply and minor legal matters.

So far non-Goths have scarcely figured into the discussion, but they
did have military obligations and occasionally fought in the front lines.
Theodoric ordered all Goths and Romans living at Dertona to fortify a
castra near the city and strengthen the villas to withstand attack.[119] At
Rome he ordered both Goths and Romans to bring in stones to rebuild
the city wall.[120] In Gaul the civil population provided provisions but
not beyond the point at which they could no longer aid in the
defense.[121] Theodoric's order to the *comes* of Salona to arm and drill
the inhabitants[122] presumably applied to the unarmed non-garrison
personnel. In general, the townsmen had a responsibility to help in a
case of attack as a militia force rarely used except in the frontier zones.
Belisarius forced the citizens of Rome to stand guard on the walls.
Since neither the Byzantines nor the Goths had enough men to defend
occupied towns, they made up the slack in part by employing civilians
and ordered the farmers to dig pits and ditches.[123] In only one instance
did Theodoric or his successors express mistrust in the Roman citizen
militias. Early in his reign, Theodoric forbid Romans at Verona to bear
arms other than small knives. Verona was in peril of invasion by barbarians from the north, and this also explains Theodoric's presence
there.[124]

There are scattered notices in Procopius to non-Gothic personnel in
the Ostrogothic army. Jewish soldiers manned the walls of Naples when

[117] Christian Courtois, *Les Vandales et l'Afrique* (Paris, 1955), pp. 216–17. His discussion
of the *chiliarchi* (*millenarii*) is based on more evidence than is available for the Ostrogoths. The
basic passage remains Procopius *B.V.* III, v, 18, that Geiseric ordered the 80 *chiliarchi* to organ-
ize their people prior to crossing the Straits of Gibraltar.

[118] E. A. Thompson, *The Goths in Spain* (Oxford, 1969), particularly pp. 137, 145.
J. Declareuil, *op. cit.*, pp. 832–33, suggested that the *thuifa* (the unit commanded by the
thuifadus) was a police force in the cities.

[119] *Variae*, i, 17.

[120] *Variae*, i, 28. Remains of the rebuilding under Theodoric have been found in excavations
of the wall. See Ian A. Richmond, *The City Wall of Imperial Rome* (Oxford, 1930), pp.
263–67.

[121] *Variae*, iii, 40.

[122] *Variae*, i, 40.

[123] *Variae*, xii, 17.

[124] Anonymus Valesianus, 83.

Belisarius besieged the city early in the war.[125] As early as Wittiges' siege of Rome, a Roman notable (Ῥωμαῖον ἄνδρα) served in the Gothic army,[126] but the large scale use of non-Goths occurred only under Totila.

Totila and the nobility, the creators and supporters of his kingship, were forced by the war to appease the native Italian population, but neither sought to abolish slavery or create a new social order.[127] The rapprochement with Romans was continuous after the settlement but along well defined social lines. The strains of war forced Totila to over-accelerate the program. No nobleman, Roman nor Goth, dreamed of the abolition of class distinction and economic inequity, but expanded cooperation without regard to nationality was hardly revolutionary.

By the late 540's manpower was so scarce that both sides employed deserters. Totila accepted Roman deserters "with full and complete equality with the Goths."[128] He eventually had to allow slaves and tenants to fight in his army — a step he was reluctant to take. The Byzantines, likewise reluctantly, recruited discontented peasants.[129] Neither side can be criticized for its recruitment. Much of the wealth accumulated by the Goths over a period of a century was irretrievably lost.[130] Supply was increasingly difficult as first one army then the other pillaged area after area. Untold misery afflicted Italy as a result of the first sweep of the bubonic plague across Europe.[131] As a result of war, pillage, and disease, the Roman tax system finally collapsed, and direct collection by treasury or military officials replaced tax farming.[132]

The shift from using Romans purely as reservists, laborers, and supply troops to placing them in the front line occurred during the grave crises of the war of Justinian. Yet except for Totila's reluctance to take tillers from the soil because their crops were so badly needed, there are no indications that Roman troops serving the Goths were distrusted or disloyal — a point the Byzantines well understood. Justi-

---

[125] Procopius, *B.G.*, V, x, 24.

[126] *Ibid.*, VI, vi, 3.

[127] See the recent article by Zinaida V. Udalcova, "La Campagne de Narsès et l'écrasement de Totila," *Corsi di cultura sull' arte ravennate e bizantina*, 18 (1971), pp. 557–64.

[128] Procopius, *B.G.*, VII, xxxvi, 24–27; VII, xxiii, 3–6.

[129] *Ibid.*, VII, xxii, 4–6, 20; VII, xvi, 15; Totila's initial reluctance, VII, xiii, 1.

[130] *Ibid.*, VII, viii, 15–25, and Agathias, A, 20.10.

[131] J. N. Biraben and J. Le Goff, "La peste dans le haut moyen âge," *Annales, économies, sociétés, civilisations*, 24 (1969), pp. 1484–1510, particularly pp. 1494–95.

[132] Procopius, *B.G.*, VII, vi, 5.

nian's ruthless paymaster in Italy, Alexander, taxed the Romans heavily for their collaboration with the Ostrogoths.[133] The employment of Romans in the army was already a fact during the Sirmium War, which witnessed Cyprianus, the son of Opilio (count of the sacred largess under Odovacar), serving with the Ostrogoths. Cyprianus later occupied the same office as his father had and was elevated to the Senate.[134] Clearly military service was never the exclusive preserve of the Ostrogoths. The concept of ethnocentricity remained weak.

The limits of centralization were largely determined by the inability of the central government to overcome the power of local leadership, not by a division of society into Goth and Roman. Gothic nobles living on villa-estates and working with Romans in almost every aspect of government rapidly merged with the Roman aristocracy, but the majority of the Ostrogoths were farmers. They forced Theodoric to seek land for them to till in the Balkans where the political and military turmoil denied them the goals they were to achieve in Italy. The Ostrogoths studiously cultivated the friendship of the Roman aristocracy, until Totila realized that many senators had betrayed his trust.[135]

Goths increasingly shared in Roman society along social lines drawn in the course of the migrations. The prolonged military necessity of the migration period produced increasingly more powerful army commands. In the course of the settlement, if not long before, the army command structure became the basis for the solidification of Gothic noble rank. The nobles were further strengthened by their importance in government at Ravenna as well as in their own dominions. The Gothic noble adopted Roman manners and customs appropriate to his rank, lived on villa-estates and shared the titular distinctions so important to the "Roman" aristocracy. The ordinary Ostrogoth shared an agricultural life with the lower strata of Roman society, and some even felt the yoke of slavery.[136]

Arianism still distinguished most Goths from Romans, but Procopius records that many Ostrogoths converted to orthodoxy.[137] Surviving papyri attest to the presence of Goths as priests, deacons, scribes and

---

[133] Procopius, *Anecdota*, xxiv, 9–10.

[134] *Variae*, viii, 22.

[135] Procopius, *B.G.*, VII, xxi, 12–15.

[136] In addition to the evidence cited above may be added an inscription set up by the son of a freedman Gutio. Found in Agro Calliense, now Cagli, south of Urbino, the name is quite likely Gothic. No definite date can be assigned. Fiebiger (1917), no. 152, *C.I.L.*, xi, 5976, and commentary, p. 90.

[137] Procopius, *B.G.*, VI, vi, 18–19.

lesser clerical functionaries of the sixth-century Orthodox church. The *Documentum Neapolitanum* lists:

> Optarit et Vitalianus praesb(yteri), Suniefridus diac(onus), Petrus subdiac(onus), Uuiliarit et Paulus clerici nec non et Minnulus et Danihel, Theudila Mirica et Sindila spodei, Costila, Gudelivus, Guderit, Hosbut et Benenatus ustiarii, Viliarit et Amalatheus idem spodei . . .[138]

Further examples can be found in the *Documentum Aretinum* which mentions Angelfrid, Alamoda, and Gudilebus.[139] Offices such as *spodei* lie beyond accurate definition since they were not typical Orthodox positions and may have represented a brief incorporation of Gothic (i.e. Arian) nomenclature after the dissolution of the Kingdom.[140] The process of conversion was incomplete at the end of the Kingdom. Intermarriage occurred.[141] Many Goths were known by their Christian (orthodox?) names as well as their Gothic.[142] If we may believe a document dated 769, not all Goths readily merged into the Italian population, for as of this late date a few isolated people or small groups still regarded themselves as living under Gothic law.[143] Such cases were rare indeed, and for the most part men ceased claiming a Gothic relationship after 554. Theodoric prophesied the course of much of the Gothic social adaptation when he noted:

> "Aurum et daemonem qui habit, non eum potest abscondere;" item "Romanus miser imitatur Gothum et utilis imitatur Romanum."[144]

---

[138] *Documentum Neapolitanum*, 82–85, as reprinted in Piergiuseppe Scardigli, *Die Goten. Sprache und Kultur* (München, 1973), p. 277. J. Tjäder informed me that this will be Papyrus no. 34 in the second volume of his edition which is in press.

[139] *Documentum Aretinum*, as in Scardigli, pp. 279–80, also available in I. B. Doni, . . . *Inscriptiones antiquae . . . editiae ab Antonio Francisco Gorio* (Firenze, 1731), p. 271, which was unavailable to me.

[140] Scardigli discusses the problems of the official nomenclature in these documents and suggests a taking over of Gothic forms by the Orthodox church, *op. cit.*, pp. 280–301, on *spodei* see pp. 287–88.

[141] For example, Fiebiger, No. 172, *C.I.L.*, xi, 5976; No. 220, *C.I.L.*, v, 7793; No. 223, *C.I.L.*, v, 6176; No. 224, *C.I.L.*, v, 1583; No. 228, *C.I.L.*, ix, 2817.

[142] For example, Fiebiger (1939), No. 45, *C.I.L.*, xi, 941 dated 570 from Moderna: Gundeberga also known as Nonnia; (1917), No. 171, *C.I.L.*, iii, 12396; and papyrus No. 13, "Ademunt who is also called Andreas."

[143] *Historiae Patriae Monumenta*, XII, "Codex diplomaticus Langobardiae" (Torino, 1873), p. xxxvii; Scardigli, pp. 300–1. Stavile [. . .] legem vivens Gothorum [. . .] civis Brixianus.

[144] Cited by the Anonymus Valesianus, 61. "One who has gold and a demon cannot hide the demon." Also, "A poor Roman plays the Goth, a rich Goth the Roman," trans., J. C. Rolfe, *op. cit.*, p. 547.

CONCLUSION

The evolution of kingship among the Ostrogoths spanned three centuries of warfare, migration and occasionally, peace. The development of kingship, the most visible social change in Ostrogothic history, is inexplicable without the constant pressures of Roman civilization. Contemporary historians and chroniclers following in the footsteps of Roman diplomats immortalized barbarian kings, yet the kingship was merely the apex of a dynamic society. At any stage between the third century regional alliances and the last kings of the sixth century, other forces in Gothic society molded leadership structures as they themselves responded to the increasing centralization accompanying the monarchy. A truculent aristocracy beneath the king remained ever ready to reassert its basic strengths. These strengths were rooted in social vistas beyond the horizon of the monarchy — in the nature of personal allegiance, the daily problems of an agrarian life periodically needing assistance from the aristocracy, the military system still largely local even in the sixth century, and religion with its origins in early regional and local structures. True tribal kingship was a fleeting episode straddling the migrations in the Balkans and to Italy and then quickly eroded after the death of Theodoric.

At the societal level Ostrogothic history appears as a chain of periods of equipose punctuated by intervals of accelerated change. The shadowy third century gave birth to a new balance between powerful and resilient kindreds and villages and the growing authority of ducal leaders. By the end of the century regional structures transcended local ties as one result of the escalating involvement with the Roman Empire. In the early fourth century the Goths experimented with temporary multi-regional alliances, but it was the nightmare of a two-pronged assault in the last quarter of the century, from the Huns and a reassertive Empire, that forever altered Gothic society. Henceforth, the Goths (now Visigoths and Ostrogoths) faced a continuous challenge to their existence. As both Hunnic and Roman antagonists sought to divide them by catering to aristocratic independence, the Goths coalesced under their kings and created a tribal kingship.

These "tribal" structures were confederations of diverse ethnic groups united in response to the more advanced Roman world. That they maintained a historical presence for centuries was because of the intense pressures exerted upon them. Many members of the Roman literary aristocracy regarded all barbarians as cultural assassins of the lowest order. Even after their settlement in Italy the Ostrogoths were a minority among the indigenous population.

The ultimate destiny of Ostrogothic society was clear even before Justinian unleashed his armies. The Ostrogoths, accustomed to ethnic assimilation, absorbed Roman civilization unevenly. The nobility, their social positions territorialized, were treading the pathways of the Roman aristocracy with whom they shared so much. The humble Goth, having returned to the soil, suffered its vagaries along with the Roman tillers. The war intervened and created another reason to champion an Ostrogothic cause. Noble and farmer stood shoulder-to-shoulder one last time.

BIBLIOGRAPHY

PRIMARY SOURCES (TEXTS AND COLLECTIONS)

Most fragmentary and minor sources found in the various collections have not been cited separately in this bibliography.

Agathias, *Historiarum Libri Quinque, CFHB*, 2, ed., R. Keydell (Berlin, 1967).

Ammianus Marcellinus, Loeb edition, trans., John C. Rolfe (Cambridge, Mass., 1935–40).

Anonymi Valesiani pars posterior, ed., T. Mommsen, *MGH.AA*, 9 (Chronica Minora, 1) (Berlin, 1892, reprint 1961).

Anonymi Valesiani pars posterior, Loeb edition, trans., John C. Rolfe (Cambridge, Mass., 1964 revision).

Arator, De Actibus Apostolorum, ed., J. P. Migne, *P.L.*, 68, cc. 45–252 (Paris, 1847).

Auxentius, bp. of Silistria, *Aus der Schule des Wulfila. Auxenti Dorostorensis Epistola de fide vita et obitu Wulfilae* . . . , ed., F. Kauffmann (Strassburg, 1899).

Cassiodori Senatoris variae, ed., T. Mommsen, *MGH.AA*, 12 (Berlin, 1894, reprint 1961).

Chronica Minora, ed., T. Mommsen, *MGH.AA*, 9 (Chronica Minora, 1) (Berlin, 1892, reprint 1961) and 11 (Chronica Minora, 2) (Berlin, 1894, reprint 1961).

Claudianus, Claudius, *Carmina*, Loeb edition, trans. M. Platnauer (Cambridge, Mass., 1922).

Codex Iustinianus, ed., P. Krüger, *Corpus Iuris Civilis* 2 (Berlin, 1915, 12th ed., 1959).

Constantius VII, *Excerpta de legationibus*, ed., J. P. Migne, *P.G.*, 113 (Paris, 1864).

Corpus inscriptionum latinarum consilio et auctoritate Academiae litterarum regiae Borussicae editum . . . , ed., (Berlin 1862–).

Delehaye, H., "Saints de Thrace et de Mésie," *Analecta Bollandiana*, 31 (1912), pp. 161–300.

Dindorf, L., *Historici Graeci Minores*, Teubner edition (Leipzig, 1870).

Diocleatis, Presbyteri, *Regnum Slavorum*, ed., J. G. Schwandther (Scriptores rerum hungaricarum veteres . . . , 3, Vinobonae, 1748).

Edictum Theodorici Regis, ed., F. Bluhme, *MGH.Legum*, 5 (Hannover, 1875–89).

Ennodius, *Opera*, ed., F. Vogel, *MGH.AA*, 7 (Berlin, 1885, reprint 1961).

Eugippius, *Vita Severini*, ed., T. Mommsen, *MGH, Scriptores rerum Germanicarum in usum scholarum* (Berlin, 1898).

Eunapius, ed., L. Dindorf, *Historici Graeci Minores*, Teubner edition (Leipzig, 1870).

Fiebiger, O., and L. Schmidt, "Inschriftensammlung zur Geschichte der Ostgermanen," *Denkschriften der kaiserlichen Akademie der Wissenschaften in Wien, philosophisch-historische Klasse*, 60, Abh. 3 (1917), continued by Fiebiger alone in 70, Abh. 3 (1939) and 72 (1944).

Frontinus, Sextus Julius, *Strategemata libri quattuor*, ed., G. Gundermann, Teubner edition (Leipzig, 1888).

Gregorius Thaumaturgus, Saint, bp. of Neocaesarea, *Opera quae reperiri potuerunt omnia*, ed., J. P. Migne, *P.G.*, 10 (Paris, 1857).

Gregorius I, Pope, *Dialogui*, 2, ed., J. P. Migne, *P.L.* 76 (Paris, 1896).

Herodian, Loeb edition, ed., C. R. Whittaker (Cambridge, Mass., 1970).

Isidorus, *Historia Gothorum Wandalorum Sueborum, MGH.AA.*, 11 (Chronica Minora, 2) (Berlin 1894, reprint 1961).

Jacoby, F., *Die Fragmente der griechischen Historiker* (Berlin, 1923–1958).

Jordanis Romana et Getica, ed., T. Mommsen, *MGH.AA.*, 5 (Berlin, 1882, reprint 1961).

Leges Visigothorum, ed., K. Zeumer, *MGH.Legum*, Sectio I,1 *Legum Nationum Germanicarum*, (Hannover, Leipzig, 1902).

Leges Burgundionum, ed., L. R. de Salis, *MGH.Legum*, Sectio I,2 pars 1 (Hannover, 1892).

Mansi, Johannes, *Sacrorum Conciliorum Nova et Amplissima Collectio*, ed., P. Labbe, G. Cossart, and G. D. Mansi (Firenze, 1758–1798, reprint Graz, 1901).

Marini, Gaetano Luigi, *I Papiri diplomatici* (Roma, 1805).

Müller, Carl, *Fragmenta Historicorum Graecorum* (Paris, 1853–1883).

Panegyrici Latini, Teubner edition, ed., W. A. Baehrens (Leipzig, 1911).

Panégyriques Latins, ed., E. Galletier, Collection G. Budé (Paris, 1949–55).

Patrick, Saint, *Confession et lettre à Coroticus*. 2ᵉ rédaction, texte critique, traduction et notes, Richard Hanson (Sources Chrétiennes, 249, Paris, 1978).

Paulinus Pellaeus, Loeb edition, trans., Hugh G. White (Cambridge, Mass., 1921).

Paulus Diaconus, *Pauli Historia Langobardorum*, ed., L. Bethmann and G. Waitz, *MGH, Scriptores rerum Langobardicarum et Italicarum, saec. vi–ix* (Hannover, 1878, reprint 1964).

Paulus Orosius, *Historiarum adversum paganos libri vii*, ed., C. Zangemeister, *Corpus Scriptorum Ecclesiasticorum Latinorum*, 5 (Wien, 1882).

Petrus Patricius, *Historiae*, ed., Niebuhr in the Bonn edition of the *Excerpta de legationibus*, 14 (Bonn, 1829).

Philostorgius, *Historia Ecclesiastica*, Kirchengeschichte, ed., J. Bidez, Die griechischen christlichen Schriftsteller der ersten Jahrhunderte (Leipzig, 1913, rev. edition by F. Winkelmann, Berlin, 1972).

Photius, *Bibliothèque*, texte établi et traduit par R. Henry, Collection G. Budé (Paris, 1959–1977).

Pithou, P., *Epigrammata vetera* (Paris, 1590).

Procopius, *History of the Wars*, Loeb edition, trans., H. B. Dewing (Cambridge, Mass., 1914–40, reprint 1953–54).

Rutilius Namatianus, in *Minor Latin Poets*, Loeb edition, trans., J. W. Duff and A. M. Duff (Cambridge, Mass., 1935).

Scheffer, J., ed., *Arriani Tactica et Mauricii Ars Militaris* (Upsala, 1664, reprint 1967).

Scriptores Historiae Augustae, Loeb edition, trans., D. Magie (Cambridge, Mass., 1921–1932).

Seeck, Otto, ed., *Notitia Dignitatum* (Berlin, 1876, reprint Frankfurt am Main, 1962).

Sextus Aurelius Victor, *Liber de Caesaribus*, Teubner edition, ed., R. Gruendel (Leipzig, 1961).

Sozomenus, *Historia Ecclesiastica*, Kirchengeschichte, ed., J. Bidez, Die griechischen christlichen Schriftsteller der ersten Jahrhunderte (Berlin, 1960).

Synesius of Cyrene, bp. of Ptolemais, *Opera*, ed., J. P. Migne, *P.G.* 66 (Paris, 1857).

Tabula Imperii Romani, Foglio L 32, Mediolanum (Aventicum-Brigantium), (Roma, 1966).

Tabula Imperii Romani, Foglio L 34 (Aquincum-Sarmizegetusa-Sirmium), (Amsterdam, 1968).

Themistius, *Orationes*, ed., W. Dindorf (Leipzig, 1832; reprint Hildesheim, 1961).

Tjäder, Jan-Olof, ed., *Die nichtliterarischen lateinischen Papyri Italiens aus der Zeit 445–700*. I. Papyri 1–28, *Srikfter utgivna av Svenska Institutet i Rom, Acta Instituti Romani Regni Sueciae*, 4, 19, 1 (Lund, 1955).

Translatio sancti Epiphani, ed., J. Pertz, *MGH, Scriptores*, 4 (Hannover, 1841, reprint 1925).

Vita S. Caesarii, ed., J. P. Migne, *P.L.*, 67 (Paris, 1865).

Zosimus, *Historia Nova*, texte établi et traduit par F. Paschoud, Collection G. Budé (Paris, 1971–).

Zosimus, *Historia Nova*, Teubner edition, ed. L. Mendelssohn (Leipzig, 1887).

SECONDARY WORKS

Åberg, N., *Die Goten und Langobarden in Italien* (Arbeten utg. med understöd af Vilhelm Ekmans universitetsfond, 29, Uppsala, 1923).

Achelis, H., "Der älteste deutsche Kalender," *Zeitschrift für die neutestamentliche Wissenschaft und die Kunde des Urchristentums*, 1 (1900), pp. 308–335.

Achelis, H., *Die Martyrologien. Ihre Geschichte und ihr Wert* Gesellschaft der Wissenschaften zu Göttingen, philologisch-historische Klasse, Abhandlungen N.F. 3,3, 1899–1901).

Alföldy, Geza, *Noricum,* trans. Anthony Birley (London, Boston, 1974).

Almren, O., *Studien über nordeuropäische Fibelformen* (Mannus-Bibliothek, 32, Leipzig 1923, reprint Bonn, 1973).

Ambrosino, G. et. Weil, A. R., "Nature et portée d'analyses nondestructives de méteux précieux," *Bulletin du Laboratoire du Musée du Louvre,* 1 (1956), pp. 53–62.

Andersson, Theodore M., "Cassiodorus and the Gothic legend of Ermanaric," *Euphorion,* 57 (1963), pp. 28–43.

Annibaldi, Giovanni and Joachim Werner, „Ostgotische Grabfunde aus Acquasanta, Prov. Ascoli Piceno (Marche)," *Germania,* 41 (1963), pp. 356–73.

Antoniervicz, J., "Tribal Territories of the Baltic Peoples in the Hallstatt-La-Tene and Roman Periods in the Light of Archaeology and Toponomy," *Acta Baltico-Slavica,* 4 (1966), pp. 7–27.

Austin, N. J. E., "In support of Ammianus' Veracity," *Historia,* 22 (1973), pp. 331–35.

Bach, E., "Théodoric, romain ou barbare?", *Byzantion,* 25–27 (1935–37), pp. 413–20.

Bachrach, Bernard S., *Merovingian Military Organization. 481–751* (Minneapolis, Minnesota, 1972).

Balg, G. H., *A Comparative Glossary of the Gothic Language* (Mayville, Wissconsin, 1887–1889).

Bang, Martin, *Die Germanen im römischen Dienst bis zum Regierungsantritt Constantins I.* (Berlin, 1906).

Barkóczi, L., "A Sixth Century Cemetery from Keszthely-Fenekpuszta," *Acta Archaeologica,* 20 (1968), pp. 275–86.

Barkóczi, L., "Transplantations of Sarmatians and Roxolans in the Danube Basin," *Acta Antiqua,* 7 (1959), pp. 443–53.

Barkóczi, L. and A. Salamon, "Remarks on the sixth century history of 'Pannonia'," *Acta Archaeologica,* 23 (1971), pp. 139–53.

Barnes, T. D., "The Lost Kaisergeschichte and the Latin Historical Tradition," *Bonner Historia-Augusta-Colloqium,* 1968/69 (Antiquitas IV, 7, Bonn, 1970), pp. 13–43.

Barrière-Flavy, C., *Les Arts industriels des peuples barbares en Gaule du Vme au VIIIme siècle* (Toulouse, 1901).

Behrens, G., "Spätrömische Kerbschnittschnallen", *Schumacher-Festschrift,* hrsg. von d. Direkt. d. römisch-german. Zentralmuseums in Mainz (Mainz, 1930), pp. 285–94.

Berger, Adolf, "Encyclopedic Dictionary of Roman Law," *Transactions of the American Philosophical Society,* n.s. 43.2 (1953).

Bersu, G., "A Sixth-century German Settlement of Foederati: Golemanoso Kale," *Antiquity,* 17 (1938), pp. 31–43.

Bichir, Gheorghe, "La Civilisation des Carpes (IIe–IIIe siècle de n.è.) à la lumière des fouilles archéologiques de Poiana-Dulcești, de Butnărești et de Pădureni," *Dacia,* n.s. 11 (1967), pp. 177–224.

Bieler, Ludwig, *Eugippius' The Life of St. Severinus,* trans., L. Bieler with collaboration of L. Krestan (Fathers of the Church, 55, Washington D.C., 1965).

Bierbrauer, Volker, "Zu den Vorkommen ostgotischer Bügelfibeln in Raetia II," *Bayerische Vorgeschichtsblätter,* 36 (1971), pp. 134–65.

Bierbrauer, Volker, *Die ostgotischen Grab- und Schatzfunde in Italien* (Biblioteca degli Studi Medievali, 7, Spoleto, 1975).

Biondi, Biondo, *Il diritto romano* (Bologna, 1957).

Biondi, Biondo, *Successione testamentaria, donazioni,* 2d. ed. (Milano, 1955).

Biraben, J. N. and J. Le Goff, "La Peste du haut moyen âge," *Annales, Économies, Sociétés, Civilisations.* 24 (1969), pp. 1484–1510.

Bloch, Marc, "Économie de nature ou économie d'argent . . .," *Annales d'histoire sociale,* 1 (1939), pp. 7–16.

Blockley, R. C., "Dexippus of Athens and Eunapius of Sardis, *Latomus*, 30 (1971), pp. 710–15.

Blume, Erich, *Die germanischen Stämme und die Kulturen zwischen Oder und Passarge zur römischen Kaiserzeit* (Mannus-Bücherei 8 and 14, Würzburg, 1912 and 1915).

Bodor, Andrei, "Emperor Aurelian and the Abandoment of Dacia," *Dacoromania*, 1 (1973), pp. 29–40.

Bolta, Lojze, "Spätantikes Gräberfeld auf Rifnik bei Sentzur," [in slovene with German summary] *Acta Archaeologica. Arheološki Vestnik. Ljubljana. Académie slovène*, 21–22 (1970–71), pp. 127–140.

Brady, C., *The Legends of Ermanaric* (Los Angeles, 1943).

Bradley, D. R., "The Composition of the Getica," *Eranos*, 64 (1966), pp. 67–79.

Brand, C. E., *Roman Military Law* (Austin, Texas, 1968).

Brašinsky, I. B., "Recherches soviétiques sur les monuments antiques des régions de la Mer Noire," *Eirene*, 7 (1968), pp. 81–118.

Bréal, Michel, "Premières influences de Rome sur le monde germanique," *Mémoires de la société de linguistique de Paris*, 7 (1892), pp. 135–48.

Brøgger, A. W. and H. Shetelig, *The Vilking Ships, their Ancestry and Evolution* (Oslo, 1953).

Brogan, O., "Trade between the Roman Empire and the Free Germans," *Journal of Roman Studies*, 26 (1936), pp. 195–223.

Broom, Leonard, et. al., "Acculturation. An Exploratory Formulation," *American Anthropologist*, 56 (1954), pp. 973–1000.

Brown, David, "The Brooches in the Pietroasa Treasure," *Antiquity*, 46 (1972), pp. 111–16.

Brown, Peter, "The Rise and Function of the Holy Man in Late Antiquity," *Journal of Roman Studies*, 61 (1971), pp. 80–101.

Bullinger, Hermann, *Spätantike Gürtelbeschläge. Typen, Herstellung, Tragweise und Datierung* (Diss. Archaeol. Gandenses 12, Brugge, 1969).

Bullough, D. A., "Early Medieval Social Groupings. The Terminology of Kinship," *Past and Present*, 45 (1969), pp. 3–18.

Bullough, D. A., "Urban Change in Early Medieval Italy. The Example of Pavia," *Papers of the British School at Rome*, 34 (1966), pp. 82–130.

Burger, A. Sz., "The Late Roman Cemetery at Ságvár," *Acta Archaeologica*, 18 (1966), pp. 99–234.

Burgundian Code, trans., Katherina F. Drew (Philadelphia, 1972).

Burns, T. S., "The Battle of Adrianople. A Reconsideration," *Historia*, 22 (1973), pp. 336–45.

Burns, T. S., "The Barbarians and the Scriptores Historiae Augustae," in: *Studies in Latin Literature and Roman History*, vol. 1 (Collection Latomus, 164, Bruxelles, 1979), pp. 521–40.

Burns, T. S., "The Alpine Frontiers and Early Medieval Italy to the Middle of the Seventh Century," in *The Frontier. Comparative Studies*, vol. 2 (Norman, Oklahoma, 1979), pp. 51–68.

Burns, T. S., "Pursuing the Early Gothic Migrations", *Acta Archaeologica*, 31 (1979), pp. 189–99.

Bury, J. B., *The Later Roman Empire* (London, 1889, reprint New York, 1958).

Calandra, C., *Di una necropoli barbarica scoperta a Testona* (Atti della Società di archeologia e belle arti per la provincia di Torino, 4, Torino, 1880).

Calasso, Francesco, *Il medio evo del diritto*, I, Le fonti (Milano, 1954).

Cameron, Alan, *Claudian. Poetry and Propaganda at the Court of Honorius* (Oxford, 1970).

Cameron, Alan, "A New Fragment of Eunapius [Suidas m.203]," *Classical Review*, 17 (1967), pp. 10–11.

Cameron, Averil, *Agathias* (Oxford, 1970).

Cameron, Averil, "Agathias on the Early Merovingians," *Annali della Scuola Normale di Pisa*, 2, 37 (1968), pp. 95–140.

Cardascia, G., "L'Apparition dans le droit des classes d'"honestiores' et d'"humiliores"," *Revue historique de droit français et étranger*, 28 (1950), pp. 305–37, 461–85.

Charles-Edwards, T. M., "Kinship, Status and the Origins of the Hide," *Past and Present*, 56 (1972), pp. 3–33.

Chastagnol, A., *Le Sénat romain sous le règne d'Odoacre. Recherches sur l'épigraphie du Colisée au Ve siècle* (Antiquitas, III, 3, Bonn, 1966).

Chastagnol, A., *Recherches sur l'histoire Auguste* avec un rapport de la Histoire Augusta-Forschung depuis 1963 (Antiquitas IV, 6, Bonn, 1970).

Chénon, Émile, "Étude historique sur le *defensor civitatis*," *Revue historique de droit*, 13 (1889), pp. 515–37.

Chrysos, Evangelos, K., "Gothia Romana. Zur Rechtslage des Föderatenlandes der Westgoten im 4. Jh.," *Dacoromania*, 1 (1973), pp. 52–64.

Cook, G. M., *The Life of Saint Epiphanius by Ennodius* (Washington D.C., 1942).

Courtois, Christian, "Auteurs et scribes. Remarques sur la chronique d'Hydace," *Byzantion*, 21 (1951), pp. 23–54.

Courtois, Christian, *Les Vandales et l'Afrique* (Paris, 1955).

Courtois, Christian, *Victor de Vita et son œuvre. Étude critique* (Alger, 1954).

Cross, Samuel H., "Gothic Loan-words in the Slavic Vocabulary," *Harvard Studies and Notes in Philology and Literature*, 16 (1934), pp. 37–49.

Crumley, Carole, *Celtic Social Structure* (Ann Arbor, Mich., 1974).

Crump, G. A., "Ammianus and the Late Roman Army," *Historia*, 22 (1973), pp. 91–103.

Czarnecki, Jan, *The Goths in Ancient Poland* (Miami, Florida, 1975).

Dagron, Gilbert, "Discours utopique et récit des origines," part 1, "Une lecture de Cassiodore-Jordanès. Les Goths de Scandza à Ravenne," *Annales, Économies, Sociétés, Civilisations*, 6 (1971), pp. 290–305.

Dahn, Felix, *Die Könige der Germanen bis auf die Feudalzeit*, Bd. 4 (Würzburg, 1866).

Davies, Oliver, *Roman Mines in Europe* (Oxford, 1935).

Declareuil, J., "Des comtes de cités à la fin du Ve siècle," *Revue historique de droit*, 34 (1910), pp. 794–836.

Degani, Mario, *Il tesoro romano-barbarico di Reggio Emilia* (Firenze, 1959).

Degrassi, N., "Rinvenimento di un tesoretto. Le oreficerie tardo-Romane di Pavia," *Notizie degli scavi di antichità* (Roma, 1941), pp. 303–10.

Deloche, M., *La Trustis et l'antrustion royale sous les deux premières races* (Paris, 1873).

Demandt, Alexander, "Magister militum," *R-E*, Suppl. 12 (1970), cc. 553–790.

Demougeot, E., *De l'unité à la division de l'empire romain 395–410*. Essai sur le gouvernement impérial (Paris, 1951).

Desjardins, Ernest, *La Table de Peutinger* (Paris, 1869).

Dessau, H., "Über die Scriptores Historiae Augustae," *Hermes*, 27 (1892), pp. 561–605.

Dessau, H., "Über Zeit und Persönlichkeit der Scriptores Historiae Augustae," *Hermes*, 24 (1889), pp. 337–92.

Diaconu, Gh., *Tîrgşor necropola din secolele III–IV* (Bucureşti, 1965).

Diculescu, C., *Die Wandalen und die Goten in Ungarn und Rumänien* (Mannus Bibl. 34, Leipzig, 1923).

Digges, Thomas G., and Samuel J. Rosenberg, *Heat Treatment and Properties of Iron and Steel* (National Bureau of Standards Monograph, 18, Washington D.C., 1960).

Dölger, F., "Byzantine Literature," *Cambridge Medieval History*, vol. 4, pt. 2, ed. J. M. Hussey (Cambridge, 1967), pp. 206–263.

Dombay, János, "Der gotische Grabfund von Domolospuszta. Der Fundort und die Umstände des Fundes," *Janus Pannonius Muzeum Evkonyve*, 1 (1956), pp. 104–30.

d'Ors, Alvaro, *Estudios visigóticos*, pt. 2: *El Código de Eurico* (Cuadernos del Instituto Jurídico Español, 12, Roma, Madrid, 1960).

Draw, Katherine Fischer, *The Burgundian Code* (Philadelphia, Penn., 1972).

Dubois, Augustin, *La Latinité d'Ennodius* (Clermont, 1903).

Dumoulin, Maurice, "Le Gouvernement de Théodoric et la domination des Ostrogoths en Italie d'après les œuvres d'Ennodius," *Revue historique*, 78 (1902), pp. 1–7, 241–65, and 79 (1902), pp. 1–22.

Durkheim, Emile, *The Division of Labor in Society* (Chicago, 1947).

Dyggve, Ejnar, *History of Salonitan Christianity* (Cambridge, 1951).

Eadie, John W., "Roman Agricultural Implements from Sirmium," *Sirmium II,* (Beograd, 1971).

Ebel, H., "Die Fremdwörter bei Ulfilas in phonetischer Hinsicht," *Zeitschrift für vergleichende Sprachforschung,* 4 (1855), pp. 282–88.

Ebert, M., "Ausgrabungen bei dem 'Gorodok Nikolajewka' am Dnjepr," *Prähistorische Zeitschrift,* 5 (1913), pp. 80–113.

Eggers, Hans Jürgen, "Das kaiserzeitliche Gräberfeld von Pollwitten, Kreis Mohrungen, Ostpreussen," *Jahrbuch des Römisch-Germanischen Zentralmuseums Mainz;* 11 (1966), pp. 154–75.

Eggers, H. J., "Zur absoluten Chronologie die römischen Kaiserzeit im freien Germanien," *Jahrbuch des Römisch-Germanischen Zentralmuseums Mainz,* 2 (1955), pp. 196–244, reprinted with an updating of sites by H. Jankuhn in *Aufstieg und Niedergang der römischen Welt,* II.5 (Berlin, New York, 1976).

Eggers, H. J., *Der römische Import im freien Germanien,* (Atlas der Urgeschichte 1, Hamburg, 1951).

Ekholm, Gunnar, *Handelsförbindelsen mellan Skandinavien och Romerska riket* (Verdandis scriftserie, 15, Stockholm, 1961).

Enmann, A., "Eine verlorene Geschichte d. röm. Kaiser," *Philologus,* Suppl. 4 (1883), pp. 335–501

Ensslin, W., *Theoderich der Grosse,* 2nd, ed. (München, 1959).

Ensslin, W., "Die Ostgoten in Pannonia," *Byzantinisch-neugriechische Jahrbücher,* 6 (1927–8), pp. 146–59.

Ensslin, W., "Zum Heermeisteramt des spätrömischen Reiches," ii, iii *Klio,* 24 (1931), pp. 102–47, 467–502.

Evans, James A.S., *Procopius* (New York, 1972).

Fagerlie, Joan M., *Late Roman and Byzantine Solidi Found in Sweden and Denmark,* (Numismatic Notes and Monographs, 157, New York, 1967).

Fertig, Michael, *Magnus Felix Ennodius' Lobrede auf Theoderich den Grossen, König der Ostgoten* (Landshut, 1858).

Fischer, Katherine M., *A Study of the Lombard Laws* (Unpublished doctoral dissertation, Cornell University, 1950).

Folz, R., *De l'Antiquité au monde médieval* (Paris, 1972).

Fowkes, R. A., "Crimean Gothic Cadarion 'Miles, Soldier'," *Journal of English and German Philology,* 45 (1946), pp. 448–49.

France-Lanord, A., "Le Polissage électrolytique et les répliques transparentes," *Conservation (Études de),* 7.4 (1962), pp. 121–33.

Freeman, J. D., "On the Concept of the Kindred," *Journal of the Royal Anthropological Institute of Great Britain and Ireland,* 91 (1961), pp. 192–220.

Fridh, Åke, *Contributions à la critique et à l'interprétation des Variae de Cassiodore* (Acta Regiae Societatis Scientiarum et Litterarum Gothoburgensis. Humaniora, 4, Göteborg, 1968).

Fridh, Åke, *Études critiques et syntaxiques sur les Variae de Cassiodore* (Göteborgs kungl. vetenskaps-och vitterhets-samhälle. Handlingar, 6. Földen, ser. A, bd. 4, No. 2, Göteborg 1950).

Fridh, Åke, *Terminologie et formules dans les Variae de Cassiodore; études sur la dévelopment du style administratif aux derniers siècles de l'antiquité* (Studia graeca et latina Gothoburgensia, 2, Stockholm, 1956).

Fried, Morton, *The Notion of Tribe* (Cummings, 1975).

Fried, Morton A., "Warfare, Military Organization, and the Evolution of Society," *Anthropologica,* 3 (1961), pp. 134–47.

Fuchs, S., *Kunst der Ostgotenzeit* (Berlin, 1944).

Gajewska, Halina, *Topographie des fortifications romaines en Dobroudja* (Wrocław, 1974).

Garnsey, Peter, *Social Status and Legal Privilege in the Roman Empire* (Oxford, 1970).

Gaudenzi, A., "Die Entstehungszeit des Edictum Theoderici," *Zeitschrift der Savigny-Stiftung für Rechtsgeschichte, Germ. Abt.*, 7 (1887), pp. 29–52.

Gaupp, Ernst Theodor, *Die germanischen Ansiedlungen und Landtheilungen in den Provinzen des römischen Westreiches im ihrer völkerrechtlichen Eigenthümlichkeit und mit Rücksicht auf verwandte Erscheinungen der alten Welt und des späteren Mittelalters dargestellt* (Breslau, 1844).

Geiss, H., *Geld-und-naturwiwssenschaftliche Erscheinungsformen im staatlichen Aufbau Italiens während der Gotenzeit*, Vierteljahrsschrift für Sozial- und Wirtschaftsgeschichte, Beiheft 27, Stuttgart 1931).

Gerov, B., "Die gotische Invasion in Mösien und Thrakien unter Decius im Lichte der Hortfunde," *Acta Antiqua Philippopolitana, Studia histor. et. philol. Serdicae*, 4 (1963), pp. 127–46.

Gerov, B., "L'aspect éthnique et linguistique dans la région entre le Danube et les Balkans à l'époque romaine (Ie–IIIe s.)," *Studi urbinati di storia, filosofia e letteratura*, n.s. B., 33 (1959), pp. 173–91.

Godłowski, Kazimierz, *The Chronology of the Late Roman and Early Migration Periods in Central Europe*, trans., Maria Wałęga (Kraków, 1970).

Goessler, Peter, "Zur Belagerungskunst der Germanen," *Klio*, 35 (1942), pp. 103–114.

Götze, Alfred, *Gotische Schnallen* (Berlin, 1913).

Goody, Jack, "Kinship. Descent Groups," *International Encyclopedia of the Social Sciences*, 8 (1968), pp. 402–8.

Gordon, C. D., *The Age of Attila* (Ann Arbor, Mich., 1966).

Grosse, Robert, *Römische Militärgeschichte von Gallienus bis zum Beginn der byzantinischen Themenverfassung* (Berlin, 1920).

Grumel, V., "L'Illyricum de la mort de Velantinian Ier (375) à la mort de Stilicon (408)," *Revue des études byzantines*, 11 (1951), pp. 5–46.

Gschwantler, O., "Zum Namen der Rosomonen und an. Jonakr.," *Die Sprache. Zeitschrift für Sprachwissenschaft*, 17 (1971), pp. 164–76.

Guillou, André, *Régionalisme et indépendance dans l'empire byzantin au VIIe siècle. L'exemple de l'Exarchat et de la Pentapole d'Italie* (Roma, 1969).

Gundel, Hans Georg, "Die Bedeutung des Geländes in der Kriegskunst der Germanen," *Neue Jahrbücher für Antike und deutsche Bildung*, 3 (1940), pp. 188–96.

Gundel, Hans Georg, *Untersuchungen zur Taktik und Strategie der Germanen nach den antiken Quellen* (Marburg, 1937).

Hachmann, Rolf, *Die Goten und Skandinavien* (Quellen und Forschungen zur Sprach- und Kulturgeschichte der germanischen Völker, 158, Berlin, 1970).

Hammond, Nicholas G. L., *A History of Macedonia*, vol. 1, *Historical Geography and Prehistory* (Oxford, 1972).

Hannestad, Knud, *L'Évolution des ressources agricoles de l'Italie du IVe au VIe siècle de notre ère* (Historisk-filosofiske Meddelelser udgivet af Det Kongelige Danske Videnskabernes Selskab, 40, 1, København, 1962).

Hannestad, Knud, "Les Forces militaires d'après la guerre gothique de Procope," *Classica et Medievalia*, 29 (1960), pp. 136–83.

Harmatta, J., "Goten und Hunnen in Pannonien," *Acta Antiqua*, 3 (1971), pp. 293–97.

Harmatta, J., "The Last Century of Pannonia," *Acta Antiqua*, 18 (1970), pp. 361–69.

Harmatta, J., *Studies on the History of the Sarmatians* (Budapest, 1950).

Hartmann, L. M., "Anonymus Valesianus," *R-E*, I,2 (1894), cc. 2333–34.

Hartmann, L. M., *Geschichte Italiens im Mittelalter* (Gotha, 1903).

Hauptmann, Ludmil, "Kroaten, Goten und Sarmaten," *Germanoslavica*, 3 (1935), pp. 95–127, 315–53.

Hawkes, Sonia Chadwick, "Soldier and settlers in Britain, Fourth to Fifth Century. With a Catalogue of Animal-ornamented Buckles and Related Belt-fittings," *Medieval Archaeology*, 5 (1961), pp. 1–71.

Helbling, Hanno, *Goten und Wandalen* (Zürich, 1954).

Herlihy, David, "The Carolingian Mansus," *Economic History Review,* 13 (1961), pp. 79–89.

Heuberger, R., "Das ostgotische Rätien," *Klio*, 30 (1937), pp. 77–109.

Heym, W., "Der ältere Abschnitt der Völkerwanderungszeit auf dem rechten Ufer der unteren Weichsel," *Mannus,* 31 (1939), pp. 3–28.

Hitzinger, P., "Der Kampf des Kaisers Theodosius gegen den Tyrannen Eugenius am Flusse Frigidus," *Mittheilungen des historischen Vereines für Krain,* 10 (1855), pp. 81 ff.

Hoddinott, R. F., *Bulgaria in Antiquity. An Archaeological Introduction* (New York, 1975).

Hodgkin, Thomas, *Italy and her Invaders, 376–814,* vol. 3, *The Ostrogothic Invasion 476–535* (New York, 1880–89).

Hodgkin, Thomas, *The Letters of Cassiodorus* (London, 1886).

Hoepffner, André, "Les 'Magistri militum praesentales' au IVe siècle," *Byzantion,* 11 (1936), pp. 483–98.

Höfler, O., "Der Sakralcharakter des germanischen Königtums," in: *Das Königtum, seine geistigen und rechtlichen Grundlagen* (Vorträge und Forschungen 3, ed. Th. Mayer, Lindau, Konstanz, 1956), pp. 75–104).

den Hollander, A. N. J., "The Great Hungarian Plain. A European Frontier Area," *Comparative Studies in Society and History,* 3 (1960), pp. 74–88, 135–169.

Huebner, R., *A History of Germanic Private Law* (The Continental Legal History Series, 4, Boston, 1918).

Jaskanis, Jan, "Human Burials with Horses in Prussia and Sudovia in the First Millennium of our Era," *Acta Baltico-Slavica,* 4 (1966), pp. 29–65.

Jellinek, Max Hermann, *Geschichte der gotischen Sprache* (Berlin, 1926).

Jones, A. H. M., "The Constitutional Position of Odoacer and Theoderic," *Journal of Roman Studies,* 52 (1962), pp. 126–130.

Jones, A. H. M., *The Later Roman Empire. A Social, Economic and Administrative Survey,* vol. 1–2. (Norman, Oklahoma, 1964).

Jones, A. H. M., et al., *The Prosopography of the Later Roman Empire,* vol. 1 (Cambridge, 1971).

Jordanes, *Gothic History in English Version,* trans., Charles C. Mierow (2 nd. ed., Princeton, N.J., 1915, reprint New York, 1960).

Kaegi, Walter Emil, *Byzantium and the Decline of Rome* (Princeton, 1968).

Kahane, Anne, Threipland, Leslie M., and Ward-Perkins, John, "The Ager Veientanus, North and East of Rome," *Papers of the British School at Rome,* 36 (1968).

Kelemina, J., "Goti na Balkanu," *Casopis za zgodovino in Narodopisje,* 27 (1932), pp. 121–36.

Kempisty, A., "Some Problems of Research on the Roman Period in Masouria and Podlachia," *Acta Baltico-Slavica,* 4 (1966), pp. 67–78.

Kitzinger, E., "A Survey of the Early Christian Town of Stobi," *Dumbarton Oaks Papers,* 3 (1946), pp. 81–182.

Kmieciński, Jerzy, "Niektofe spoleczne aspekty epizodu goekiego w orkesie środknworzymskim na Pomorzu," *Zeszyty Naukowe Uniwersytetu Lódzkiego, Nauki Humanist-Spol.,* Ser., 1,12 (1959), pp. 3–22.

Kmieciński, J., ed., *Odry Cmentarzysko kurhanowe z okresu rzymskiego* (Łódź, 1968).

Kmieciński, Jerzy, "Problem of the So-called Gotho-Gepidian Culture in the Light of Recent Research," *Archaeologia Polona,* 4 (1962), pp. 270–85.

Kmieciński, Jerzy, *Zagadnienie tzw. Kultury gocko-gepid-zkiej na Pomorzu Wschodnim w okresie wczesnorzymsk'n* (Societas Scientiarum Lodziensis. Sectio 2, 46, Acta Archaeologica Lodziendzia, 11, Łódź, 1962).

Korkkanen, Irma, *The Peoples of Hermanaric. Jordanes, Getica 116* (Suomalainen tiedeakatemian toimituksia. Annales Academiae Scientiarum Fennicae, Ser. B., 187, Helsinki, 1975).

Korsunskij, A. R., "The Visigoths and the Roman Empire in the late Fourth to Early Fifth Century," [in Russian], *Vestnik Moskovskogo Universiteta* (istor. sexcija), 3 (1963), pp. 87–95.

Korsunskij, A. R., "Visigothic Social Structure in the Fourth Century," [in Russian], *Vestnik Drevnej Istorii*, 93 (1965), pp. 54–74.

Korsunskij, A. R., "Small Landed Property in the Western Provinces of the Late Roman Empire," [in Russian], *Vestnik Drevnej Istorii*, 112 (1970), pp. 167–74.

Kossina, Gustaf, "Die ethnologische Stellung der Ostgermanen," *Indogermanische Forschungen*, 7 (1897), pp. 276–312.

Kossina, Gustaf, *Das Weichselland, ein uralter Heimatboden der Germanen* (Danzig, 1919).

Kostrzewski, Józef, "Le problème du séjour des Germains sur les terres de Pologne," *Archaeologia Polona*, 4 (1962), pp. 7–44.

Kovačevič, Jovan, *Varvarska Kolonizacija Južnoslovenskih Oblasti od iv do početka vii veka* (Musée de Voivodina Monographie, 2 Novi Sad, 1960).

Kovács, István, "A. M. Marosszentannai népvándozlaskori temetö," *Dolgozatok (Cluj)*, 3 (1912), pp. 250–367.

Kraus, Franz F., *Die Münzen Odovacars und des Ostgotenreiches in Italien* (Halle, 1928).

Kropotkin, V. V., "Topografija rimskich i rannevizantijskich monet na territorii SSSR," *Vestnik Drevnei Istorii*, 3, 49 (1954), pp. 152–80.

Kuharenko, Iurij V., "Le Problème de la civilisation gotho-gépide en Polésie et en Volhynie," *Acta Baltico-Slavica*, 5 (1967), pp. 19–40.

Kühn, Herbert, *Die germanischen Bügelfibeln der Völkerwanderungszeit in der Rheinprovinz*, part 1. (Bonn, 1940), rev. reprint Graz, 1962).

de Laet, S. J., Dhondt, J., and Nenquin, J., "Les Laeti du Namurois et l'origine de la civilisation mérovingienne," *Études d'histoire et d'archéologie dediées à Ferdinand Courtoy* (1952), p. 149ff.

Lammert, Friedrich, "Zum Kampf der Goten bei Abrittus im J. 251," *Klio*, 34 (1942), pp. 125–6.

Langenfelt, Gösta, "On the Origin of Tribal Names," *Anthropos*, 14/15 (1919–20), pp. 295–313.

Laqueur, Richard, "Suidas (Lexikograph)," *R-E*, IV, A 1 (1931), cc. 675–717.

Lattimore, Owen, *Studies in Frontier History* (Paris, 1962).

Lavagnini, B., *Belisario in Italia, I: Storia di un anno (533–36).* (Atti Accad. di Scienze, Lett. & Arti di Palermo Ser. 4 VIII, 2, 1947–48, Palermo, 1948).

Leach, E. R., *Political Systems of Highland Burma. A study of Kachin Social Structure* (Cambridge, Mass., 1954).

Lecce, M., "La vita economica dell'Italia durante la dominazione dei Goti nelle 'Variae' di Cassidoro," *Economia e Storia, Rivista Italiana di Storia Economica e Sociale*, 3, 4 (1956), pp. 354–408.

Léglise, M. Stanislas, *Œuvres complètes de Saint Ennodius évêque de Pavie*, vol. 1, *Lettres* (Paris, 1906).

Léglise, M. Stanislas, "Saint Ennodius et la haute éducation littéraire dans la monde romain au commencement du VIe siècle," *Revue des facultés catholiques (l'université catholique)*, 5 (1892), pp. 209–228, 375–397, 568–90.

Léglise, M. Stanislas, "Saint Ennodius et la suprématie pontificale au VIe siècle (499–503)," *Revue des facultés catholiques (l'université catholique)*, 2, 1889, pp. 220–242, 400–415, 569–593; 3 (1890), pp. 513–523; 4 (1891), pp. 55–66.

Le Goff, Jacques, "Travail, techniques et artisans dan les systèmes de valeur du haut moyen âge (V^e–Xe siècles)," *Settimane di Studio*, 18 (1971), pp. 239–66.

Leighton, Albert C., *Transport and Communication in Early Medieval Europe A.D. 500–1100* (New York, 1972).

Lengyel, I., "Chemico-analytical Aspects of Human Bone Finds from the Sixth Century 'Pannonian' Cemeteries," *Acta Archaeologica*, 23 (1971), pp. 155–66.

Levy, Ernst, Review of Alvaro d'Ors, *El Código de Eurico*, in *Zeitschrift der Savigny-Stiftung für Rechtsgeschichte, Rom. Abt.*, 79 (1962), pp. 479–88.

Lewicki, T., "Zagandnienie Gotów na Krymie," *Przegląd Zachodni*, 7 (1951), pp. 78–99.

Lewis, I. M., "Tribal Society," *International Encyclopedia of the Social Sciences,* 16 (1968), pp. 146–51.

Liber Pontificalis, trans. with introduction by Louise R. Loomis (New York, 1916, reprint 1965).

Loewe, Richard, "Der gotische Kalender," *Zeitschrift für deutsches Altertum und deutsche Litteratur,* 59 (1922), pp. 245–90.

Lot, F., "Du Régime de l'hospitalité," *Revue belge de philologie et d'histoire,* 7 (1928), pp. 975–1011.

Lotter, Friedrich, "Zur Rolle der Donausueben in der Völkerwanderungzeit," *Mitteilungen des Instituts für österreichische Geschichtsforschung,* 76 (1968), pp. 275–98.

Lotter, Friedrich, *Severinus von Noricum, Legende und historische Wirklichkeit.* Untersuchungen zur Phase des Übergangs von spätantiken zu mittelalterlichen Denk- und Lebensformen (Monographien zur Geschichte des Mittelalters, Bd. 12, Stuttgart 1976).

MacMullen, R., *Soldier and Civilian in the Later Roman Empire* (Cambridge, Mass., 1963).

Magoun, Francis P., Jr., "On the Old-Germanic Altar- or Oath-Ring (Stallahringr)," *Acta Philologica Scandinavica,* 20 (1949), pp. 277–93.

Mann, J. C., "The Role of the Frontier Zones in Army Recruitment," *Quintus Congressus Internationalis Limitis Romani Studiosorum,* 1961 (Zagreb, 1963), pp. 145–50.

Manso-Zisi, Dorde, "O Granicama Periodizacije anticke kulture", *Materjali IV. VII Kongres archeologa Jugoslavije. Actes IV. VIIᵉ Congrès des archéologiques yugoslaves.* Herceg-Novi, 1966 (Boegrad, 1967), pp. 225–28.

Matthews, J. F., "Olympiodorus of Thebes and the History of the West (407–425)," *Journal of Roman Studies,* 60 (1970), pp. 79–97.

Menner, R. J., "Crimean Gothic cadarion (cadariou), Latin centurio, Greek κεντύριον," *Journal of English and Germanic Philology,* 36 (1937), pp. 168–75.

Merwe, N. J. van der, *The Carbon-14 Dating of Iron* (Chicago, 1969).

Mierow, C. C., *The Gothic History of Jordanes in English Version* (2nd ed., Princeton, 1915, reprint Cambridge, New York, 1960).

Millar, Fergus, "P. Herennius Dexippus. The Greek World and the Third-century Invasions," *Journal of Roman Studies,* 59 (1969), pp. 12–29.

Miller, K., *Die Peutingersche Tafel* (Stuttgart, 1962).

Mirković, Miroslava, "Die Ostgoten in Pannonien nach dem Jahre 455," *Recueil des travaux de la faculté de philosophie,* 10.1 (Beograd, 1968), pp. 119–28.

Mirković, Miroslava, "Sirmium. Its History from the First Century A.D. to 582 A.D.," *Sirmium I,* (Beograd, 1961), pp. 5–90.

Mitrea, Bucur, "La Migration des Goths reflétée par les trésors de monnaies romaines enfouis en Moldavie," *Dacia,* n.s. 1 (1957), pp. 229–36.

Mócsy, András, "Der Name Flavius als Rangbezeichnung in der Spätantike," *Akten des IV. internationalen Kongresses für griechische und lateinische Epigraphik* (Wien, 1962), pp. 257–63.

Mócsy, András, *Pannonia and Upper Moesia* (London, 1974).

Mohler, S. L., "The Iuvenes and Roman Education," *Transactions of the American Philological Association,* 68 (1937), pp. 442–79.

Momigliano, A. D., "An Unsolved Problem of Historical Forgery. The Scriptores Historiae Augustae," *Journal of the Warburg and Courtauld Institutes,* 17 (1954), pp. 22–46.

Momigliano, A. D., "Cassiodorus and Italian Culture of His Time," reprinted in his *Studies in Historiography* (New York, 1966).

Mommsen, Theodor, "Der Begriff des Limes", *Westdeutsche Zeitschrift für Geschichte und Kunst,* 13, (1894), pp. 134–143, reprinted in *Gesammelte Schriften,* 5 (*Historische Schriften,* 2), (Berlin, 1908), pp. 456–64.

Mommsen, Theodor, "Ostgothische Studien," *Neues Archiv der Gesellschaft für ältere deutsche Geschichtskunde,* 14 (1888), pp. 225–243, 453–544, Nachträge 15 (1890) pp. 181–186, reprinted in *Gesammelte Schriften,* 6 (Historische Schriften, 3), (Berlin, 1908), pp. 372–482.

Mongait, A. L., *Archaeology in the USSR*, trans., M. W. Thompson (Harmondsworth, 1961).

Moss, H. St. L. B., *The Birth of the Middle Ages* (Oxford, 1935).

Mossé, Fernand, "Bibliographia Gotica, A Bibliography of writings on the Gothic Language to the end to 1949," *Mediaeval Studies*, 12 (1950), pp. 237-320. First Supplement, Corrections and Additions to the middle of 1953, 15 (1953), pp. 169-83).

Munz, Peter, "Medieval History in Australasia or the End of the Ancient World," *Historical Studies, Australia and New Zealand*, 11 (1963), No. 41.

Musset, Lucien, *Les Invasions. Les vagues germaniques* (Nouvelle Clio. L'Histoire et ses problèmes, 12, Paris 1965).

Nagy, T., "The Last Century of Pannonia in the Judgement of a New Monograph", *Acta Antiqua*, 19 (1971), pp. 299-345.

Nagy, T., "Reoccupation of Pannonia from the Huns in 427 (Did Jordanes use the Chronicon of Marcellinus Comes at the Writing of the Getica?)," *Acta Antiqua*, 15 (1967), pp. 159-86.

Nef, J. V., "Mining and Metallurgy in Medieval Civilization," *Cambridge Economic History*, vol. 2, ed., M. Postan and E. E. Rich (Cambridge, 1952), pp. 429-89.

Nenquin, Jacques A., *La Nécropole de Furfooz* (Brugge, 1953).

Nestor, "La Fin du monde ancien et les 'Barbares'," *XIIIe Congrès International des Sciences Historiques* (Moscou, 1970).

Nischer, E., "The Army Reforms of Diocletian and Constantine and their Modifications up to the Time of the Notitia Dignitatum," *Journal of Roman Studies*, 13 (1923), pp. 1-55.

Nixon, Charles E. V., *Historiographical Study of the Caesares of Sextus Aurelius Victor* (Unpublished, Ph. D. Thesis, University of Michigan, 1971).

Odobescu, A., *Le Trésor de Pétrossa* (Paris, 1895-1900).

Okulicz, Lucja and Jerzy Okulicz, "The La Tène and the Roman periods in northern Masovia and in the southern Mazurian area in the light of new discoveries," *Archaeologia Polona*, 4 (1962), pp. 286-94.

Oost, Stewart I., *Galla Placidia Augusta* (Chicago, 1968).

Ostrogorsky, Georg, *Geschichte des Byzantinischen Staates*, 3d. ed. (Handbuch der Altertumswissenschaft, Abt. 12, pt. 1, Bd. 2, München, 1963).

Oxenstierna, E., *Die Urheimat der Goten* (Leipzig, 1945).

Parducz, Mihály, "Der gotische Fund von Csongrád," *Dolgozatok*, 14 (1938), pp. 124-38.

Parker, H. M. D., *A History of the Roman World A.D. 138-337* (2nd ed., London 1958).

Pašalić, Esad, "Die Wirtschaftsbeziehungen zwischen dem Hinterland der Adria und dem römischen Limes an der Donau," *Quintus Congressus Internationalis Limitis Romani Studiosorum*, 1961 (Zagreb, 1963), pp. 167-75.

Patsch, K., *Die Völkerwanderung an der unteren Donau in der Zeit von Diocletian bis Heraclius* (Wien, 1928).

Pepe, Gabriele, *Le Moyen Âge barbare en Italie*, trans., Jéan Gonnet (Paris, 1956).

Percival, John, "Seigneurial Aspects of the Late Roman Estate Management," *English Historical Review*, 84 (1969), pp. 449-73.

Percival, John, *The Roman Villa. A Historical Introduction* (Berkeley, 1976).

Petrescu-Dîmbovita, Mircea, "Die wichtigsten Ergebnisse der archäologischen Forschung über den Zeitraum vom 3.-10. Jh. östlich der Karpaten," *Dacoromania*, 1 (1973), pp. 162-173.

Pfeilschifter, Georg, *Der Ostgotenkönig Theoderich der Grosse und die katholische Kirche* (Kirchengeschichtliche Studien, 3, Bd. 2, Münster, 1896).

Phillpotts, Bertha S., *Kindred and Clan in the Middle Ages and After. A Study on the Sociology of the Teutonic Races* (Cambridge, 1913).

Piétri, C., "Le Sénat, le peuple chrétien et les partis du cirque à Rome sous le pape Symmaque (498-514)," *Mélanges d'archéologie et d'histoire*, 78 (1966), pp. 123-39.

Piotrowicz, Ludwik, "Goci i Gepidowie nad dolna wisla i ich wedrówka ku morzu Czarnemu i Dacji," *Przeglad Zachodni, Miesiecznik*, 5/6 (1951), pp. 60-76.

Pleiner, R., "Experimental Smelting of Steel in Early Medieval Furnaces," *Památky Arch.*, 60 (1969), pp. 458-87.

Pontieri, Ernesto, *Le Invasioni barbariche e l'Italia del V a VI secolo* (Napoli, 1959–60).

Popescu, Emilian, "Das Problem der Kontinuität in Rumänien im Lichte der Epigraphischen Entdeckungen," *Dacoromania*, 1 (1973), pp. 69–77.

Protase, D., *Problema continuiţăţii în Dacia în lumina arheologii şi numiismaticii* (Bucureşti, 1966).

Przewoźna, D., "Osafa i cmentarzysko z okresu rzymskiego w Słopanowie, pow. Szamotuly," *Fontes Archaeologici Posnanienses*, 5 (1954), pp. 60–140.

Rappaport, B., *Die Einfälle der Goten in das römische Reich* (Leipzig, 1899).

Rasi, Piero, "Ancora sulla paternità del c.d. 'Edictum Theodorici'," *Annali di Storia del Diritto*, 5/6 (1961–62), pp. 113–136.

Rasi, Piero, "Sulla paternità de c.d. Edictum Theodorici regis," *Archivio Giuridico*, 145, sesta serie, 14 (1953), pp. 105–162.

Reinecke, P., "Aus der russischen archäologischen Litteratur," *Mainzer Zeitschrift* 1 (1906), pp. 42–50.

Remennikov, A. M., *Borba plemen Severnogo Pričenomorja s Rimom v III veke n.e.* (Moskva, 1954).

Revillout, Charles-Jules, *L'Arianisme des peuples germaniques* (Ph. D. Thesis, Paris, 1850).

Riché, Pierre, *Éducation et culture dans l'Occident barbare, VIe–VIIIe siècles* (Paris, 1962).

Richmond, Ian A., *The City Wall of Imperial Rome* (Oxford, 1930).

Riépnikoff, N., "Quelques cimetières du pays des Goths de Crimée," *Bull. de la com. impériale archéol.*, 19 (1906), pp. 1–80.

Rostovtzeff, M., *Iranians and Greeks in South Russia* (Oxford, 1922).

Rougé, J., "Quelques aspects de la navigation en Méditerranéee au Ve siècle et dans la première moitié du VIe siècle," *Cahiers d'histoire*, 6 (1961), pp. 129–54.

Rowell, Henry T., *Ammianus Marcellinus Soldier-Historian of the Late Roman Empire* (Semple Lectures, University of Cincinnati, 1964).

Ruggini, L., *Economia e società nell. "Italia annonaria." Rapporti fra agricultura e commercio dal IV al VI secolo d.c.* (Milano, 1961).

Ruggini, L., "Vicende rurali dell'Italia antica dall'età tetrarchica ai Longobardi," *Rivista Storica Italiana*, 76 (1964), pp. 261–86.

Russell, J. C., "That Earlier Plague," *Demography*, 5 (1968), pp. 174–84.

Sahlins, Marshall D., *Tribesmen* (Englewood Cliffs, N.J., 1968).

Salamon, Maciej, "The Chronology of Gothic Incursions into Asia Minor," *Eos*, 59 (1971), pp. 109–39.

Salin, B., *Die altgermanische Thierornamentik* (Stockholm, 1904).

Salin, E., "Le Forgeron du haut moyen-âge, ses ancêtres, sa descendance," *Archaeologia*, 14 (1967), pp. 78–81.

Salin, E., and A. France-Lanord, *Le Fer à l'époque mérovingienne*, vol. 2 of *Rhin et Orient* (Paris, 1943).

Šašel, J., *Claustra Alpium Iuliarum*, pt. 1, *Fontes* (Ljubljana, 1971).

Scardigli, Piergiuseppe, *Die Goten. Sprache und Kultur* (München, 1973).

Scavone, Daniel C., "Zosimus and His Historical Models," *Greek, Roman and Byzantine Studies*, 11 (1970), pp. 57–67.

Schaffran, E., "Zur Nordgrenze des ostgotischen Reiches in Kärnten," *Österreichisches Archäologisches Institut in Wien. Jahreshefte* (Beiblatt), 42 (1955), pp. 111–130.

Schindler, R., *Die Besiedlungsgeschichte der Goten und Gepiden im unteren Weichselraum auf Grund der Tongefässe* (Quellenschriften zur ostdeutschen Vor- und Frühgeschichte, Bd. 6, Leipzig, 1940).

Schlesinger, Walter, "Das Heerkönigtum," in: *Das Königtum, seine geistigen und rechtlichen Grundlagen* (Vorträge und Forschungen, 3, ed., Th. Mayer, Lindau, Konstanz, 1956), pp. 105–141.

Schlesinger, Walter, "Herrschaft und Gefolgschaft in der germanisch-deutschen Verfassungsgeschichte," *Historische Zeitschrift*, 176 (1953), pp. 225–75.

Schmidt, B., "Theoderich der Grosse und die damaszierten Schwerter der Thüringer," *Ausgrabungen und Funde,* 14 (1969), pp. 38–40.

Schmidt, L., "Die Comites Gothorum," *Mitteilungen des österreichischen Instituts für Geschichtsforschung,* 40 (1925), pp. 127–34.

Schramm, P. E., *Herrschaftszeichen und Staatssymbolik* (Schriften der MGH, 13.1, Stuttgart, 1954).

Schroff, Helmut, *Claudians Gedicht vom Gotenkrieg* (Berlin, 1927).

Schwartz, Jacques, "Le Limes selon l'Histoire Auguste," *Bonner Historia-Augusta-Colloquium,* 1968–69 (Antiquitas IV, 7, Bonn, 1970), p. 233–8.

Seeck, Otto, *Geschichte des Untergangs der Antiken Welt* (Vol. 1, 4th ed. 1921, Vol. 2–6, 2nd ed. 1920–22, reprint Stuttgart, 1966).

Seeck, Otto, and G. Veith, "Die Schlacht am Frigidus," *Klio,* 13 (1913), pp. 451–467.

Seyfarth, Wolfgang, "Nomadenvölker an den Grenzen des spätrömischen Reiches. Beobachtungen des Ammianus Marcellinus über Hunnen und Sarazenen," *Das Verhältnis von Bodenbauern und Viehzüchtern in historischer Sicht* (Deutsche Akademie der Wissenschaften zu Berlin, Institut für Orientforschung, 69, Berlin 1969), pp. 207–13.

Sinnigen, William G., "Comites Consistoriani in Ostrogothic Italy," *Classica et Mediaevalia,* 24 (1963), pp. 158–65.

Sinnigen, William G., "Administrative Shifts of Competence under Theoderic," *Traditio,* 21 (1965), pp. 456–467.

Sjövold, T., "The Iron Age Settlements of Arctic Norway. A Study in the Expansion of European Iron Age Culture within the Arctic Circle, pt. 1, Early Iron Age. Roman and Migration Periods," *Tromsö Museums Skrifter,* 10.1 (1962).

Skjelsvik, E., "The Stone Circles and Related Monuments of Norway," *Tirada a parte de la Cronica del IV Congresso Internacional de Ciencas Prehistoricas y Protohistoricas,* Madrid, 1954 (Zaragoza, 1956), pp. 579–583.

Slabe, Marijan, "La Nécropole de la période de la migration des peuples à Davlje" [in Slovène with French résumé], *Acta Archaeologica Arheološki Vestnik. Académie slovène,* 21–22 (1970–71), pp. 141–50.

Sophokles, E. A., *Greek Lexicon of the Roman and Byzantine Periods* (Cambridge, Mass., 1887, reprint New York, 1957).

Spicer, Edward H., "Acculturation," *International Encyclopedia of the Social Sciences,* 1 (1968), pp. 21–27.

Sprandel, Rolf, "Dux and comes in der Merovingerzeit," *Zeitschrift der Savigny-Stiftung für Rechtsgeschichte, Germ. Abt.,* 74 (1957), pp. 41–84.

Sprandel, Rolf, "La production du fer au moyen âge," *Annales, Économies, Sociétés, Civlisations,* 24 (1969), pp. 305–21.

Sprandel, Rolf, "Struktur und Geschichte des merovingischen Adels," *Historische Zeitschrift,* 193 (1961), pp. 33–71.

Stefan, Friedrich, *Die Münzstätte Sirmium unter den Ostgoten und Gepiden. Ein Beitrag zur Geschichte des germanischen Münzwesens in der Zeit der Völkerwanderung* (Halle, 1925).

Ştefan, G., "Une Tombe de l'époque des migrations à Aldeni (Dep. de Buzau)," *Dacia,* 7–8 (1941), pp. 217–21.

Stein, Ernst, *Histoire du bas-empire,* II, De la disparition de l'empire d'occident à la mort de Justinien (476–565), ed., J. R. Palanque (Bruges, 1950).

Stenberger, M., *Valhagar. A Migration Period Settlement on Gotland, Sveden* (København, 1955).

Stjernquist, Berta, *Simris: On cultural connections of Scania in the Roman Iron Age* (Acta Archaeologica Lundensia, series in 4º, 2, Lund, 1955).

Streitberg, Wilhelm August, *Die gotische Bibel* (Heidelberg, 1908, reprint 1965).

Stroheker, K. F., *Germanentum und Spätantike* (Zürich, Stuttgart, 1965).

Sturms, E., "Das Problem der ethnischen Deutung der kaiserzeitlichen Gräberfelder in der Ukraine (mit einer Karte)" *Zeitschrift für Ostforschung,* 2 (1953), pp. 424–432.

Suceveanu, Al., "Observations sur la stratigraphie des cités de la Dobrogea aux IIe–IVe siècle à la lumière des fouilles d'Histria," *Dacia*, n.s. 13 (1969), pp. 327–365.

Sulimirski, Tadeusz, *The Sarmatians* (London, 1970).

Sundwall, Johannes, *Abhandlungen zur Geschichte des ausgehenden Römertums* (Suemen Tiedeseura. Oversikt av Finska vetenskaps – societetens förhandlingar, 60, Helsinki, 1919, reprint New York, 1975).

Svennung, Josef Gusten Algot, *Jordanes and Scandia. Kritisch-exegetische Studien* (Acta Soc. Litt. Hum. Upsal. 44, 2 A, Stockholm, 1967).

Syme, Ronald, *Emperors and Biography,* Studies in the Historia Augusta, (Oxford, 1971).

Syme, Ronald, *The Historia Augusta.* A call of clerity (Antiquitas IV, 8, Bonn, 1971).

Szádeczky-Kardoss, S., "Zur Interpretation zweier Hydatius-Stellen," *Helikon,* 1 (1961), pp. 148–52.

Täckholm, U., "Aetius and the Battle of the Catalaunian Fields," *Opuscula Romana,* 7 (1969), pp. 259–76.

Theodosian Code, trans., Clyde Pharr (Princeton, N.J., 1952).

Thibault, Fabien, "L'Impôt direct dans les royaumes des Ostrogoths, des Wisigoths et des Burgundes," *Nouvelle Revue historique de droit français et étranger*, 25 (1901), pp. 698–728. 26 (1902), pp. 32–48.

Thomas, B., *Römische Villen in Pannonien.* Beiträge zur pannonischen Siedlungsgeschichte. (Budapest, 1964).

Thompson, E. A. "Constantine, Constantius II, and the Lower Danube Frontier," *Hermes,* 84 (1956), pp. 372–81.

Thompson, E. A., "Olympiodorus of Thebes," *Classical Quarterly,* 38 (1944), pp. 43–52.

Thompson, E. A., "Christianity and the Northern Barbarians," in: *The Conflict between Paganism and Christianity in the Fourth Century,* ed., A. G. Momigliano (Oxford, 1963), pp. 56–78.

Thompson, E. A., *The Early Germans* (Oxford, 1965).

Thompson, E. A., *The Goths in Spain* (Oxford, 1969).

Thompson, E. A., *The Historical Work of Ammianus* (Cambridge, 1947).

Thompson, E. A., *History of Attila and the Huns* (Oxford, 1948).

Thompson, E. A., Review of *Die Auswanderung der Goten aus Schweden* by Curt Weibull, *Journal of Roman Studies,* 50 (1960), p. 288.

Thompson, E. A., "The Settlement of the Barbarians in Southern Gaul," *Journal of Roman Studies,* 46 (1956), pp. 65–76.

Thompson, E. A., *The Visigoths in the Time of Ulfila* (Oxford, 1966).

Thompson, E. A., "The Visigoths from Fritigern to Euric," *Historia,* 12 (1963), pp. 105–26.

Thomsen, Rudi, *The Italic Regions from Augustus to the Lombard Invasion* (Classica et Mediaevalia, Dissertationes, 4, København, 1947).

Todd, Malcolm, *Everyday Life of the Barbarians. Goths, Franks, and Vandals* (Putnam, N.Y., 1972).

Todorov, Yanko, *Le grandi strade romane in Bulgaria* (Roma. Istituto di Studi Romani, Quaderni dell'Impero, II, 16, Le grandi strade del mondo romano, 1937).

Tudor, Dimitru, "Preuves archéologiques attestant la continuité de la domination romaine au nord du Danube après l'abandon de la Dacie sous Aurélian (IIIe–Ve siècles)," *Dacoromania,* 1 (1973), pp. 149–61.

Tudor, Dimitru, *Sucidava, une cité daco-romaine et byzantine en Dacie* (Bruxelles, 1965).

Turney-High, Harry H.,*Primitive War. Its Practice and Concepts* 2nd ed. (Columbia, S.C., 1971).

Udalcova, Zinaida V., "La Campagne de Narsès et l'écrasement de Totila," *Corsi di Cultura. sull' arte ravennate e bizantina,* 18 (1971), pp. 557–64.

Udalcova, Z. V. et E. V. Goutnova, "La Genèse du féodalisme dans les pays d'Europe," *XIII Congrès international des sciences historiques* (1970).

Utšenko, S. L., and D'jaknoff, I. M., "Social Stratification of Ancient Society," *13th International Congress of Historians* (Moscow, 1970).

Valentin, L. Chanoine, *Saint Prosper de l'Aquitaine. Étude sur la littérature latine ecclésiastique au cinquième siècle en Gaule* (Toulouse, 1900).

Várady, László, *Das letzte Jahrhundert Pannoniens, 376—476* (Amsterdam, 1969).

Vasiliev, A. A., *The Goths in Crimea* (Cambridge, Mass., 1936).

Vernadsky, George, "The Eurasian Nomads and their Impact on Medieval Europe," *Studi Medievali*, Ser. 3, pt. 4, 2 (1963), pp. 401—34.

Vinskí, Zdenko, "Die völkerwanderungszeitliche Nekropole in Kranj und der Reihengräberfelder Horizont des 6. Jahrhunderts im westlichen Jugoslawien," *Actes du VIIIᵉ congrès international des sciences préhistoriques et protohistoriques* (Beograd, 1971), pp. 253—65.

Vinskí, Z., "Kranj et l'horizon de necropoles en rangées du VIᵉ S. en Yougoslavie occidentale," [en slovène avec résumé en france] *Acta Archaeologica. Arheoloski Vestnik. Académie Slovène*, 21—22 (1970—71), pp. 151—52.

Vinskí, Z., "Zikadenschmuck aus Jugoslawien," *Jahrbuch des Römisch-Germanischen Zentralmuseums Mainz*, 4 (1957), pp. 136—160.

Vismara, Giulio, *Edictum Theoderici*, (Ius Romanum Medii Aevi, Pars 1, 2b, aa, α, (Milano, 1967).

Vismara, Giulio, "El 'Edictum Theororici'," in: *Estudios visogóticos* (Roma, Madrid, 1956), pt. 1, pp. 49—89 (Cuadernos del Instituto Juridico Espanol, 5).

Vismara, Giulio, "Romani e Goti di fronte al diritto nel Regno Ostrogoto," *Settimane di Studio* 3 (1955), pp. 409—63.

Vogel, F., "Chronologische Untersuchungen zu Ennodius," *Neues Archiv der Gesellschaft für ältere deutsche Geschichtskunde*, 23 (1898), pp. 53—74.

Vogt, Joseph, *Kulturwelt und Barbaren. Zum Menschheitsbild der spätantiken Gesellschaft* (Abhandl. der Akad. der Wiss. in Mainz, Geistes- und Sozial-Wissen. Klasse, 1967, No. 1).

Vries, J. de, *Altgermanische Religionsgeschichte*, 2nd. ed. (Berlin, 1956).

Vries, J. de, "Das Königtum bei den Germanen," *Saeculum*, 7 (1956), pp. 289—309.

Vučkovič-Todorovič, D., "Recherches récentes sur le Limes Danubien en Servie," *Quintus Congressus Internationalis Limitis Romani Studiosorum*, 1961 (Zagreb, 1963), pp. 183—194.

Vulič, Nikola, *Il Limes Romano in Jugoslavia*, 2nd., ed. (Roma, Istituto di Studi Romani, Quaderni dell'Impero, 1, Il Limes romano (1938).

Vulpe, Radu, *Le Vallum de la Moldavie inférieure et le "mur" d'Athanric* (La Hage, 1957).

Vulpe, Radu, "Les *valla* de la Valachie, de la Basse-Moldavie et du Boudjak," *Actes du IXᵉ congrès international d'études sur les frontières romaines* (Mamia, Sep. 1972, éd. par D. M. Pippidi, Bucureşti, Köln, Wien, 1974), pp. 267—76.

Vyver, A. van der, "Cassiodore et son œuvre," *Speculum*, 6 (1931), pp. 244—92.

Wagner, Norbert, *Getica. Untersuchungen zum Leben des Jordanes und zur frühen Geschichte der Goten* (Berlin, 1967).

Wallace-Hadrill, J. M., *Early Germanic Kingship in England and on the Continent* (Oxford, 1971).

Weibull, Curt, *Die Auswanderung der Goten aus Schweden* (Göteborgs kungl. vetenskapsoch vitthetssamhälles handlingar, 6 följden, ser. A, bd. 6, No. 5, Göteborg, 1958).

Weill, A. R., "L'Analyse critique au service de l'histoire des métaux anciens," Symposium de chimie historique et archéologique, Atlantic City, 1962. *Archeological Chemistry*, 1 (1967), pp. 313—46.

Weill, A. R., "Examens de surfaces par l'intermédiarire de répliques transparentes," *Bull. Lab. Musée du Louvre*, 4 (1959), pp. 21—29.

Welkov, I., "Eine Gotenfestung bei Sadowetz (Nordbulgarien)," *Germania*, 19 (1935), pp. 149—58.

Wenskus, Reinhard, *Stammesbildung und Verfassung: das Werden der frühmittelalterlichen gentes* (Köln, Graz, 1961).

Werner, J., "Kriegergräber aus der ersten Hälfte des 5. Jahrhunderts zwischen Schelde und Weser," *Bonner Jahrbücher*, 157 (1958), pp. 372—413.

Werner, J., "Zur Entstehung der Reihengräberzivilisation," *Archaeologica Geographica*, 1 (1950), pp. 23–32.

Werner, J., Review of *Funde aus der Hunnenzeit und ihre ethnische Sonderung*, by A. Alföldi (*Archaeologia Hungarica*, 9, 1932) in *Germania*, 18 (1934), pp. 236–8.

Werner, Joachim, "Die archäologischen Zeugnisse der Goten in Südrussland, Ungarn, Italien und Spanien," *Settimane di Studio*, 3 (1956), pp. 127–30.

Werner, Joachim, *Die Langobarden in Pannonien. Beiträge zur Kenntnis der langobardischen Bodenfunde vor 568.* (Bayerische Akad. d. Wissenschaften, phil.-hist. Klasse, Abh., Neue Folge, Heft 55A, München, 1962).

Werner, Joachim, "Ostgotische Bügelfibeln aus bajuwarischen Reihengräbern," *Bayerische Vorgeschichtsblätter*, 26 (1961), pp. 68–75.

Werner, Joachim, "Studien zu Grabfunden des V. Jahrhunderts aus der Slowakei und der Karpatenukraine," *Slovenská Archeologia*, 7 (1959), pp. 422–38.

Werner, Joachim, "Zur Herkunft und Zeitstellung der Hemmorer Eimer und der Eimer mit gewellter Kannelure," *Bonner Jahrbücher* 140/141 (1936), pp. 395–410.

Wes, M. A., *Das Ende des Kaisertums im Westen des römischen Reichs* (Archeologische Studien van het Nederlands Historisch Instituut te Rome, 3, 's-Gravenhage, 1967).

Wheeler, Mortimer, *Rome beyond the Imperial Frontiers* (London, 1954).

Wilkes, John J., *Dalmatia* (London, 1969).

Wiseman, James, *Stobi. A Guide to the Excavations* (Beograd, 1973).

Woloch, G. Michael, "A Survey of Scholarship on Ostrogothic Italy (A.D. 489–552)," *Classical Folia*, 25 (1971), pp. 320–56.

Wrede, Ferdinand, *Über die Sprache der Ostgoten in Italien* (Quellen und Forschungen zur Sprach- und Culturgeschichte der Germanischen Völker, 68, Strassburg, 1891).

Wroth, W., *Catalogue of the Coins of the Vandals, Ostrogoths and Lombards. . . , in the British Museum* (London, 1911).

Yü, Ying-shih, *Trade and Expansion in Han China. A Study in the Structure of Sino-barbarian Economic Relations* (Berkeley, Cal., 1967).

Zaharia, Emilia and N. Zaharia, "Contributii la cunvasterea cultirii materiale din secolul al V-lea e.n. din Moldova, in lumina sápáturilor de la Botoşari," *Arheologia Moldovei*, 6 (1969), pp. 167ff.

Zeiss, H., "Zur ethnischen Deutung frühmittelalterlicher Funde," *Germania*, 14 (1930), pp. 11–24.

Zeiss, H., "Die Donaugermanen und ihr Verhältnis zur römischen Kultur nach der Vita Severini,", *Ostbayerische Grenzmarken*, 17 (1928), pp. 9–13.

Zeiss, H., "Die Nordgrenze des Ostgotenreiches," *Germania*, 12 (1928), pp. 25–34.

Zeiller, Jacques, "Étude sur l'arianisme en Italie à l'époque ostrogotique et à l'époque lombarde," *Mélanges d'archéologie et d'histoire publiés par l'école française de Rome*, 25 (1905), pp. 127–46.

Zeiller, J., *Les Origines chrétiennes dans les provinces danubiennes de l'empire romain* (Studia Historica, 48, Paris, 1918, reprint Roma, 1967).

Zimmermann, Odo John, *The Late Latin Vocabulary of the Variae of Cassiodorus* (Washington, D.C., 1944).

Zosimus, *Historia Nova*, trans., J. Buchanan and Harold T. Davis (San Antonio, Texas, 1967).

Zwikker, W., *Studien zur Markussäule* (Archeologisch-historische bijdragen, 8, Amsterdam, 1941).